HUDSON RIVER
Day Line

Hudson River Day Line

*The story of a
great American
steamboat company*

By DONALD C. RINGWALD

HOWELL-NORTH BOOKS · BERKELEY, CALIFORNIA · 1965

HUDSON RIVER DAY LINE

Printed and bound in the United States of America.

Library of Congress Catalog Card No. 65-18744

Endsheets from Harper's Weekly

Collection of Lucius Beebe

Published by Howell-North Books

1050 Parker Street, Berkeley, California 94710

PREFACE

Steamboats have been running on the Hudson River for well over a century and a half. In that period, there has been a vast number of them, of all sizes and shapes, operating on a wide variety of lines.

There is a tendency to think of Albany, the capital of New York State, as having been the head of navigation for passenger steamboats. Here the wharves were about 143 miles from the mouth of the Hudson at New York City. Actually, there was service to Troy, a few miles above. During the heyday of steamboating, every landing along the approximately 150 miles of tidal water of the Hudson from its mouth to Troy, was served by a steam-propelled vessel of some kind.

Of the many Hudson River steamboat lines, the one which became the best known in this country and abroad, was the Hudson River Day Line. Its "white flyers" were famous for their speed and their appointments, and represented the acme of elegance in water travel. No one had seen America until he had seen the Hudson River, and no one had seen the Hudson River properly unless he had done so from the deck of a Day Line steamer.

This is primarily the story of the formation of the Day Line in 1863, of its development into the greatest organization of its kind, and of its decline through the closing season of operations, 1948. Then, as an epilogue, there is an account of the Day Line under new owners, from 1949 to the present.

DONALD C. RINGWALD

Albany
New York
1965

Arthur Helmke.

ACKNOWLEDGMENTS

A prime difficulty in preparing a work on the Hudson River Day Line is not the lack of material, but the superabundance of it. The management of the line from its formation in 1863 until the sale in 1949, was in the hands of one family, so probably much more was retained in the way of records and other material of all kinds than would otherwise have been the case.

After the old company ceased operations, the late Alfred Van Santvoord Olcott, with great wisdom stemming from his inherited regard for the history of Hudson River steamboating, presented to the New-York Historical Society in New York City a vast amount of Day Line material, including ledgers, letter books, scrapbooks, timetables, picture postcards and even Bibles that were at one time carried on the steamers. Recently, Mrs. Alfred V. S. Olcott has presented still more material to the Steamship Historical Society of America, Inc., for its reference library in Staten Island, New York. Neither of these Day Line collections has been catalogued.

In addition, the Day Line has always been attractive to collectors of steamboat material, and much exists both in private hands and in marine collections in museums.

To explore thoroughly all of this would obviously be an impossibility without having years of free time available. What I have tried to do is set down an over-all account which is reasonably comprehensive, but which will not tell you how much money the Day Line spent for bunting in 1913 or many of the other facts so dear to the heart of the esoteric marine historian. This can be left for some following student who may one day write a definitive account of the line that, with the existing material, could run through several volumes.

Having been delving into the history of Hudson River steamboating for many years, I am not so sanguine as to lay claim for utter accuracy. Wherever possible, original sources or the closest things thereto have been used.

The New-York Historical Society kindly permitted full utilization of its Hudson River Day Line collection. I am particularly indebted to Arthur B. Carlson, Curator of Maps and Prints, and Wilmer R. Leech, Curator of Manuscripts, for enabling me to accomplish the most possible in periods when time was limited. Likewise, thanks to Mrs. Alice S. Wilson, secretary and librarian of the Steamship Historical Society of America, Inc., for her help when using the Hudson River Day Line collection in the SSHSA library.

The writer also used information gleaned from Hudson Valley newspapers over a period of many years, from official documents in the National Archives, and had access to private collections. Amongst the latter are the major collection of steamboat material of Elwin M. Eldredge of Clermont, New York, and the extensive Hudson River steamboat collections of Captain William O. Benson of Sleightsburgh, New York, and Roger W. Mabie of Port Ewen, New York. Also very helpful were a number of old and fruitful scrapbooks owned by Fred J. Johnston of Kingston, New York.

I appreciate, too, the critical reading of the manuscript by Elwin M. Eldredge, Roger W. Mabie and C. Bradford Mitchell.

Amongst the many other kind people who rendered esteemed assistance in various ways, are: Francis J. Barry, present operator of the Day Line; Herman F. Boyle, collector of Hudson River steamboat material; Frank O. Braynard, marine historian and author; the late Captain Frank E. Brown, who approved the portion on the loss of the *Washington Irving;* Captain George Carroll; Edward O. Clark, marine historian and photographer; De Witt Clinton, who participated in the christening of the *De Witt Clinton;* Harold C. Collins of the University of Vermont; Harry Cotterell, Jr., marine historian specializing in ferryboats; William King Covell, marine historian specializing in the Fall River Line; Richard V. Elliott, J. Joseph Fitzgerald, David G. Forrest, Thomas Garvey, all Hudson

River Day Line enthusiasts; Captain Edward M. Grady; R. Loren Graham, marine photographer; Dr. John I. Griffin of City College, New York; Kenneth R. Hall of the National Archives; Douglas L. Haverly, who rendered great assistance in research; Arthur Helmke; Erik Heyl, marine historian and author; Forrest R. Holdcamper, National Archives; the late Captain Maurice A. Howard; George V. W. Kelly; Thomas Kraljic, formerly Day Line First Mate; Charles O. L. Lawesson; the late Captain Grant B. Lezatte; John L. Lochhead, librarian of the Mariners Museum, Newport News, Virginia; Mrs. Sophie Miller, newspaper columnist; Conrad Milster, Jr., student of marine engines; William G. Muller, who, amongst other things, did the jacket; Alexander P. Olcott, son of Alfred V. S. Olcott and once a Day Line employee; Mrs. Alfred V. S. Olcott; Chief Engineer Elvoid E. Post; George Sanders, formerly president of the Hudson River Day Line, Inc.; the late A. Fred Saunders; Victor E. Scrivens; Frederick C. Shipley; Miss Jane F. Smith, National Archives; Alan J. Staight, Marine Board, Hamilton, Bermuda; W. du Barry Thomas, marine historian; Walter A. Tuttle.

Finally, I would like to thank the two men who are responsible for your reading this volume: William H. Ewen, Hudson River steamboat historian of Hastings-on-Hudson, New York, who urged me to write it; and George W. Hilton, author of *The Great Lakes Car Ferries* and *The Staten Island Ferry*, who urged me to submit the manuscript to Howell-North Books.

THE AUTHOR

Edward O. Clark

vii

The forward smokestack of the Alexander Hamilton.—*Edward O. Clark*

TABLE OF CONTENTS

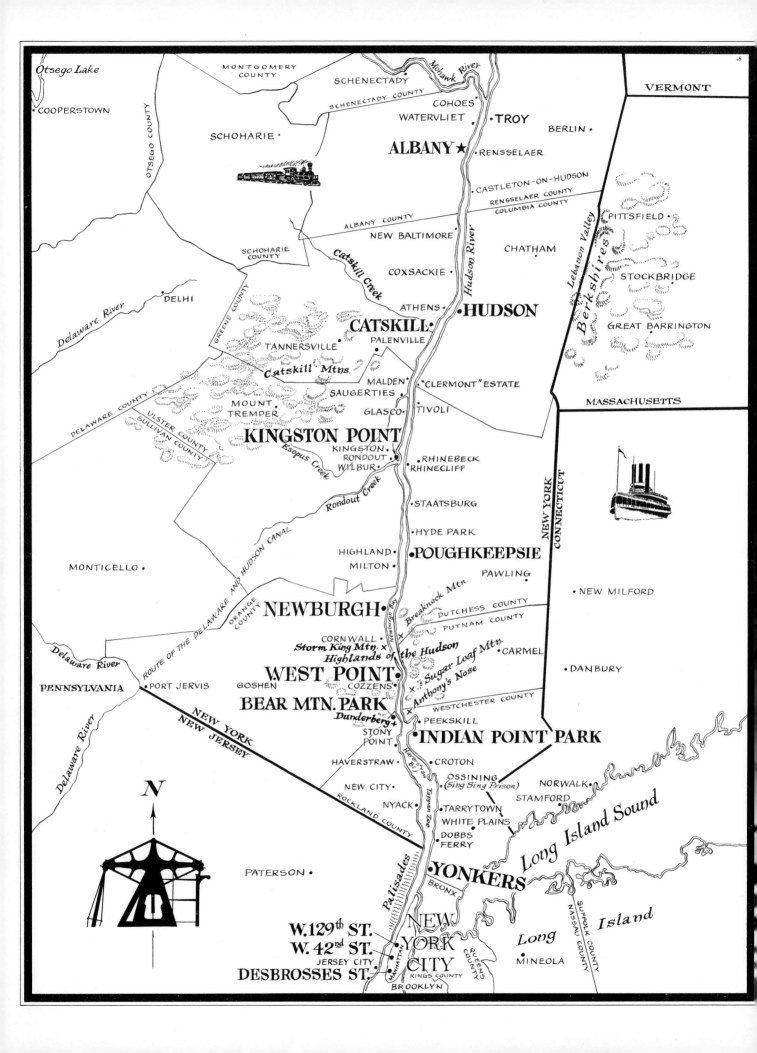

Chapter 1

EARLY YEARS ON THE RIVER

On September 13, 1948, the steamboat *Robert Fulton* of the Hudson River Day Line cast off her lines at Albany and started down the river for New York. There was nothing particularly unusual about her departure, except that she was making the last sailing of that year from Albany. Traditionally last trips were always regarded with melancholy interest by the followers of Hudson River steamboating, for they marked the beginning of a bleak interval until the first trip of the year was made the following spring. But in the spring of 1949 there was no first trip of the season to Albany. There was never again to be a first trip of the season to Albany, for regular steamboat service between that place and New York had died.

It was appropriate that the *Robert Fulton* had ended it, since Robert Fulton began it in 1807 with his first Hudson River steamboat. That he did so was due to Robert R. Livingston, of a wealthy and prominent New York State family. Livingston was a political power and in 1798 had in his hands a New York State monopoly for the operation of a steamboat provided he could produce a vessel of a required size and speed on the Hudson River within one year. This he was unable to do. When he was minister to France, he met Robert Fulton, the artist who became an engineer and inventor, and from that association came the first steamboat to ply between New York and Albany. There had, of course, been steamboats operating earlier, both in the United States and abroad, but the success of Fulton and Livingston was to mark the beginning of the unbroken development of steam navigation in America.

The initial trip to Albany and back gained for Fulton and Livingston a twenty-year monopoly of steamboat operations on New York State waters. The legislature, by an act of 1803, granted it to them provided they were able to meet the requirements within two years, and then by an act of April 1807, gave them another two years from that date. This time the conditions were met.

The steamboat was a sidewheeler, built at New York, powered with an engine imported from England, and fitted with sails to help her along when the wind was favorable. On her first experimental trip to Albany, she left New York on Monday, August 17, and reached Albany on Wednesday, August 19. She had lain over about 20 hours at Clermont, Livingston's residence on the Hudson. Her running time was approximately 32 hours. Leaving Albany on Thursday, August 20, she arrived back in New York on Friday, about 30 hours running time.

Fulton then set to work to make the vessel suitable for passenger service, and enrolled her on September 3, giving her name as *North River Steam Boat*. Here was a purely practical designation, for she was a steamboat and she ran on the North River—then an optional name for the Hudson River.

On September 4 the *North River Steam Boat* formally entered commercial service and ran through to Albany in 28 hours 45 minutes. The initial fare from New York to Albany was seven dollars; to Hudson, five dollars; to Poughkeepsie, four dollars; and to Newburgh, three dollars.

Considering that the steamboat was completely an experiment, it is not surprising that she experienced accidents during her operation in 1807. But she was favorably patronized, nonetheless.

In order to remedy flaws in her design and to improve her passenger accommodations, the *North River Steam Boat* was rebuilt and enlarged between the operating seasons of 1807 and 1808. This changed the dimensions, and the new statutory measurements* were recorded when she was

---

*Statutory measurements are the official length, breadth, and depth of hold of a vessel as entered in government records. They are discussed in Appendix A. In the same appendix are two tables detailing facts and figures—including statutory measurements—concerning steamboats prominently mentioned in this book. The *North River Steam Boat*, together with other vessels not operated by the Day Line, is listed in Appendix A-3.

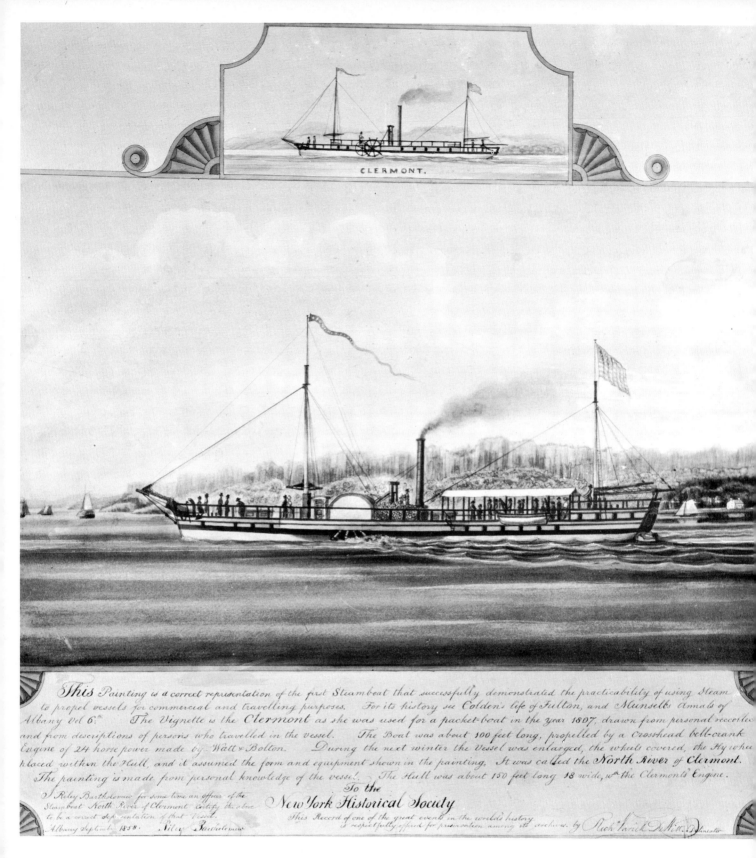

CLERMONT.

This Painting is a correct representation of the first Steamboat that successfully demonstrated the practicability of using Steam to propel vessels for commercial and travelling purposes. For its history see Colden's life of Fulton, and Munsell's Annals of Albany Vol 6th. The Vignette is the Clermont as she was used for a packet-boat in the year 1807, drawn from personal recollection and from descriptions of persons who travelled in the vessel. The Boat was about 100 feet long, propelled by a crosshead bell-crank Engine of 24 horse power made by Watt & Bolton. During the next winter the Vessel was enlarged, the wheels covered, the Fly wheel placed within the Hull, and it assumed the form and equipment shown in the painting, It was called the North River of Clermont. The painting is made from personal knowledge of the vessel. The Hull was about 150 feet long 18 wide, with the Clermont's Engine.

I Riley Bartholomew for some time an officer of the
Steam boat North River of Clermont certify the above
to be a correct representation of that Vessel.
Albany September 1858. Riley Bartholomew

To the
New York Historical Society

This Record of one of the great events in the world's history
is respectfully offered for preservation among its archives. by Rich Varick DeWitt Delineator

These views of the *North River Steam Boat* are from a watercolor done by Richard Varick De Witt about 1858. They were intended to show the vessel as she appeared in regular service in 1807, and after she had been enlarged between the seasons of 1807 and 1808. In the lower left-hand corner, Riley Bartholomew, a former officer of the *North River Steam Boat*, signed a statement as to authenticity. Because over forty years had elapsed since the vessel was withdrawn from service, the views should be taken as general approximations of her appearance and not as definitive portrayals. The treatment of the name in De Witt's caption is in keeping with historical acceptance at that time. In the lower picture, wood for fuel is piled high abaft the paddle box and the pilot stands at the wheel forward of the smokestack. Originally the vessel was steered by a tiller, as shown in the upper picture.—*Courtesy of The New-York Historical Society, New York City.*

enrolled again on May 14, 1808. Her length was now 149 feet, an increase of seven feet. The first hailing port had been New York, but on the new enrollment it was set down as Clermont. This was because Livingston, who the day before had officially purchased a half-interest in the vessel from Fulton, took care of the enrolling at that time.

Inasmuch as a hailing port is in no sense a part of the name, the fact that *North River Steam Boat* of New York became *North River Steam Boat* of Clermont would normally be of little interest. She continued to paddle her way up and down the river and was still *North River Steam Boat* when she made her last trip in 1814.

In 1817, two years after Robert Fulton's death, *The Life of Robert Fulton* by Cadwallader D. Colden was published, and in that work the author called the vessel the *Clermont*. Colden was a lawyer who afterwards became mayor of New York City, and, because of his association with Fulton and Livingston, his book had about it the aura of an official biography. Regardless of how he reasoned or the basis for his thinking, Colden in effect renamed the steamboat, for later historians regarded him as such a firm source that *Clermont* came to be generally accepted as the original name.

While confusion was to surround the name of the pioneer steamboat, the line which Fulton and Livingston had begun added more steamers through the years and successfully thwarted attempts of others to infringe on the monopoly. Finally in 1824, the Supreme Court of the United States declared unconstitutional all the New York State laws that prohibited steam vessels licensed under United States laws from running on water of New York State. Soon the Hudson was open to all comers. The monopoly line, since it had no reason to be otherwise, was highly conservative. Competition was now to spur rapid strides in the design and machinery of Hudson River steamboats.

Before long there had evolved what might be called a general type for the larger Hudson River steamboats built for the New York-Albany trade. The wooden hulls were flat-bottomed and of shallow draft because of the shoal water in the upper river. Since the paddle wheels had to project beyond the line of the hull, the main deck was extended to the outer extremity of the paddle-wheel housing—the paddle boxes or wheelhouses—to form wheel guards both ahead of and behind the paddles. This practice had been begun by Fulton and the guards were eventually continued all the

way to the bow and around the stern, tapering off from their greatest width at the paddle boxes and supported underneath by struts from the hull.

In addition to providing much more space than would otherwise be available, the guards also afforded a practical place to put the boilers, and steamboats with two boilers generally had one on either guard, behind the paddle box. Setting the boilers there allowed greater room in the hold and in the area above through which the smokestacks passed. Also, the arrangement made for convenience in the loading and stowing of fuel, which in the early years was wood and then coal. In the days when prospective passengers were extremely boiler-explosion conscious, it was possible to allay their fears by pointing out that the boat really didn't have any boilers. They were stuck out over the water where they couldn't harm anyone! Boilers-on-the-guards steamboats were built for service on the Hudson as late as the 1870s and the final survivor of the style last ran in 1917.

Our general type vessel, besides having boilers on the guards, would also have a vertical beam engine, which came to be favored as the most satisfactory engine for powering Hudson River steamers. Since it was placed close to the boilers, it was abaft the shafts of the paddle wheels. Rocking up and down above the top deck was the walking beam, at the apex of a massive gallows frame which rose up from the keelsons in the hull. One end of the walking beam was linked to the crosshead on the piston rod of the vertical cylinder. At the other end of the walking beam, a long connecting rod ran down to a crankpin joining the cranks on the inner ends of the paddle-wheel shafts. The shafts thus united could be referred to as a unit—the paddle-wheel shaft—or in the plural if one preferred them to retain their separate identity.

The light wooden hulls, fitted with more and more powerful engines, required strengthening to maintain their shape. Two methods by which this was done had a decided effect on the external appearance of the vessels and in the larger steamers both were employed. There was a heavy timber truss running fore and aft on either side with the highest point sometimes higher than the tops of the paddle boxes. These were the hogframes, so called because their function was to prevent the vessel from hogging—that is, from drooping forward and aft and so changing in shape to an upward curve. Also, they averted sagging elsewhere.

As a further preventive against distortion of the hull, there were tie or guy rods running down from pole masts or spars. These rods and spars served to distribute the strain, and were in addition employed to afford further support for the guards and to support the bow and the stern, since the hogframes did not run the full length of the vessel.

This method seems to have been first used by fastening a chain to the bow and running it over a spar in the center of the vessel. Iron tie rods replaced chains and were fitted with turnbuckles so that they could be tightened when necessary. When one said a steamer had spars for strengthening, he meant not the spars alone, of course, but the tie rods connected to them. The largest of the boilers-on-the-guards steamboats built for the Hudson had no less than eight spars.

In a further employment of the spar principle, there were also shorter king posts, set at the sides of the hull and therefore in pairs. They and their tie rods were used particularly to maintain the guards in the area of the paddle wheels. Indeed, rods ran in wonderful abandon on the old side-wheelers, from the hogframes, the spars and the king posts to members of the hull, the guards or the boilers.

As for passenger accommodations, our general type steamboat of the earlier years would probably have a cabin for female passengers, the ladies' saloon, on the main deck aft and cabins in the hold for the men. The after cabin in the hold was also utilized as the dining room of the vessel.

From 1807 onward, the speed of Hudson River steamboats steadily increased, but it was to be many years before they were capable of going all the way between New York and Albany by daylight or overnight. A latter-day writer concluded that the steamboat *Richmond* was the ". . . first boat to make regular trips from New York to Albany by *daylight*. . . .," and based his statement purely on the fact that in 1822 the *Richmond* was advertised to sail from New York at 6 a.m. Since she had been built in 1814 and later in the 1820s was advertised as "Slow but Sure," it is unlikely that she arrived at Albany until well into the following day.

In 1823 the line established by Fulton and Livingston placed in service the new *James Kent*. On May 12, 1824, that steamer left New York at 5 p.m. and made the trip to Albany in 15 hours 30 minutes. Said a press correspondent, "This, I believe, is speed unequalled in steam boat navigation."

The line was then maintaining six sailings a week, Monday through Saturday, from New York at 5 p.m. and Albany at 10 a.m. Effective May 31

The *James Kent* was so celebrated in her day that her likeness was placed on chinaware.—*Photograph, Elwin M. Eldredge coll.*

the schedule was revised so that the *James Kent* departed from either New York or Albany at 5 a.m. and the Albany departures of the other vessels were at 11 a.m. The change in Albany sailings was made, the line advertised, "In order to accommodate the citizens of the western part of the state, who travel by the canal boats. . . ." and added, "Passengers leaving Albany or New-York in the JAMES KENT, will be landed the same evening."

The *James Kent* made her first sailing under the new timetable on May 31 and the next day the *Albany Daily Advertiser* reported that she had ". . . left New-York yesterday morning at a quarter past 5 o'clock, and arrived here last evening at eight, affording the passengers the gratification of viewing the beautiful and sublime scenery of the Hudson by day light. There was but the common pressure of steam kept up on the passage, so that the passengers were exposed to no hazard."

This was indeed a regular trip through by daylight. The *James Kent* left New York about 45 minutes after sunrise and although she completed her run approximately half an hour after sunset, there was still over an hour and a half of twilight left. But the arrangement continued for only a short time. By a new schedule the *James Kent* left Albany at 9 a.m.; and New York at 10 a.m. on two of her weekly sailings and at 5 p.m. on the third.

Two years later, in May of 1826, advertisements appeared reading, "The Steam Boat *Sun*, Capt. Henry Drake—the only Daily Line between New York and Albany—through in one day, and by day light." The *Sun* left New York and Albany at 6 a.m. and arrived at the opposite terminus the "same afternoon."

The advertisement also assured the public that the *Sun* would land passengers only at Newburgh, Poughkeepsie, Catskill and Hudson and at those places would stop at the wharves. How could a steamboat "land" at a place without stopping at the wharf? Well, on the Hudson River to save time there had come into being a type of landing made while the vessel was "on the fly." When only a few passengers were getting off or on at a landing, the vessel's small boat was brought into use. Attached to a long line, it was cast off and the momentum imparted to it by the moving steamboat enabled the steersman to head it into the dock. Here the passengers being landed had to jump out in an instant, with their luggage tossed out after them. Embarking passengers leaped in, ready to fend off their baggage as it was tumbled in on top of them. Then the small boat was hauled rapidly back to the steamboat and it was not uncommon for the revolving paddle-wheel shaft to be utilized to supply the pull to the line. The fly landing was of course dangerous and eventually outlawed. It is little wonder that passengers lacking the agility of antelopes were not happy at the prospect of boarding or leaving by this means.

The *Sun* held to her daylight schedule for only a short time. Then the arrangements were altered so that she made most of her passages by night. In June 1826 she apparently established a new record of 12 hours 13 minutes, between New York and Albany. One editor, who thought "remarkable" best described the trip, printed a poem which went,

"Who can out 'clipse the *Sun*,
When she from port to port hath run,
In hours twelve and minutes few;
The time is short, the fact is true."*

The constant increase in speed so that steamboats were able to make the New York-Albany run either overnight or by day, resulted in two types of lines—the day lines, on which one went through by day, and the night lines. Originally, the service into which a vessel was to be placed had little effect on the design. All had the same general facilities and could be used in either trade. Then, as specialization advanced, two definite breeds began to take form. The night boats had staterooms built on the second deck to provide added accommodations. The day boats were largely open on the second deck except perhaps for a small saloon.

---

* *Albany Daily Advertiser*, June 12, 1826. The time has also been set at 12 hours 16 minutes.

While the steamboat monopoly granted to Fulton and Livingston had been broken legally, there was no reason why a new monopoly could not be rigged. Some years after the end of the original monopoly, the Hudson River Steamboat Association set its sights on domination of the through passenger business. The Association was a powerful organization of important steamboat owners who had banded together for monopolistic purposes and whose methods were simple. If anyone dared compete with them, they slashed their fares to the point that the interloper usually gave up in despair, for the Association was sufficiently stable financially that it could lose money longer than a single competitor. If this didn't work, they then proceeded to buy out or buy off the competitor. Cornelius Vanderbilt opposed them with what he came to call the People's Line, a name calculated to have a good anti-monopoly ring to it. Vanderbilt was bought off, but in his place appeared another People's Line in which Daniel Drew was an important factor.

Drew was a shrewd individual who had made a tidy sum as a drover before entering the steamboat business. Like Vanderbilt, he also went into railroading. Drew was a rich mine for anecdotes and one stemmed from the fact that apparently he never dressed the part of the man of wealth that he became. Thinking Drew was a member of the crew, a passenger on board a steamboat of his is said to have approached him with the question, "Do you belong to the boat?" Drew replied, "No, the boat belongs to me."

In the summer of 1836, the People's Line had added a new steamboat named the *Rochester*, owned by Drew and Eli Kelly (or Kelley). She was operated at first as a day boat and proved to be a fast vessel. A few days after the advent of the *Rochester*, the new *Swallow* made an experimental trip to Albany prior to entering the service of the Association. Her elapsed time of ten hours led to her being returned to shipyard to be lengthened and altered in the hopes that this would improve her speed. It did. She was placed in regular service as a night boat on September 30 and on October 7-8 ran from New York to Albany in the "unparalleled" elapsed time of 9 hours 10 minutes, with one landing en route.

Meantime, the *Rochester* had commenced to run as a night boat for the People's Line. In speed she and the *Swallow* were well matched and a fierce rivalry developed. In a race on November 8-9, 1836, arranged to take place without passengers on board, the two vessels ran from New York

The brothers James and John Bard, and later James Bard alone, painted portraits of a long list of Hudson River steamboats during the nineteenth century. This J. and J. Bard watercolor of the fast *Swallow* shows her in 1837, a year after she was built. Her wreck in 1845, with initial reports of lives lost far too high, brought forth several prints, of which the view used here is one. By then the *Swallow* had been lengthened for the second time and carried many staterooms on her upper deck.—*Above: New-York Historical Society.*

to Van Wies Point, less than five miles below their Albany landings. The People's Line claimed the *Rochester* had won in 8 hours 57 minutes—five minutes better than the time of the *Swallow*. The *Swallow's* people insisted that the time of the *Rochester* had actually been nine hours, or only one minute better than *their* figure for the *Swallow*, and that the *Rochester* had left her New York wharf two to three minutes before the *Swallow*. The average speed of the two boats would have been, roughly, 15.3 statute miles an hour. The race had no effect on the heat of the rivalry and for years the two boats raced whenever the opportunity presented itself. For a considerable time they were reputed to be the fastest steamboats in the United States.

The *Swallow* was wrecked on the night of April 7, 1845, in one of the major disasters of Hudson River steamboating. Then running between Troy, Albany and New York, she sailed from Albany with about 250 passengers on board, in company with the *Rochester* and the *Express*. While going down Athens channel in a snow squall, she ran on a rocky islet. Her hull broke open and the stern sank back into the river. Fifteen lives were lost. At the time, the *Swallow* was partly owned by the People's Line, for that organization had emerged victorious in its opposition and there had come to be a People's Line Association to carry on the monopolistic aims of its predecessor.

In the 1840s Hudson River steamboating was at its peak as far as the number of steamers in the New York-Albany service was concerned. When there was competition, fares sometimes dropped to nothing. When there was no competition, they increased to the maximum the traffic would bear and the quality of the service declined. The same old tactics were employed. Competitors were to be beaten off, raced off, foxed off or bought off.

In 1847, the *Niagara*, running as a day boat and with the opposition day boat *Roger Williams* astern, burst a steam chimney, whereby seven passengers were injured and two firemen killed. Fumed an editor:

> It is notorious that the *Niagara* has been racing for six weeks past, and a calamity of this kind has been confidently predicted. It is the game of the old monopoly line to either buy or drive from the river every opposition boat; and the *Roger Williams* not being in the market to be bought off, the *Niagara* was pitted against her to drive her from the river by reducing the fare to nothing, and beating her every trip. But the *Roger* could beat the *Niagara* without an effort,

and hence the necessity of crowding steam upon the latter to the utmost pressure. . . .*

A steamboat passenger who signed himself "R." wrote a letter describing his experiences which were typical of the period. Having occasion to take a night boat at Albany for New York, he looked over the posted handbills and found that there was a People's Line boat with a fifty-cent fare and an opposition steamer at twenty-five cents. He went down to see if the opposition boat was safe to sail on and discovered that she wasn't sailing at all until the following night. Upon going aboard the People's Line steamer, R. found, too, that the fare wasn't fifty cents any more. Now it was one dollar.

He also cited another common practice. A fellow passenger had boarded the boat after being assured that the vessel would stop at the way landing to which he was bound. The steamer sailed right by and he had to get back to his destination on another boat. Wrote R.:

> There does not appear to be any regard to faith or honor in some who conduct the travelling trade. Let one class of (good boats,) . . . keep up the fair [*sic*] inevitably at one dollar, and they need never fear of a good patronage, but in the shameful manner in which opposition and anti-opposition is carried on sometimes on the North River Boats—why its [*sic*] a disgrace to *Mexico*. I would not stand in the mean position of making a living by any trickery upon travellers for the best boat on the waters. But the fellows have got so callous to it, that it has become second nature to them.†

In those periods when the People's Line was unopposed on its night service, an editor said, "Old worn out boats are used, while their best vessels are laid up in ordinary."

The two finest night boats on the river at this point (1847) were the *Hendrik Hudson* and the *Isaac Newton* of the People's Line. They were also the largest steamboats on the river and had long and elaborate grand saloons on the second or promenade deck, with a range of staterooms on either side. The *Hendrik Hudson*, which sailed from New York on October 8, 1845, on her first trip to Albany, had been enrolled months before as the *Hendrick Hudson* and was so carried in Government records. This may have been due to a clerical error or because the line intended to spell the name that way. If the latter were true, there

Ulster Republican, Kingston, N. Y., August 4, 1847.
†*Mechanics' Journal*, Albany, N. Y., June 26, 1847.

was a change of mind between the enrollment and the completion of the vessel. The *Isaac Newton*, named for a major figure in the line, not the famous scientist, entered service exactly a year to the day after the *Hendrik Hudson* and was equipped with a machine for generating illuminating gas for the chandeliers in the grand saloon. Both vessels carried boilers on the guards and a vertical beam engine and were advertised as the "new steam palaces."

Large as the *Hendrik Hudson* (329′9″) and the *Isaac Newton* (320′7″) may have been, they were soon to be eclipsed by the still larger *New World* (352′8″), enrolled in December 1848 and placed in service on the People's Line day line in June of 1849. The New York *Herald* reported that she was the largest vessel afloat in the world. When she appeared on the Hudson, crowds turned out to see this giant of a steamboat and were properly impressed by her size and her costly fittings and furnishings. Not until 1906 was a day boat longer than the *New World* to be built for the Hudson.

A traveler described her as ". . . a filigree framework of white wood surrounding a huge engine, which is much too conspicuous." But he also found the *New World* ". . . a very pleasant place. It has a light, airy, open and clean deck, whence you may spy the shyest nook of scenery upon the banks, and a spacious cabin, where you do not dine at a huge table, with eager men plunging their forks into dishes before you, and their elbows into your sides, but quietly and pleasantly as at a Parisian cafe. . . ."*

Early in the autumn of 1851 the Hudson River Railroad was opened for business along the east bank of the river between New York City and Greenbush, opposite Albany. No longer did the steamboats dominate the New York-Albany trade, for the trains could puff up and down all year 'round, winter and summer. The man who was in a hurry was not likely to buy a ticket on a steamboat that had just won the last race. Instead, he would head for the railroad station.

Railroad or not, competition continued keen on the river in 1852. A new steamer to enter service that year on the day route was the *Francis Skiddy* (312′7″). Her appearance was most unusual, for into her was incorporated a rarely used boiler arrangement. Instead of two on the guards, she had four—one ahead of and one abaft the paddle box on either side, giving her a quartet of smoke-

stacks. Later on the *Francis Skiddy* was converted to a night boat and for a time in 1853 ran between New York and Albany in a dual capacity, going one way as a day boat and returning as a night boat.

For the day lines 1852 was far from a happy year. In fact, it was a black one in river history. On July 28, the day boat *Henry Clay*, Captain John F. Tallman, southbound and the winner in a race with the *Armenia*, took fire. She was run ashore at Riverdale to be consumed by the flames, with a loss of life that has been placed at about seventy. On September 4, the northbound *Reindeer* had started her engine to leave Bristol Landing, Malden, about 1:15 in the afternoon, when the flue-box connection of a boiler exploded. In all, 36 died. The *Reindeer* could not be accused of racing, for she was the only through northbound day boat that day, and at the time of the accident was about an hour late. The *Reindeer* was not much damaged and was to have been towed to New York for repairs on September 10. About four that morning she was discovered to be afire and was destroyed. Spurred by the *Henry Clay* disaster, Congress passed a bill for a more rigorous inspection of steam vessels and a broader control over the manner in which they were operated.

The New Jersey Steamboat Co. was formed in 1854 to carry on the business of the People's Line. The name was not indicative of any change in the route, for the company's principal tie to New Jersey was that it had been incorporated under the laws of that state. The People's Line under the new organization was to be operated exclusively as an express night line for freight and passengers between New York and Albany. It was to maintain its supremacy of that trade and to continue as the most important of the night lines on the Hudson. Isaac Newton was the first president of the New Jersey Steamboat Co. and Daniel Drew the treasurer. Newton died in 1858 and Drew succeeded to the presidency.

The company held onto the three "giants" of the old People's Line Association, the *Isaac Newton*, *Hendrik Hudson* and *New World*, the latter of which had previously done some duty as a night boat. To retain the patronage of first class passengers and to meet the competition of the railroad, the company decided to rebuild the *New World* so in proportions and splendor she would be unlike any night boat heretofore seen on the river. In the course of this work the hull was widened by about one-third. Besides a tier of staterooms on the second deck, she had another tier above that. The

---

*George William Curtis, *Lotus Eating: A Summer Book*, pp. 29-30.

PEOPLES LINE BETWEEN NEW YORK AND ALBANY.

New Steamer Hendrik Hudson, the largest now in America.

This Endicott lithograph of the *Hendrik Hudson* shows well the method employed to strengthen the long wooden hull. The heavy timber truss or hogframe runs fore and aft; tie rods descend from the spars to give further support to the hull, and to the overhanging guards at critical points. The boilers are on the guards; the walking beam is linked at its after end to the crosshead of the piston rod, and connected at its forward end to the crank of the paddle-wheel shaft. The two ovals near the top of the paddle box are breathers to relieve inside pressure, and in the center of the paddle box is a decorative painting of the Hudson River. Although built as a night boat and used primarily as such, the *Hendrik Hudson* saw some service on the New York-Albany day route. The larger *New World*, depicted here as a day boat, was also operated by the People's Line which, as may be seen in the caption on the lithograph above, sometimes eliminated the apostrophe in its name.—*Photographs, Elwin M. Eldredge coll.*

The four-boilered *Francis Skiddy* first appeared on the river as a day boat *(above)*. When she was later altered into a night boat, the Endicott & Company advertising lithograph was similarly altered. Notice the same top-hatted gentleman reclining on shore and waving leisurely in both pictures, and many of the day passengers continuing their never-ending journey on the night boat.—*Photographs, Elwin M. Eldredge coll.*

grand saloon rose from the second deck to the shelter deck over the upper tier, with a gallery around it on the third deck. Her interior ornamentation was considered magnificent, with carvings, gilt-work, mirrors, oil paintings and expensive carpetry. After the rebuilding, she reentered service on September 6, 1855, and was the talk of the river. To have a suitable companion boat for the *New World*, the company rebuilt the *Isaac Newton* on the same grand scale after the season of 1855. Since the *Isaac Newton* was cut in two and lengthened, she exceeded the *New World* in massiveness. The two made an impressive pair of night boats.

While we have thus far mentioned only service between New York and Albany, there were many other lines on the river. Water connections from Albany up to Troy by small steamer began early and not long after the break-up of the Fulton-Livingston monopoly, Troy had through service of its own. Likewise, communities of size along the river were soon supporting steamboat lines from their wharves to New York City. Eventually there was not a landing worthy of the name which was not a port of call for at least one steamboat. At first the steamboats on the more local lines were vessels which were too small for service on the through run to Albany, or had been supplanted on that or some other major route on other waters by newer and faster craft. As the local lines prospered, they were able in time to boast of steamboats built exclusively for such routes.

Steamboats were everywhere—a common but glorious sight.

The night boat *Isaac Newton*, which entered service in 1846 a year after the *Hendrik Hudson*, is shown in this Endicott lithograph as she appeared then. Measurements given in the lower margin are figures arrived at by the Line, which also included for the benefit of prospective passengers the information that the vessel had "wrought iron shafts and cranks."—*Photograph, Elwin M. Eldredge coll.*

PEOPLES LINE BETWEEN NEW YORK AND ALBANY.

New Low pressure Steamer Isaac Newton, the largest in the new or old world.

W. H. Peck, Commander.

COMMERCIAL LINE
OF
Steam-Boats,
AND
SAFETY-BARGES.

The public are respectfully informed, that the new Steam-Boat *Commerce*, to which is at tached the spacious Safety-Barge *Lady Clinton*, is now employed in transporting freight an passengers upon the Hudson River.

The *Commerce* is an elegant and stanch built Boat of 270 tons burthen, drawing 46 inches water, with an engine of great power and upon the most improved construction, and has genteel accommodations for about sixty passengers. Many more can be accommodated if necessary. The Cabins are remarkably safe and pleasant; and that on deck is covered by a substantial roof, forming a promenade of upwards of 60 feet in length by 40 in breadth. The Boat has also a forward and after hold for the accommodation of freight, with all necessary apparatus for receiving and discharging the same with advantage, and is capable of carrying 150 tons of merchandise or produce with convenience.

To attain that degree of safety and comfort for passengers which has long been considered a desideratum, the proprietors have been induced to build and equip the Safety-Barge *Lady Clinton*, which is towed by the *Commerce* in such a manner and with such speed, as to remove all reasonable objections to this mode of conveyance.

This Boat is near 200 tons burthen, and fitted exclusively for passengers, with a dining Cabin of nearly 90 feet in length, a deck Cabin for the accommodation of ladies, a range of state rooms for private families, a reading room, and all the usual accommodations found in the best steam boats. Over the whole, is a promenade deck, more than 100 feet in length, furnished with settees, and covered with a good awning; the whole forming, perhaps, the best and most inviting establishment, for the purpose, ever offered to the public.

Passengers on board the Safety-Barge, will not be in the least expose to any accident which may happen by reason of the fire or steam board of the Steam-Boat; the noise of the machinery, the tremblin of the boat, the heat from the furnace, boilers and kitchen, and ever thing which may be considered as unpleasant or dangerous on board a Steam-Boat, are entirely avoided in the Safety-Barge.

It is the intention of the proprietors to establish a daily line of th description between New-York, and the cities of Albany and Troy.

For this purpose, the new Steam-Boat *Swiftsure*, of the same dime sions with the *Commerce*, will soon be put in operation, and will be a tended by a Safety-Barge, equal in accommodations to the *Lady Clinto*

The proprietors having been duly incorporated by the name a style of the **STEAM NAVIGATION COMPANY**, with a capital three hundred thousand dollars, "for the purpose of transporting freig and passengers, and transacting other business incident thereto," hav established an agency at 137 Washington-street, where the bus ness of the concern will be transacted. Arrangements will soon be mad by the Company, for the forwarding of merchandize on the Canals, a to almost any part of the United States.

The attention of Merchants, and others, is respectfully invited to th establishment.

New-York, July 30th, 1825.

W. C. REDFIELD,
Agent for the Steam Navigation Company

Clayton & Van Norden, Printers, 64 Pine-street.

Advertisement for the Steam Navigation Co.—*Photograph, Elwin M. Eldredge coll.*

Chapter 2

THE VAN SANTVOORDS ARRIVE

INTO THE ARENA of Hudson River steamboating at the beginning of its busiest days came Abraham Van Santvoord. Of Dutch ancestry, he had been born in Schenectady, New York, on December 18, 1784, and at the age of 14 was established in the home of his granduncle, John Post, who was in the shipping business at Utica, New York. Van Santvoord later succeeded to the business of freight transportation on the Mohawk River, expanded the operations and prospered. During the War of 1812 he served as a subcontractor for supplying provisions and as a Government storekeeper. In 1815 and 1816 he was a prominent municipal official of Utica and at this period entered into a glass manufacturing business which was not successful. He then went to Schenectady and again became engaged in the shipping and freighting business. Van Santvoord was a supporter of the Erie Canal and became an operator on it after it was built.

In 1825 the Steam Navigation Co. placed into service on the Hudson River the "safety barge" *Lady Clinton.* She had been planned for passengers exclusively and offered all the luxury of steamboat travel without the necessity of being in proximity to an engine and boilers, for the *Lady Clinton* moved sedately along between New York and Albany off the stern of the steamboat *Commerce*, which towed her. The *Commerce* also had passenger accommodations and could stow up to 150 tons of freight. Soon the Steam Navigation Co., which had been incorporated ". . . for the purpose of transporting freight and passengers and towing vessels by the power of Steam. . . .," added another safety barge and steamboat, the *Lady Van Rensselaer* and the *Swiftsure*. Even the names of the safety barges were intended to inspire visions of decorum and comfort.

The Steam Navigation Co., although not the first to do so, next established a line of steam towboats in 1826. At that time "steam towboat" did not mean a towing steamer, but rather a boat that was towed by a steamer. In this case the towboats

were freight barges with limited passenger accommodations, suitable for carrying everything from general merchandise and produce to livestock and carriages. The safety barges were to be a relatively short-lived experiment, because a steamboat towing one of them obviously could not make as good time as a steamboat running unencumbered. Speed was as important then as it is today and those who preferred to travel safely and leisurely were in the minority. The business of operating freight barges and towing steamers became a lucrative one. The opening of the Erie Canal in 1825 resulted in a steady increase in the amount of freight moving on the Hudson and through the years long tows of barges and canal boats became a familiar sight.

Abraham Van Santvoord was the New York agent for the Steam Navigation Co. in 1826. While of course he became involved in other phases of steam navigation, his interest in the towing business was continuing and in 1845 he was one of the organizers and the first president of the Hudson River Steamboat Co., which was formed in February of that year to carry on the towing trade as the "Old Line Steam Tow Boats."

Van Santvoord had married Sarah Hitchcock, a daughter of Alfred Hitchcock of Utica, on December 24, 1812, and fathered three sons—Cornelius, Abraham and Alfred. Alfred had been born in Utica on January 23, 1819, and after being educated in public schools in Jersey City, New Jersey and Farmington, Connecticut, followed his father into the steamboat business. He was connected with the towing industry and for a time with the People's Line.

The large towing steamers on the Hudson had all been former passenger steamboats which had been superseded by faster and better vessels. In 1848 the Hudson River Steamboat Co. built the first of the large sidewheel towing steamers to be designed specifically for that work. She was the *Oswego* and Alfred Van Santvoord is said to have had a hand in the planning of her. She was not by

These J. and J. Bard paintings show the *Alida* and the *Armenia* as they appeared when they entered New York-Albany day service in 1847 and 1848 respectively. While the *Alida* was initially used largely on the route for some years, the smaller *Armenia* was often withdrawn for other service. A number of years passed before she commenced a span of uninterrupted seasons on the run.—Alida: *photograph, Elwin M. Eldredge coll.;* Armenia: *Shelburne Museum, Shelburne, Vermont, where the painting is exhibited on the preserved steamboat* Ticonderoga.

any means the first vessel to be constructed exclusively for towing, but was the first large steamer to be built for this duty on the Hudson.

Alfred Van Santvoord has been described as an energetic man, with sound financial judgment, a dominating personality and a high sense of honor. He became the Albany agent for the Hudson River Steamboat Co., married Anna Margaret Townsend—daughter of Absalom Townsend of Albany—in 1852 and remained in Albany for years before moving to New York City. Like his father, he had other interests in steamboating besides the towing trade.

One of these interests was to be the steamboat *Alida* (249'5"), built in 1847 at New York City. Placed in service as a day boat between New York and Albany, she proved both speedy and popular. A waltz was written in her honor. In November 1852 the *Alida* went into service between New York City and Wilbur on Rondout Creek, a tributary of the Hudson. Although the terminus was later changed from Wilbur to the village of Rondout, the *Alida* continued to ply out of the creek through her 1855 season. Then, in November, she was sold at auction and acquired by Alfred Van Santvoord for an amount in excess of $20,000. In 1856 Van Santvoord placed her again on the day line between New York and Albany. She ran with the *Armenia* (181'9"), which was independently owned, but the two boats together formed a regular line. One went up when the other went down, except on Sunday when there was no service.

The *Armenia* originally had one boiler in the hold with a single tall smokestack abaft the pilothouse, but later had two boilers and two smokestacks. Because of her 14-foot cylinder stroke, the gallows frame for the walking beam was extremely high in comparison with her length. She was first enrolled on April 21, 1848, under the ownership of Captain John F. Tallman, who then commanded her; Thomas Collyer, who built her hull; and two other men. The next day she was placed on the New York and Albany route as an opposition day boat. She was a fast vessel, but not particularly impressive in dimensions for that service. She had a succession of shareholders and in the fall of 1848 was enrolled for the fifth time that year with Isaac P., Abraham P., D.D. and Tunis Smith of Nyack among the nine men who owned her and of whom Thomas Collyer was still one. In the summer of 1849 she was enrolled with the Smiths alone as owners and these were finally whittled to Isaac P. Smith who commanded her.

Before the close of the season of 1856, Captain Smith announced that he was going to have new boilers installed in the *Armenia* and that she would be lengthened and otherwise improved to make her more in keeping with the larger *Alida*. A contract for the boilers was made and they were duly fitted, but the lengthening did not come to pass. As it developed, this mattered little, for the *Alida* did not continue as a day boat in 1857. Instead, she became a towing steamer in the fleet of the Hudson River Steamboat Co., to which her ownership was subsequently transferred. Abraham Van Santvoord was still president of the company and continued to serve until his death on August 12, 1858.

On the day route between New York and Albany in 1857, the *Armenia* ran in line with the *Broadway*, built in 1837 as the *Arrow*. After a rebuilding she had been given a new name, but not officially, for by enrollment she remained the *Arrow*. And in 1858 and 1859, the *Armenia* ran with the *Metamora*. The latter vessel was commanded at this time by Captain John F. Tallman.

In 1858 it had been reported that a new sidewheeler, the *Daniel Drew*, had been contracted for and would run in place of the *Metamora* in 1859. This was premature, for the *Daniel Drew* was not ready for service until 1860.

In view of the fact that this vessel would be over sixty feet longer than the *Armenia* Captain Smith decided that he now at last must lengthen his steamer. Although two vessels might be independently owned and run together to form a line, that did not mean competition between them was nonexistent. Passengers could arrange their travelling to coincide with the sailing of the larger or faster vessel; the steamer that offered the most would probably get more of the business. The competition at times bordered on the senseless. For example, on a day in 1859 the *Armenia* and the *Metamora*, going of course in opposite directions, both raced madly for the landing at Poughkeepsie, with one giving way only at the last moment.

Captain Smith had previously installed a steam calliope on the *Armenia*, so that his passengers were ". . . entertained by the Musical Wonder. . . ." Now he needed increased size. Between the 1859 and 1860 seasons the boat was cut in half forward of the paddle wheels and drawn out to an even 200 feet in length. She was improved otherwise and smokers learned ". . . with satisfaction that a room expressly for fumigating has been fitted up on board." On her first up-trip of the season, April

4, 1860, this "Queen of the Waters" ran from New York to Albany in a claimed 7 hours 14 minutes running time.

By June the new *Daniel Drew* was ready for service. She was named for the same Daniel Drew who was president of the New Jersey Steamboat Co., operating the People's Line. Drew appeared on her first papers as sole owner, although Thomas Collyer who built her hull had an investment in her. On June 4, by prior agreement, the *Daniel Drew* and the *Armenia* raced from New York to Newburgh without passengers. The newcomer won by anywhere from four to seven minutes and the following day entered regular service.

Her vertical beam engine is said to have been constructed originally by the Morgan Iron Works for the Sandy Hook towing steamer *Titan*, also built by Thomas Collyer, which was subsequently wrecked. The Neptune Iron Works installed this engine in the *Daniel Drew*. She had two boilers on the guards and carried hogframes and two spars, one forward and the other aft. On the second or promenade deck there was little but the pilothouse with quarters behind it. A light shelter deck ran aft from the top of the quarters to abaft the after spar. From there to the stern was a framework for an awning to protect those passengers who chose to sit on the after promenade. Later on a saloon was built on this deck forward and the pilothouse placed atop it on the third deck. These top or hurricane decks on the day steamers of the period were exclusively a shelter deck and were not intended for use by the passengers. As far as design was concerned, a deficiency of the 244-foot *Daniel Drew* seems to have been that she tended to be cranky—that is, she listed easily.

The new and swift *Daniel Drew* entered service in 1860.—*Photograph of painting, Elwin M. Eldredge coll.*

A traveller described her as plain but tasteful, without either gingerbread or overgilding. He found her handsomely furnished and roomy, with a large and well-ventilated dining room where the tables were plentifully loaded. The dining room, of course, was in the after hold. Also available on board were a smoking room, hot and cold baths and a few staterooms. These last were carried on the day boats for rental by invalids, the otherwise sick and the dead tired.

In 1860 Alfred Van Santvoord again entered the Hudson River passenger business, once more using the *Alida* on which he had expended about $22,000 for repairs, alterations and furnishings. He ran her on round trips between New York and Poughkeepsie, with stops at Newburgh and other way landings. Besides the usual traffic and the excursionists, he hoped to attract travellers and tourists who wanted to include a trip on the Hudson in their itinerary, but were reluctant to spend a whole day on the river. These could go on the *Alida* to Poughkeepsie and continue from there by train, with a free baggage transfer provided.

The *Alida* was advertised to commence running on June 23, leaving Jay Street, New York, at 8:30 a.m. and arriving back in New York about 6:30 p.m. She closed her season in the latter half of September and afterwards returned to the more humble role of a towing steamer. Alfred Van Santvoord's second venture in running day boats on the Hudson had ended.

The *Daniel Drew* made her last through up-trip of the season on October 13 and was pushed in quest of a record. She made it in 7 hours 20 minutes elapsed time, with a claimed landing allowance of 30 minutes.

In that year of 1860 the Prince of Wales—later King Edward VII—made a tour of Canada and the United States as Lord Renfrew and on October 16 the *Daniel Drew* carried the royal party from West Point to Albany. Preparatory to the auspicious occasion, new carpets and crockery had been placed on board and the paintwork touched up so that the steamer would appear at her best. It was reported that Daniel Drew had placed the steamer at the disposal of the mayors of New York and Albany for the occasion. Then, carried away by the magnificence of the event, he apparently invited a hundred friends to go along and planned a sumptuous collation to be served aboard. At this point the Duke of Newcastle communicated with Mr. Drew and told him that it was the policy of the royal party to pay all expenses while in the

United States and that they would charter the steamer. Drew had no alternative but to withdraw his invitations and received an amount said to have been $1,300 for the use of his boat.

The *Daniel Drew* was now the cock of the river. She had made her record run on October 13 and three days later carried the most distinguished personage to travel on the Hudson that season. On October 17 there was handed to the press a challenge, the wording of which varied slightly in the papers in which it appeared:

> Notice to Steamboat Proprietors.—The steamboat *Daniel Drew* having discontinued her trips on the day route for the season, will, for the purpose of gratifying the curiosity of certain individuals, hold herself in readiness until the 27th of the present month to make a Trial Trip from New York to Albany with any steamer now built, for One Thousand Dollars or upwards, on one week's notice from this date; the boats to start from the foot of 30th street, North River, at 8 o'clock A.M.; to run with the same tackle as used in their ordinary business.
>
> Any person or persons that have a steamer which they think can beat her, can have an opportunity to make a profitable trip, by calling on the subscriber, 283 Broadway, Albany.
>
> J. W. Harcourt
>
> October 17th, 1860.

Since the *Daniel Drew* had already bested the *Armenia*, this challenge was taken to be aimed at the *Alida*. But it may have been directed as well at the *Thomas Powell*, a speedy day boat operating in round-trip service between Rondout and New York. In any event, the 27th came and went and no one accepted the challenge.

Daniel Drew in time sold out his interest in the steamer which bore his name, but the *Daniel Drew* continued to run as a day boat between New York and Albany. In her first season on the Hudson and again in 1862, she was commanded by Captain John F. Tallman, who came to dub her the "Honey Cooler."

She still ran with the *Armenia* to form a regular line. The latter had been lengthened again, this time aft of the paddle wheels, between the seasons of 1860 and 1861. Perhaps that was the only case in steamboat history where a vessel was lengthened first ahead of the paddle wheels and then behind them in such rapid succession.

The *Daniel Drew* and the *Armenia* plied through the seasons of 1861 and 1862 with no apparent competition to disturb them.

For this painting of the *City of Albany* in 1863, James Bard charged $20. Today his works are treasured museum pieces.—*Photograph, Hudson River Day Line coll., Steamship Historical Society of America, Inc.*

When the *New World* came back to the river in 1855 after an extensive rebuilding, she carried two tiers of staterooms. As so shown in a lithograph, she was far different in appearance from the day boat illustrated on page 9.—*Photograph, Elwin M. Eldredge coll.*

Chapter 3

THE BEGINNINGS OF A NEW DAY LINE

O F THE STEAMBOAT LINES running on the Hudson in the 1860s and not having a terminal in New York City, the hardiest was the Newburgh and Albany day line. Indeed, it was sufficiently hardy to survive after a fashion through 1928.

The Newburgh and Albany day line was little like the New York and Albany day line. The small steamboats which plied on it took much of the day to cover the route, and called for freight and passengers at most of the landings along the way. It was probably a historic event when a passenger went completely through from one terminus to the other. He would have been a man who either delighted in a leisurely jaunt on the river, or gained satisfaction from watching freight being hauled on and off all day long. In short, he would have been something like a nineteenth century version of the tramp-ship tourist.

One similarity between the Newburgh and Albany and the New York and Albany day lines in the early 1860s was that they had come to be operated in the same manner. Daily service in either direction was afforded by separately owned steamboats. The stronger operator in the Newburgh-Albany field was the well-known Rondout firm of Romer & Tremper, running the *Eagle.*

In the fall of 1861 announcement was made that a new and superior sidewheeler was being built at D. C. Terry's shipyard at Keyport, New Jersey, for the Newburgh and Albany route. She was being constructed for Alfred Van Santvoord, Jacob Leonard and Captain David H. Hitchcock. Leonard was an Albany businessman and, like Van Santvoord, was to supply 40% of the capital. The remaining 20% was invested by Captain Hitchcock, who was pushing open the door to days of glory. We shall hear more of him in pages to come.

The three men seem to have toyed with the idea of naming their new steamboat *City of Albany,* but decided on *Jesse Hoyt.* Under the command of Captain Hitchcock, she was placed on the Newburgh and Albany day line on May 14,

1862, running opposite the *Eagle* in place of a smaller vessel which had been withdrawn for Government charter, this being the time of the Civil War.

The *Jesse Hoyt* was the most impressive vessel ever placed on this route up to that time. As a result of her excellence, she made her last trip in the service on June 2, for she had been snapped up by new owners to run between New York City and the north shore of Long Island. Van Santvoord, Leonard and Hitchcock had gained about $6,800 for division amongst them.

The *Jesse Hoyt* had not been long disposed of before Van Santvoord was having another passenger steamboat built. Once more Jacob Leonard and Captain Hitchcock were in the business with him, with each of the three holding a one-quarter interest. The rest of the partnership was Captain John P. Acker and Captain George H. Power, who held one-eighth interests. Both Power and Acker were experienced steamboatmen. Captain Power had commanded steamboats in the Poughkeepsie-Albany and Newburgh-Albany day line trade in the 1840s, while amongst Captain Acker's past accomplishments was commanding the big *New World* on the New York and Albany day line.

Just what these men had in mind when they laid plans for this boat cannot now be determined. From her general design and her light draft, it would appear that they intended to run her on the upper Hudson. Perhaps they constructed her with the idea of using her on the Newburgh and Albany day line, or the Catskill and Albany day line, a route similar in operation to the Newburgh and Albany day line, but sufficiently short so that one boat could cover it in both directions in a day. A new steamer, the *City of Hudson,* had gone into service on the Catskill-Albany route in August of 1862 and had barely had time to become acquainted with it before she was taken over by the Government. Indeed, their prime motive may have been to sell their steamer to the Government. They well knew that wherever they ran her, they could probably dispose of her to the Government before long at a handsome profit. At times the Government was interested in almost anything that would float and the Civil War was a bonanza to many a steamboat operator.

Late in November of 1862, the hull of the new steamboat was quietly launched from the shipyard of Brainard & Lawlor at East Albany, New York. There was not even a christening to brighten the occasion. On Saturday night, November 29, the towing steamer *Anna* hauled the hull off to New York where the building was to be completed.

Whatever the original intentions of Van Santvoord and his associates may have been, they had made up their minds by late March of 1863. They let it be known that the new steamboat, which would be called the *City of Albany,* would run as a day boat between New York and Albany.

It seems unlikely that they were deluding themselves into believing that they could make a go of it in that service with the *City of Albany.* She was exactly 200 feet in length, which would give her little drawing power against the *Daniel Drew.* The *Armenia* was only about 14 feet longer and growing old, but she was still a fast stepper with a considerable following. If they had originally had the New York and Albany day line in mind when they commenced the *City of Albany,* in all probability they would have planned something more impressive than she.

The *Daniel Drew,* in her first three seasons on the river, had not commenced operations until many weeks after the *Armenia* appeared, and went into winter hibernation before that boat. Since the *Armenia* was likely cheaper to operate, Captain Smith seems to have found it worth his while to run up the Hudson with the first whiff of spring, and to keep running to Albany as long as practical. The *Daniel Drew's* owners were content to confine their vessel to the period of the heavier movement of passengers.

The year of 1863 was no exception and, in fact, the *Daniel Drew* was apparently involved in the settlement of the affairs of one of her owners, Thomas Collyer, who had died. In May she was to be sold at auction evidently so that the estate could be satisfied. Van Santvoord and his colleagues, therefore, could feel perfectly safe in arranging to run the *City of Albany* on opposite days to the *Armenia.* They would have ample time to do such things as testing the capabilities of the steamer and when the *Daniel Drew* appeared. . . . Well, that was for the future.

The *City of Albany* arrived at Albany for the first time on Sunday morning, May 3. She had come up from New York without passengers so that she could be put to an initial test, and probably because Van Santvoord wanted to have her first regular trip commence from Albany. The citizens of that place were proud of the fact that her hull had been built just across the river at East Albany, and that a businessman of their city was guiding the enterprise.

On her first trip to Albany, it was announced that she had covered the distance from New York to Poughkeepsie in less than 3 hours 40 minutes. This was not sensational, but of course her engine was brand-new.

The *City of Albany* was typical of the smaller beam-engined sidewheel steamboats then com-

Here is a James Bard painting of the *Daniel Drew* in her early days on the river, with a fine assortment of flags flying in the breeze.—*Photograph, Elwin M. Eldredge coll.*

mon in eastern waters. The main deck forward was open, but could be covered by a canvas awning to afford shade for the passengers who cared to sit there. Her saloon on the second deck was commodious. A few staterooms were also available, fitted with rosewood couch bedsteads. The steamer had one spar forward and one aft, and her single smokestack was abaft the cabin behind the pilothouse. Catering to passengers exclusively, she carried no freight.

Needless to say, her captain was "Dave" Hitchcock, who proudly sailed her away from Albany on her first trip in business on Monday morning, May 4. She used the same New York pier at the foot of Harrison Street as the *Armenia* and ran on the same schedule, leaving Albany at 9 a.m. and New York at 7 a.m. She was advertised to stop at 30th Street in New York, connect with the Tarrytown-Nyack ferryboat (later omitted) and call at West Point, Newburgh, Poughkeepsie, Rhinebeck landing (Rhinecliff), Malden, Catskill and Hudson. At this time the *Armenia* made those same landings and also called at Cozzens' and Haverstraw.

Before mid-May it was announced from Washington that Van Santvoord had offered the *City of Albany* to the Government for $85,000—about $29,000 over her net cost. Later on came another report that Captain I. P. Smith had also offered his *Armenia* to the Government for $75,000. The *Armenia* was to be passed over, but the new *City of Albany* was considered desirable. On June 1 she made her last trip on this short-lived Van Santvoord day line and two days later was acquired by the Quartermaster's Department for $82,000.

While she was in service, the *City of Albany* took in over $4,900, including at least eight dollars in counterfeit money, but the disbursements came to about $5,575. That was a minor matter. When all was done, the partners had approximately $24,000 for division. In those days, it wasn't a bad take at all, and the *City of Albany* had proved a good investment.

When the *City of Albany* went off to the war, the *Armenia* was left to run alone until June 16 when the *Daniel Drew* went into commission.

Van Santvoord was once more out of the New York and Albany day line picture, but his absence was not to be for long. Soon he was closing in again, and this time he had allied with him John McB. Davidson and Chauncey Vibbard. Negotiations for the *Daniel Drew* bore fruit and on Saturday, September 5, 1863, she made her first trip up the river under their proprietorship.

The purchase had been made from James T. and George B. Collyer, and H. W. Johnson, who held respectively 11/16, 4/16 and 1/16 of the shares in the *Daniel Drew*. On Monday, September 7, there was recorded in Van Santvoord's ledger the issuance of three separate checks in favor of George B. Collyer in the total amount of $77,500. Van Santvoord supplied half and Davidson and Vibbard equally the other half.

Immediately the new owners announced that they would build a larger boat to run with the *Daniel Drew* in 1864. This meant that they would have a complete line of their own, independent of any other operator, and that they would be competing directly with the *Armenia*. The news must have given Captain Smith considerable food for

The *Armenia* sports two stacks abreast in a painting by an unknown artist.—*Eldredge coll., Mariners Museum, Newport News, Va.*

thought. He knew that he could not oppose the *Daniel Drew* for long if she ran against his steamer, and he would be in an even worse position if the new boat were pitted against him. He had been in a selling mood earlier in the year and the latest development probably increased his inclination in that direction.

Soon he sold the *Armenia* to Van Santvoord and Davidson for $53,000. The total acquisition cost was $55,000 to include "barges," presumably coal barges used in refueling. The first trip of the *Armenia* under the new management was on October 6, one day before the bill of sale was signed.

Now that at last Van Santvoord had achieved his ambition to control the New York and Albany day line, it may be well to cast an eye at the two men who were at this time associated with him.

Chauncey Vibbard had been born in Galway, New York, on November 11, 1811. He clerked for a time in a wholesale grocery in Albany, in a wholesale dry-goods house in New York and then worked for about two years in Montgomery, Alabama, as a bookkeeper. Returning to New York State in 1836, he became chief clerk of the new Utica & Schenectady Railroad, which came to be considered one of the best-run railroads in the country.

Vibbard was an early advocate of consolidation of the short railroads like the Utica & Schenectady which together connected Albany and Buffalo. This was finally accomplished in 1853 with the formation of the New York Central Rail Road Co., of which Vibbard was the first superintendent.

Amongst other things, he was a large holder in a liquor business. Here was a conflict of interest, because as a railroadman he killed off his liquor customers! Each year he included in the annual report of the railroad a required listing of all people who met their death on the New York Central. Always there was a goodly representation of drunks who either injudiciously walked in front of his trains or went to sleep on the tracks.

The New York Central was important to the New York and Albany day line. The railroad could steer passengers from the west down the Hudson on steamboats instead of on the Hudson River Railroad. Therefore Vibbard's position was all to the good. Vibbard himself probably regarded the New York and Albany day line only as an investment and had no great interest in it otherwise. Years later he wrote to Van Santvoord to inquire as to when the *Daniel Drew* and the *Armenia* had been purchased.

John McB. Davidson has come to be the forgotten man of the line. He was born on August 29, 1824, as the posthumous son of Alexander Davidson of the firm of Root & Davidson, an Albany mercantile house of the early nineteenth century. At the age of 15, young John McB. Davidson went to work in the hardware store of Erastus Corning & Co., where an elder brother, Gilbert C. Davidson, also worked. John chose to challenge life on his own and eventually purchased a small Albany foundry where he manufactured hollow ware. He prospered and next branched into what was then an infant industry: the making of fireproof and burglarproof safes. Davidson's safes were apparently just that, for his orders in time so exceeded his capacity for production that he moved to a larger foundry.

Now he had room to spare and delved into another unlikely business by building an iron railroad freight car, said to have been the first one built in this country. The car was tested by President Corning of the New York Central and found so satisfactory that Davidson was given orders for hundreds of them. From 1860 through 1864 the Central added some 719 iron freight cars to its equipment, although there is no indication as to whether Davidson built them all. The cars that he did build had to be hauled by horses from Davidson's foundry through the streets of Albany to the railroad. Once one of them was in collision with the wagon of a farmer who probably couldn't believe his eyes.

Davidson was a sociable man who had a wide circle of friends and entertained generously. Perhaps he was too socially minded, for it was afterwards said of him that with his opportunities he could have become one of the wealthiest men in New York State. In any event, he became just plain wealthy, which he was when he joined Van Santvoord in the day line in 1863. Eventually he left Albany, usually making his home in New York during the winter and in Saratoga Springs in the summer.

Before long Van Santvoord and Davidson were dividing the profits from the *Daniel Drew* equally. It may be that Vibbard's quarter-interest was simply turned over to Davidson for administration and that some of Davidson's capital remained Vibbard capital. There is no particular reason to doubt that Davidson early bought out Vibbard. So far as its internal workings were concerned, the New York and Albany day line became largely a Van Santvoord-Davidson enterprise, with Van Santvoord as manager.

Chapter 4

ADVENT OF THE *Chauncey Vibbard*

As far as actual operations were concerned, the change in ownership of the *Daniel Drew* and the *Armenia* made no difference to the ordinary passenger. The boats, of course, continued to operate as they had been running.

Since the new owners' talk about a new steamboat was no bluff, one might ask why they bothered to buy the *Armenia* at all. The season of 1863 was drawing to a close and by 1864 they would be able to run her off the river with ease. But by purchasing her peacefully they accomplished two things. They put Captain Smith out of the field painlessly and acquired the goodwill he had built up during years on the New York-Albany route. They gained in the *Armenia* a splendid spare boat, which in those days was a handy thing to have around. A mechanical breakdown was not uncommon and, although there were usually steamboats that could be chartered, these were often inferior and ill-suited to the demands of the trade. This was particularly true during the busy season of the year when, in the case of a serious accident, the securing of a good replacement was almost impossible.

The previous owners of the *Daniel Drew* and the *Armenia* seem always to have operated placidly. Although there was some slight difference in the landing places, they ran on more or less the same schedule and had the same agents at many of the way landings and at Albany. At times, they even ran combined advertisements in the New York papers, but they often inserted separate notices, each headed "Day Boat. . . ." This last was the usual practice in local papers along the Hudson, where the notices were generally carried on a seasonal basis. Consequently, these were continued until the end of the 1863 season.

What must have been the first advertisement of Van Santvoord and his associates in the New York papers appeared on September 30. Although Van Santvoord had previously advertised the *City of Albany* briefly as "Day Line for Albany," this one had the traditional "Day Boat for Albany"

heading. Thereafter it differed by listing the fares. These were: to Yonkers, 20¢; to West Point or Newburgh, 75¢; to Poughkeepsie, $1.00; to Rhinebeck, Tivoli, Catskill or Hudson, $1.25; to Albany, $1.50.

This advertisement was, of course, only for the *Daniel Drew*, which continued as before to leave Jay Street on Tuesdays, Thursdays and Saturdays at 7 a.m. and 30th Street at 7:10 a.m. Then, on October 8, the advertisement was expanded slightly to include the information that the *Armenia* left on the alternate days of Monday, Wednesday and Friday from the foot of Harrison Street.

At the time of these first public notices of what would officially become, decades afterward, the Hudson River Day Line, the line used no particular name. It was still the New York and Albany day line, the day boat line, the day steamboat line, or whatever else one might choose. When it got around to having stationery printed up, the heading ran, "Office of the Day Line of Steamers on the Hudson River." More important than what it called itself was the fact that it was now also largely Van Santvoord and Davidson's line. Hereafter, for simplicity, we shall call it the Day Line.

As soon as the *Daniel Drew* was acquired, Captain David H. Hitchcock strode aboard to take command, like a herald of better days to come. Captain Dave had staked out a claim to be senior captain of the new Day Line through his command of the *City of Albany* earlier in the year. Now that he had the *Daniel Drew*, there was no doubt about it. He was often said to have been "as happy as a lark," and on this occasion he doubtless was.

When Captain Isaac P. Smith sold the *Armenia*, he either was not asked to work for the new proprietors or felt it beneath his dignity to do so. He left the *Armenia* and her steam calliope forever and the command passed to his son, John Perry Smith, who was then in his early thirties. John Perry Smith was a practicing marine engineer and

The great *St. John* of 1864 was the first vessel built by the People's Line in a fleet-renewal project. Wittingly or not, members of the crew standing on the decks accentuate the massiveness of the steamboat. Notice the man standing in the walking beam, and the recessed effect of the elaborately designed paddle box. Next to be constructed was the *Dean Richmond,* shorter by forty-five feet than the *St. John.* The peculiar appearance of the tops of the smokestacks in the *Dean Richmond* picture was due to discoloration by smoke.—*Below: Elwin M. Eldredge coll.*

is said to have been an engineer on the *Armenia* prior to assuming the captaincy. He stayed with her as master until the season ended.

The Day Line kept the *Daniel Drew* in operation in 1863 later than she had ever run. She did not make her final sailing of the year from Albany until November 6. The following day the *Armenia* closed the season and the new Day Line shut up shop for the winter.

Considering the fact that it had not gotten into business until the heavy summer traffic was almost over, the results were not bad. Altogether 21,784 passengers were carried. The *Daniel Drew,* making 54 trips, had taken in over $19,000 in receipts. The *Armenia,* coming into the line only a month before the end of the season and making but 29 trips for her new owners, realized almost $8,000. The net operating earnings for the short period of operation, exclusive of course of any deduction for the cost of acquisition, were about $7,500.

The proprietors had decided ideas as to what they wanted the Day Line to be, and it became obvious that they were not short on capital. In addition to going ahead with the building of the promised new boat, they made preparations to have the *Daniel Drew* lengthened 16 feet so they would have a well-matched pair of steamboats for the 1864 season.

The contract for the hull of the new steamboat was awarded to the firm of Lawrence & Foulks, who had a shipyard in Brooklyn and who launched her during the winter of 1863-1864. When the *Daniel Drew* had first been acquired and announcement was made that a new boat was to be built to run with her, it was said that the steamer would be named for Dean Richmond, the vice president of the New York Central and later the successor of Erastus Corning as president. The name selected, however, was none other than that of Chauncey Vibbard.

For those with an abiding interest in Hudson River steamboating, it is just as well that Dean Richmond's name was not used. In 1864 the New Jersey Steamboat Co., operating the People's Line (New York-Albany night line), built the first of three new sidewheelers in a badly needed replacement program. The newcomer was the mammoth *St. John,* named not for the saint but for Captain A. P. St. John, an important figure in the line. She was 393 feet in length, which allegedly made her the longest steamboat in United States waters, and was about 14 feet longer than one of the giants of the North Atlantic, the new Cunard liner *Scotia.*

The company named its second steamer—348 feet and built in 1865—the *Dean Richmond* and finished its program in 1866 with the 366.5-foot *Drew.* The latter was named of course for Daniel Drew, who was still president of the New Jersey Steamboat Co. While the short form was probably used partly to avoid undue confusion with the day boat, such confusion did and still does exist. Boatmen promptly dubbed the night boat the "big" *Drew* to keep their own minds clear. Having the *Daniel Drew* on the Day Line and the *Drew* on the People's Line was bad enough, but it would have been considerably worse with two *Dean Richmonds.*

All of the new People's Line steamers carried on the same general style of the *New World* and the *Isaac Newton* before them, with boilers on the guards; a vertical beam engine; main deck used largely for freight; two tiers of staterooms above it; elaborate grand saloon.

The Day Line's *Chauncey Vibbard* was not yet ready when the season of 1864 opened. The *Daniel Drew* made the first trip on May 4, sailing from the Desbrosses Street pier where the Day Line had established its New York base. Besides having had 16 feet added to her length, she had been renovated and refurnished at a total cost of $22,500. Her sailing days from New York had been changed to Mondays, Wednesdays and Fridays so that the *Chauncey Vibbard* would have the Tuesday, Thursday and Saturday sailings. These sailing days of the two boats were to remain in effect for it was usually desirable to have the larger steamer available for the Saturday up-trip on which northbound traffic would be heaviest during a good part of the season. The Day Line continued the practice of not operating on Sundays, and in fact did not commence to do so until 1918.

Captain Hitchcock naturally was to have the new boat, so on the *Daniel Drew* was Captain John F. Tallman, who had once again returned to command his beloved "Honey Cooler." She ran alone until May 19, when the *Armenia* was placed in commission to serve until the *Chauncey Vibbard* was ready.

Not even the *Armenia* had been neglected by the new proprietors, for she too had been renovated. Her main saloon on the second deck had been enlarged and she had been fitted with a new pair of boilers at a total cost of $28,000.

The eagerly anticipated first trip of the *Chauncey Vibbard* was finally set for Saturday, June 18. In honor of the occasion, the owners arranged

In paintings by James Bard, here are the *Daniel Drew* after she had been cut in two aft of the paddle boxes and lengthened at the shipyard of D. Burtis, and the *Chauncey Vibbard* when she was new.—*Photographs, Elwin M. Eldredge coll.*

an excursion from Albany to which many in the transportation and newspaper business were invited. The party sailed down as far as Catskill on the *Daniel Drew*. There they disembarked and went to the Catskill House to be treated in "a most liberal manner" until the time for the arrival of the *Chauncey Vibbard* drew near.

As she approached Catskill Point with her colors flying, an assemblage on the landing burst into cheers and cannon fired a salute of welcome. Captain Hitchcock, who had been playing host to a delegation of New York newspapermen, bade the excursion party welcome. They were treated to a tour of the new steamboat and then ushered to the dining saloon, where the tables were laden with seasonal delicacies. The most was made of the opportunity and many a glass was emptied and reemptied in honor of the *Chauncey Vibbard*. Albany, perhaps a little bit blurry, came all too soon. Here the welcome was loud, with whistles blowing, cannon firing and bells ringing a merry greeting. It was hard to imagine the Civil War was far from over.

The *Chauncey Vibbard* (267') was several feet longer than the lengthened *Daniel Drew* and the two vessels were similar in general arrangement and appearance. The wooden hull was strengthened by the usual hogframes and spars. In the case of the *Chauncey Vibbard*, there were originally three spars, two of which were aft and one forward. The latter passed through the center of the pilothouse on the third deck and gave it the appearance of being nailed firmly into place.

With its forward end immediately beneath the pilothouse, the main saloon was plentifully supplied with windows to afford a view of the Hudson scenery. The decorations included a medallion of Erastus Corning cut from marble.

As an innovation, an extension of the deckhouse on the main deck ran forward from the deckhouse proper. Windows were placed around this projection to afford another fine spot from which to watch the river without being exposed to the strong head wind on the open bow.

The ladies' cabin or saloon on the main deck aft was the height of opulence. Here were rosewood furniture, curtains of French lace, and medallion carpeting. Soft and mellow light filtered through the stained glass of a skylight overhead, and both the ceiling of the cabin and the skylight were frescoed in oil, ". . . so perfect one would think he was in an art gallery."

In the forward hold were a number of staterooms, with Brussels carpet, more lace curtains

and black walnut bedsteads. The thickly carpeted dining room was in the after hold, with separate tables seating from six to eight.

The final cost of the *Chauncey Vibbard*, reckoned at $144,000, was a sizeable sum for a vessel of her type and in part was due to the wartime increase in shipbuilding costs. Davidson was half-owner, with the other half divided between Van Santvoord and Captain Hitchcock. Eventually the partners acquired the captain's share and by 1879 had so adjusted their holdings that each owned a half-interest in all three vessels.

Although the official name of the new steamboat was *Chauncey Vibbard*, this name appeared on neither her paddle boxes nor her pilothouse. There it was simply *C. Vibbard*. Perhaps this was done because Mr. Vibbard preferred the abbreviation for his signature. On the other hand, Stephen Rogers, the painting contractor, may have decided that *Chauncey Vibbard* was too long to look presentable in limited space. Whoever made the decision, it was never questioned as long as the steamboat ran on the Hudson, for the name on the paddle boxes and pilothouse and often in printed matter, remained *C. Vibbard*. Decades later the steamboat was sold for service on the Delaware River, where the bulk of her passengers had probably never heard of Chauncey Vibbard. Then, at last, the full name was spread on her paddle boxes and looked quite well, at that.

One other point regarding her is worthy of some comment. All people who have traveled in ships and steamboats of the United States are familiar with the fact that the pilothouse or bridge is the holy of holies from which all but properly qualified persons are barred. The immediate area is studded with prohibiting signs. But that was not always so.

In the earlier days of Hudson River steamboating, passengers could wander in and out of the pilothouse at will. Many preferred it as the best spot on the boat from which to watch the scenery. How the pilots liked this depended upon their personalities. Some welcomed company and regaled them with tales of the river, while less sociable souls hated the intruders. On one boat which had her pilot wheel set well back in the pilothouse, the pilot always found making a landing difficult because passengers blocked off his vision by standing between him and the windows.

The Day Line seems to have realized the peril of having the pilot constantly distracted from his duties before passengers were legally barred from

Hudson River pilothouses. This was not the case, though, when the *Chauncey Vibbard* came out. It is said that her pilothouse was fitted in particularly luxurious fashion, with easy chairs specifically for the benefit of those passengers who liked to travel in pilothouses. These chairs rented for a substantial fee and to get one it was usually necessary to make a reservation weeks in advance.

With the coming of the *Chauncey Vibbard*, Van Santvoord and Davidson made it apparent that advertising was another of the many things about which they had marked ideas. Prospective travellers for years had been treated to nothing but a dull recitation of landings and leaving time. Now, suddenly, they found confronting them something more alluring—"Pleasure travel." The Day Line for Albany wanted you to know that it could do more than simply carry you up or down the river. It offered the enticement of far-away places and exotic spots on the landscape, the jour-ney to which you could begin on its steamers. "Pleasure travel to Catskill Mountain House, Lebanon Springs, Saratoga, Montreal, and all points North and West, via the Hudson river." You could buy your ticket on board and your baggage would be checked either west or north.

The Day Line was now as Van Santvoord and Davidson had visualized it, but it had not come cheaply. In less than a year, the new owners had expended or committed themselves to a total of $327,000.

Fortunately, the season of 1864 moved along placidly. It was marred but slightly by a minor collision between the *Chauncey Vibbard* and another new steamboat, the *Magenta*, which was running on the Newburgh and Albany day line. September came, marking an end to the heavy traffic of summer. Now was the time to test fully the *Chauncey Vibbard* to see of what she was capable in the way of high speed.

With the *Drew* of 1866, the People's Line completed the building of a new and magnificent trio of night boats for New York-Albany service.—*Elwin M. Eldredge coll.*

Chapter 5

HIGH SPEED

HIGH SPEED" provided fuel for endless debates in pilothouses, engine rooms, barrooms and newspapers during the nineteenth century. Its fascination never flagged, for rarely was anything definitely decided.

At an early date a newspaperman dug into his back files and compiled a list of fast trips on the Hudson River as reported by his paper. His initiative gave the idea to other papers so that there came to be several such lists. When a new trip of unusual speed was made by some steamboat, it was added in its proper place and a less impressive run deleted.

Let us take two mythical steamboats, the *Sauerbraten* and the *Mincemeat*. In 1847, we will assume, the *Sauerbraten* ran between two given points in 2 hours 17 minutes. Fifteen years later the *Mincemeat* ran between the same two points in 2 hours 15 minutes. That made the *Mincemeat* the faster boat.

To the uninitiated, this was fine. It's too bad it isn't as fine as it looks, for it would have spared countless people endless amounts of trouble. Unfortunately, there were a number of other factors to be considered. These factors usually cannot be ascertained today for the very good reason that they often couldn't even be ascertained at the time a fast run was made. They were known, of course, by the officers of the boat involved, but it was all part of the game to release them in the most sketchy fashion. That made it much harder to beat them down at a later date.

The only thing definite about these fast runs was that they were all made with a favorable tide, or, as boatmen put it, "with the tide underfoot." If any steamboat ever made a record run against the tide, she would have been so fast with it that the high-speed debate would have withered and died at once. That part is easy to deduce, but the strength of the tide—whether strong, average or poor—was generally the captain's opinion. The wind direction and approximate velocity can often be found, but the wind had a different effect on different steamboats, depending on the type of deckhousing they carried.

We are rarely told how many passengers or how much freight was carried on any of these fast trips. The time lost at landings was computed by the captain and is beyond all checking. Some claimed deductions of such size that one is tempted to wonder whether or not they went ashore for a constitutional everytime their steamboat stopped. On the other hand, a very small landing deduction is a hallmark of authentic figures. It might be added, too, that not often were the landings listed, and sometimes not even the number was given.

But above all, the most difficult point to determine is the actual distance covered by the steamboat. To find the distance between two points on the river right up the middle of the channel is simplicity itself. But all landings resulted in the addition of mileage—sometimes slight, sometimes considerable. One pilot might run a particular course in a certain way, while another could traverse it more cagily and save distance by so doing. There is no record as to how far out of their way any of the steamers had to go to accomplish passing situations encountered en route.

The seeker of truth soon found that steamboatmen were more prejudiced than anyone else, and further, much more convincing in their arguments for a particular steamboat than the laymen. If you ever got involved in the high-speed debate with a steamboatman, you found such things as steam pressure carried, type of fuel burned, proficiency of the engine-room crew and a score of other factors being thrown at you so rapidly that you agreed to anything.

Another complication was that many of the old-timers had been particularly impressed with one special steamboat in the days of their youth. This boat became to them a paragon that grew better with each passing year. The newer boats they regarded as mere whippersnappers, completely unable to come anywhere near the time their favorites had once made.

Born in 1812, Captain Absalom L. Anderson was a bold figure in Hudson River steamboating as commander of his beloved *Mary Powell.—Commemorative Biographical Record of Ulster County, N. Y., copied by W. du Barry Thomas.*

What these high-speed runs did more than anything else was to separate the men from the boys, so to speak. Although individual fast runs in themselves could not determine to absolute definitiveness which member of a small group of steamboats was fastest, they could indicate what steamboats were in the elite bracket of high-speed boats.

As we have seen, on October 13, 1860, the *Daniel Drew* made a run from New York to Albany specifically planned to test her speed. She covered the distance from Jay Street, New York, to Albany in 7 hours 20 minutes elapsed time. A deduction of 30 minutes was claimed for landings and another 30 minutes for the fact that she is said to have had a strong head wind all the way up the river. The latter allowance has never been seriously considered, since if one gave cognizance to the force of nature opposing her, he would also have to make an addition to the running time for the force of nature—the tide—in her favor. Her average rate of speed to Hudson was perhaps

about 22¾ miles per hour or at least, probably over 22 miles per hour. Above Hudson navigation was difficult because of the numerous bars and shoals, so that the average for the entire trip from New York to Albany may have been about 20.9 miles per hour with the half-hour landing deduction unquestioned.

Now the *Chauncey Vibbard* was to have her mettle tried on the through run. Already there had been skirmishing between her and the *Daniel Drew* on short runs. Favorable tides would occur in mid-September of 1864 and the fifteenth was selected as the day. This was not announced in advance, because it would have been too embarrassing if something went wrong.

In New York, on the morning of September 15, Andrew Fletcher of the firm of Fletcher, Harrison & Co. went aboard the *Chauncey Vibbard*. Since Fletcher, Harrison & Co. had built the engine, the appearance of Andrew Fletcher was sufficient indication to anyone not already in the know that something was about to happen. Having an engine builder on board on a fast run was regarded by the public as tantamount to having God on the passenger list and gave an air of complete authenticity to any figures released.

It seems that in those great days of steamboating, engine builders were regarded as men of unquestioned integrity. Most of them were, of course, but it is hard to imagine more interested observers of a fast run. Their presence on board also gave a decided advantage to the boat, since they could probably offer an occasional suggestion as to how to get just a trifle more speed out of the engine. And in the event of a breakdown, they knew better than anyone else what to do about it. Perhaps the secret of the great regard in which they were held was that, as practicing businessmen, they had to be diplomatic. At the end of any fast run in which they participated, they were usually able to phrase their remarks so that their present and previous customers would still be their future customers.

Thus it was that on September 15, 1864, the *Chauncey Vibbard* "left New York" at 8:09 a.m. and arrived in Albany at 3:31 p.m., making her elapsed time 7 hours 22 minutes, or two minutes more than the time of the *Daniel Drew* in 1860. But Captain Hitchcock claimed a deduction of 40 minutes for an unspecified number of landings, likely seven, bringing the running time down to 6 hours 42 minutes, or eight minutes better than the *Daniel Drew's*. Perhaps the deduction was inflated by about ten minutes. The departure time from New York was from the 30th Street landing, while in 1860 the *Daniel Drew's* time had been taken from Jay Street, about 2⅝ miles south of 30th Street. Using Captain Hitchcock's time for the run from 30th Street to Albany, the average speed of the *Chauncey Vibbard* comes very close to 21 miles per hour.

In reporting the event, one newspaper included the information that Mr. Fletcher said he had never seen a faster steamer than the *Chauncey Vibbard* and added that Mr. Fletcher's firm had also built the engine for the *Mary Powell*. The next day the paper corrected some errors in the times it had given for the fast run and noted—probably at the behest of Mr. Fletcher—that what that gentleman had actually said was that he never went faster than he did on the *Chauncey Vibbard*. That covered the point nicely, for Mr. Fletcher does not seem to have been aboard on an earlier fast run of the *Mary Powell*.

At that time the *Mary Powell* was the largest day steamer running on the Hudson River and was not exceeded in length in that category until 1887. Like the *Daniel Drew* and the *Chauncey Vibbard*, she was a wooden-hulled, beam-engined side-wheeler with boilers on the guards. The *Mary Powell* had been built in 1861 for a day line for passengers only, operated by Captain Absalom L.

Anderson between Rondout, now part of Kingston, and New York City. Early every morning except Sunday she left Rondout for New York and sailed on the return trip from New York in the afternoon. In her day's work she covered roughly 180 miles, or considerably more than the one-way distance between New York and Albany.

As originally built, the *Mary Powell* had been 267 feet in length. She proved to be less fast than had been anticipated and after the season of 1862 was lengthened 21 feet. This refined her lines and balance to the desired degree and early in the season of 1863 she commenced to turn up runs of unusual speed.

If ever a man loved a steamboat, Captain Anderson loved the *Mary Powell*. He operated her strictly as a "family boat," which meant that the passengers were expected to conduct themselves with the same decorum that they would in their own home. While she was tastefully fitted out, she did not carry needless frills. Captain Anderson felt that such things were unnecessary weight to be carried along, and to him that was something to be avoided like the plague. Those familiar with him could almost accept the legend that he regularly detailed one of the waiters to go around whisking flies off the railings, lest their added weight slow down his steamer!

The *Mary Powell* looked like this after her lengthening in the fall of 1862. She is bound up the river, with the Palisades in the background.—*Photograph of painting, Elwin M. Eldredge coll.*

Captain Anderson also believed that the scenery and fresh air of the Hudson could best be enjoyed with plenty of open deck space. While the *Daniel Drew* and the *Chauncey Vibbard* had their upper saloons well forward, the *Mary Powell's* was located aft of amidships, leaving the whole forward promenade deck unobstructed. The captain considered this the best part of the steamer from which to view the scenery and felt you could see it best unsheltered. You might be chilled to the bone in the seeing, but you had the satisfaction of knowing that you were being chilled in the best of surroundings.

Shortly after the *Chauncey Vibbard's* fast run of September 15, 1864, Captain Tallman of the *Daniel Drew* let it be known that he was not impressed. He had been captain of the *Daniel Drew* when she made her fast run in 1860, and he vowed that before the season of 1864 ended he would top the *Chauncey Vibbard's* time.

Captain Anderson was not impressed, either. There was not a doubt in his mind but that his own *Mary Powell* was the better—or the best—boat. Shortly after the *Chauncey Vibbard's* fast trip he made another fast trip of his own, on which the *Mary Powell* seems to have bettered as far as Newburgh both the time of the *Chauncey Vibbard* and the October 13, 1860 time of the *Daniel Drew* to that place.

Immediately afterwards it was understood that Captain Anderson had proposed a sweepstakes to be held after the close of the season. Everyone was welcome, but a deposit of from a thousand to five thousand dollars was to be made for each boat entered, with the winner to take all. If only one boat, here the finger pointed straight at the *Chauncey Vibbard*, were interested, then a match race could be arranged. Whether or not such a challenge actually went out, the story had sufficient credence to persist for half a century, and nothing seems to have been done to deny reports of it that appeared in the press.

It was said that some of their brethren in the steamboat fraternity strongly urged Van Santvoord and Davidson to enter both the *Daniel Drew* and the *Chauncey Vibbard* against the *Mary Powell*. Here was a rare chance to gain added glory. But nothing happened. That is unfortunate, for thereby for all time was lost the golden opportunity to see which of the three was then the fastest steamboat on the Hudson River.

The *Mary Powell* ended her season on October 18, but the *Daniel Drew* and the *Chauncey Vibbard* continued to run until early November. Cap-

tain Tallman was still determined to make his promised fast run and, after considering the tides, chose almost the last possible day for it, October 28. Not to be outdone by Captain Hitchcock, he invited an engine builder who had either been in charge of the construction of the engine or the installation of it in the *Daniel Drew*, to come along to do the timing.

The *Daniel Drew* "left New York" at the same magical hour of 8:09 a.m. as the *Chauncey Vibbard* and arrived at Albany in the elapsed time of 7 hours 16 minutes. Captain Tallman claimed a 39-minute allowance for seven landings to make the running time 6 hours 37 minutes, or five minutes better than the *Chauncey Vibbard's*. The captain's engine builder, who had no connection with the engine of either the *Chauncey Vibbard* or the *Mary Powell*, was quite willing to give his unbiased opinion. He said that no steamer into which he had put an engine had ever made such fine time as the *Daniel Drew*. Taking 30th Street as the starting point and using the 39-minute allowance, the average to Albany would be about a quarter of a mile an hour better than that of the *Chauncey Vibbard*.

Naturally, neither the *Chauncey Vibbard* nor the *Daniel Drew* could have made the speed they had to maintain as far as Hudson on their 1864 trips without help from the tide. Their timetable, based on normal operations, permitted them roughly nine hours to run between their termini, or a far cry from their elapsed time on these fast runs.

Although claims were often made that the *Daniel Drew* or the *Chauncey Vibbard* or the *Mary Powell* had on one occasion or another covered some course at the rate of 30 miles an hour, it was generally felt in dispassionate circles that 25 miles an hour would be almost the maximum for any of them over a comparatively short stretch under ideal conditions. Under unusual conditions of wind and tide they might have been capable of something more than that, but probably not much or for long.

This should not be considered derogatory. Actually, they were all remarkably fast vessels. Throughout the long history of American steamboating or steamboating anywhere, vessels of their capabilities were the exception rather than the rule.

These test trips of the *Chauncey Vibbard* and the *Daniel Drew* represented practically the best to be attained by steamboats running between New York and Albany and making way landings in the course of regular business. No such trips could be attempted by steamers of more recent years even if they had disregarded strict adherence to schedule, which in the Day Line came to be beyond the pale. In the 1860s there was no requirement for steamers to check their speed when passing either tows or boats lying at landings, no matter how near they came. Such damage as might be caused by the suction and swells created had to be borne by the owners of the damaged vessels. Towing was an important business on the Hudson and on a trip between New York and Albany many tows would be encountered en route.

In the 1870s a case involving the *Daniel Drew* entered the courts and resulted in one of the first decisions on this point. The *Daniel Drew* had passed close to and at full speed a tow in charge of the towing steamer *Ohio*. The suction and swell had damaged three canal boats. The owner, Michael Moran, sued for damages and was awarded $233.22, but the case was appealed and the judgment reversed. The court decided that since there was no law prescribing the speed of a steamer, the swell it might make or the distance at which it must pass, the action of the *Daniel Drew* in passing close at high speed was proper.

This left the situation as it had been. Any slowing was left to the orders of the owner or the discretion of the captain or the pilot. Almost without exception, they apparently passed tows at full speed, for as late as 1879 Captain A. L. Anderson of the *Mary Powell* was being widely applauded by towboat operators as the only captain on the river who slowed his steamer when passing tows. In the 1880s the legal point of view was reversed and it has since been upheld that a large steamer can be held liable for swell damage under certain circumstances. In this case, which involved a Day Line steamer, it was adjudged that even though the steamboat was at dead slow speed and making only five or six miles an hour when passing close to a scow loading at a landing, she should have stopped her engine entirely and drifted past.

As a result of this about-face of the courts, Hudson River steamers slowed at the proper time or their owners literally paid the consequences. The Day Line was as fastidious about this as were other steamboat operators, but the result was a long succession of claims and lawsuits which plagued the line thereafter.

As counter-ammunition in the courts, the Day Line came to have prepared long log sheets listing all of the landings along the river, with columns for entering when necessary the time at which the vessel slowed or stopped while passing and the time she resumed full speed. In addition, similar information was compiled for all tows passed. A latter-day captain who attempted a run of the type made by the *Daniel Drew* and the *Chauncey Vibbard* in 1864 would probably have automatically been dismissed when he reached Albany.

In the sixties things were different, and the *Daniel Drew's* trip on October 28 was not the end of the Hitchcock-Tallman rivalry.

Captain Hitchcock received the news of the fast run of the *Daniel Drew* promptly. Perhaps Captain Tallman saw to that. The following morning, with what Captain Dave described as a poor flood or favorable tide and a strong north or head wind, he left Desbrosses Street at 8:00 a.m. with the *Chauncey Vibbard* and sailed to Yonkers at a rate of speed which, based on his own announcement of time and distance, would have been 27 miles per hour. This, he announced gleefully, was the best time any boat had yet made between New York and Yonkers. Captain Tallman, who has been described as being "jolly" and "good natured," was probably anything but when he read that.

Thereafter, he and Captain Hitchcock seem to have decided upon the stretch between New York and Yonkers as their own private feuding grounds. The *Mary Powell* didn't land at Yonkers in those days, so they had the dock-to-dock field all to themselves and kept it nicely in the Day Line family. They were still at it in 1866. By this time Captain Tallman had increased the mileage enough so that he was able to cover the run with the *Daniel Drew* at over 30 miles an hour. Now let Dave Hitchcock beat that!

But through it all Captain Dave still swore he could beat the *Daniel Drew's* time to Albany and he finally did, although it was many years before he could prove his point. And by that time his steamboat was considerably changed from what she had been in 1864 and Captain Tallman had ceased to pace the decks of the *Daniel Drew*.

In the spring of 1876 the Day Line planned to send the *Chauncey Vibbard* to Albany to be painted prior to the opening of regular service. This was Captain Dave's golden opportunity. The *Chauncey Vibbard* "left New York" on April 18 at 5:20 in the morning and arrived at Albany at 11:40, in 6 hours 20 minutes.

At face value, that seems to have been just about the all-time steamboat record between New York and Albany.

Chapter 6

THE ROUTE

As the Day Line's first full season was drawing to a close, the quality of its service and the fine accommodations available on its boats were attracting public notice. On October 28, 1864, the following item appeared in the Albany *Evening Journal:*

> The river travel by the day boats is drawing to a close. . . . These boats have had a profitable season of it, but nothing more than their courteous, liberal and public spirited owners were justly entitled. The people are becoming yearly more and more fascinated with the beauty of the scenery on the Hudson, and are preferring a water route in summer to the rail road, where they are treated to a covering of dust or almost sufficated [*sic*] with the heat. Another week is given to those who have desired and have never yet embraced the opportunity offered of seeing the scenery on the Hudson, and sailing on safe commodious boats.

Here was truth. The greater speed of the railroad had for a time drawn patronage away from the river. During the 1850s when traveling along the Hudson by train was yet a novelty, day passengers on the boats had dwindled. But in the 1860s they commenced to return to the river. With the building of the *Daniel Drew* and the *Chauncey Vibbard*, first-rate steamers were available, and the added time en route was more than offset by the scenery and the opportunity to relax aboard luxurious and swift boats.

As the Day Line came to say, it was "the most charming inland water trip on the American continent." The scenery was usually more than ample to stimulate even blasé passengers. But nature within required as much consideration as nature without. When hunger gnawed, there was good food available in comfortable dining rooms and wine or stronger liquors to whet the taste for it. For those who required whetting over a longer period, there was a bar to serve the proper spirits at the needed time.

Vacationists again came to favor the day route in increasing numbers, and travellers from other parts of the country and from abroad found it as it had always been, the only way to view fully the entire panorama of Hudson River scenery.

At first the Day Line permitted them to view it until early November, for in 1863 and 1864 two-boat operations were continued that late. In 1864, its first full season, one-boat service began on May 4 and two-boat service was available from May 19 onward. A season extending over that period of time was to prove longer than the traffic warranted, and it soon became the general rule not to open service until late May or early June, and to close in October.

In the 1860s and 1870s, the timetable of the Day Line varied. Changes were even made during the season, and in the early years at least were probably governed by the operation of connecting railroads at Albany. The leaving time from New York at first was 7:00 a.m., which was generally thought to be too early and was eventually advanced to the more convenient time of about 8:30 a.m. From Albany, the departure time ranged from 7:45 to 10:00 in the morning, until it came to be 8:30.

The Day Line liked to say that the *Daniel Drew* and the *Chauncey Vibbard* operated under the "nine hour system," which was quite true if one ignored the minutes. Although the southbound steamer was for a while scheduled at nine hours, the northbound steamer was generally allowed more elapsed time. This may have been due to the fact that if the southbound vessel were late, it could be let out in the lower reaches of the river. The northbound steamer, on the other hand, would under any condition have her speed retarded by the restricted channel of the upper Hudson. It was not until 1885, with increasingly heavy traffic, that the same elapsed time of nine and a half hours was scheduled for both directions.

The timetables, after they developed into what was to become a standard pattern, placed the passing point of the steamers at just above Poughkeepsie landing, with the up-boat leaving there only five minutes before the down-boat. Poughkeepsie was almost at the mid-point of the trip and the arrangement was splendid if both vessels were on time. But if the northbound boat was bucking a strong tide with a sizeable load of passengers and consequently running late, this considerably delayed the southbound boat which, except in the case of an accident to the other vessel, had to wait. The round trip to Poughkeepsie represented the maximum one-day sail up the Hudson available to New Yorkers and was a popular outing. These passengers obviously couldn't be left stranded at Poughkeepsie.

Like the scheduled times, the way landings between New York and Albany which were served by the Day Line also varied. During the 1860s and 1870s, sometimes as few as six were advertised and as many as twelve.

Part of this was experimentation on the part of the new company. If one landing failed to produce ticket sales, it would be abandoned in favor of another. The intent was to keep the landings sufficiently few so as not to increase the running time, and to make these selected landings the ones that would bring the most business.

Were we to call at all of the landings that were served by the Day Line at one time or another in the 1860s and 1870s, we would have to spread our travelling over several years. We might depart from the downtown New York terminus, which was at the Desbrosses Street pier, 1864-1869 and then at the adjacent pier at Vestry Street, approximately 1¼ miles from the mouth of the river. Or we might go aboard at the "up-town" landing, which at first was at the foot of 30th Street and then successively at West 34th, West 23d and West 24th Street.

With the busy traffic of New York's Hudson River waterfront dropping astern, we would have our first taste of the varied scenery in store for us as the high cliffs on the west bank develop into unbroken miles of wall-like, perpendicular face which gave to them the name of the Palisades.

Our first landing along the river might be Yonkers, then a bustling Westchester County town popular as a residence for those in business in New York and affluent enough to live elsewhere. Although Yonkers served Captains Hitchcock and Tallman nobly when those worthies were carrying on their high-speed feud, it was later dropped from the timetables for a number of years.

A few miles above Yonkers, on the west shore, is the boundary line between the states of New York and New Jersey. This was a boundary that was

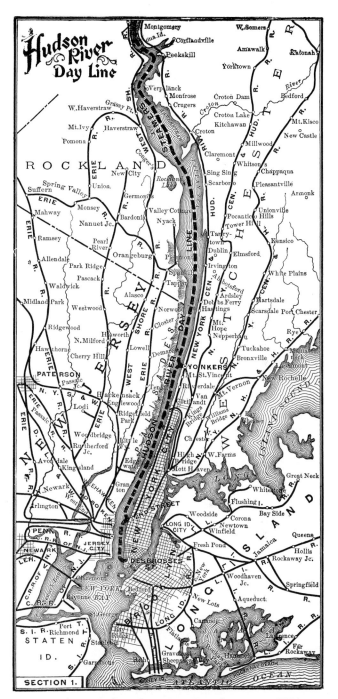

Map from Hudson River Day Line literature, 1911.

rarely respected by generations of New York City dwellers who patronized the Day Line. To them, the west shore was always the "Jersey shore," no matter how far up the river they happened to be.

Twenty-seven miles from the mouth of the river, on the east bank, is Tarrytown, made immortal through the writings of Washington Irving, whose last home was nearby. Off Tarrytown was the next landing, guaranteed to fascinate those who reveled in the unusual because it was not a true landing at all. Rather, it was a connection or "meet" with the Tarrytown-Nyack ferryboat out in the river. By this method passengers for or from either Tarrytown or Nyack could be disembarked or picked up without the detour necessary to land properly at either place. It was a practical way to serve both sides of the river in a minimum of time and was also employed by the smaller, local steamboats running on the lower Hudson. Although the *Armenia* and the *Daniel Drew* had made connections with the ferry under previous ownership, the Day Line eliminated the arrangement and did not restore it to its published schedules until 1870.

One would think that it must have been a somewhat hazardous maneuver for the lumbering ferryboat to come alongside for the transfer, particularly with a strong wind raising rollers on the river. But apparently it was executed without any more dire results than the occasional loss of dignity on the part of the passengers involved. A writer of the period observed generally that ". . . the transfer . . . is effected with such ease and good humor that it seems a pleasant episode of the trip, rather than that usually much-dreaded and hateful thing—*a change.*"

Off Tarrytown, we would already be in the Tappan Zee and, after pulling away from the ferryboat, would continue on across its broad expanse and into the even wider Haverstraw Bay, where the Hudson reaches its greatest width of about 3½ miles. Then it narrows rapidly and, rounding Dunderberg Mountain on the west, we would enter the storied Highlands of the Hudson. Rising abruptly on either side are high and rugged hills, dwarfing our steamer and seeming at one point to be cutting off our passage completely. The Hudson runs for over twelve miles through the Highlands, past a succession of peaks that bear such widely known names as Anthony's Nose, Bear Mountain, Sugar Loaf, Crows Nest, Mount Taurus, Breakneck and Storm King. The restricted width of the river is compensated by the great depth, which in one spot is over two hundred feet.

In the Highlands a Mr. Cozzens had built a popular summer hotel, and this was once served by the Day Line. General Winfield Scott had favored the place for many years and chose to make it his summer headquarters. The landing here was simply Cozzens', which on the river was usually pronounced "Cozzenses," or better still, "Cozzenseses."

Less than a mile above it was West Point landing. There was never any question about West Point being on the timetable. Luminaries of the army and even the Secretary of War himself might be encountered on Day Line steamers going to or from "the Point." And it was always a popular attraction for tourists.

On up through the Highlands we would sail to pass out through the northern gate marked by Storm King on the west and Breakneck Mountain on the east. Now we would be at the southern end of beautiful Newburgh Bay and here, at the

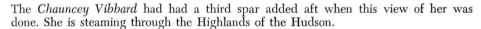

The *Chauncey Vibbard* had had a third spar added aft when this view of her was done. She is steaming through the Highlands of the Hudson.

base of Storm King Mountain, we might touch at Cornwall Landing.

Cornwall owed a lot to Nathaniel P. Willis. Little remembered today, he was a figure in the literary world of the last century. Willis had moved to the Cornwall region in an attempt to regain his health and established a home which he called Idlewild. Through his writings in the old *Home Journal,* he was better than several chambers of commerce in publicizing the area. Although he never moved any mountains in this phase of his activity, he did succeed in renaming one. A man of letters, he felt that "Storm King" was a far more appropriate name for the local mountain than "Butter Hill" and in time his choice came to be accepted.

Said an old guidebook:

Cornwall is a great summer resort; and, seeing how small and scattered a place it looks, the traveller will be surprised at the large number of persons that leave the boat here, and at the crowd of people and vehicles, some of the latter quite stylish, that assemble on the wharf to meet the new arrivals and convoy, or carry, them away. Cornwall is just far enough up the river to make the sail a pleasant one; it is situated at the very point where the river reaches its climax of beauty and interest; and it is, in itself, an attractive place for quiet people, with its pleasant wood-walks, its drives, its coolness, and its nearness to the river and West Point.*

Another remarked:

Cornwall, where the hillsides are crowned with villas and summer homes. This is one of the pleasantest and healthiest places on the Hudson.**

A few miles above Cornwall and likewise on the west bank is the city of Newburgh (incorporated 1865), about sixty miles from the mouth of the river. On the east bank, about fifteen miles up from Newburgh, is the city of Poughkeepsie, the "Queen City of the Hudson." These two places were sufficiently important so that they were always Day Line landings. There are several villages in between, in country that is characterized by low hills skirting the river. One of these, Milton, on the west bank, was served briefly by the Albany day boats. Milton was a minor summering spot in the heart of a fruit-growing region.

Miller's New Guide to the Hudson River, p. 85.

**Thursty McQuill (pseud. of Wallace Bruce), *The Hudson River by Daylight,* 1875, p. 54.

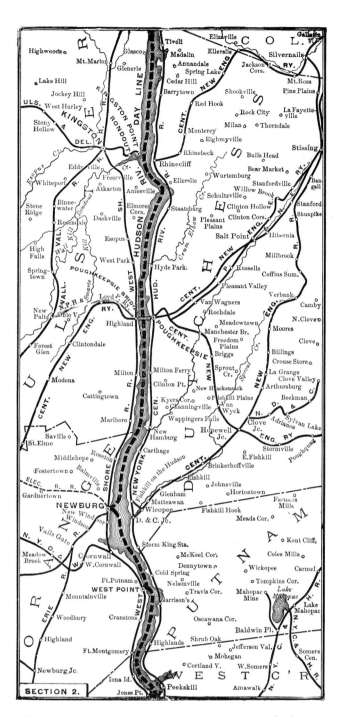

The landing at Cozzens', mentioned opposite, had been renamed Cranston's when the map was executed.

Immediately after leaving Poughkeepsie we would have the thrill of passing the down-boat, a thrill that never dulled. There was magic in the fleeting moment when one stood on deck and watched the other steamboat glide swiftly by, with paddles chunking the water and bright flags wav-

A modern view of West Point, looking up the Hudson through the northern gateway of the Highlands with Newburgh in the far distance. The river in the foreground bends sharply around Gees Point and reappears above the right-hand buildings of the United States Military Academy. The nearer mountain on the west bank (left-hand side of the picture) is Crows Nest, with Storm King showing slightly darker beyond it. Opposite Storm King is Breakneck Point and Breakneck Mountain. The island in the background is Pollepel (spelling varies), the site for many years of Bannerman's Island Arsenal.—*New York State Department of Commerce photograph.*

ing in the breeze. A kindred feeling enveloped both vessels as handkerchiefs fluttered and arms waved in greeting. Everyone felt like a proprietor and little boys decided there could be no career for them but steamboating.

In those days of simpler pleasures, passengers looked forward to the passing long before it came to be and kept a sharp eye out so as to be the first to sight the other steamer. Cries of, "There's the down-boat!" or ". . . the up-boat!" would be followed by "No, it's not!" or "Yes, it is!" until the steamers got sufficiently close so that there could be no doubt.

The owners, the real owners that is, were not above appreciating or capitalizing on this high-point of the trip. Whether or not the steamers did so originally, they came in time to accord each other a full-blown salute on the whistle. The standard practice in the Day Line of later years was for the up-boat to salute the down-boat and to hold closely to navigational rules in so doing. A port-to-port passing meant one long blast from each steamer, and a starboard-to-starboard passing, two blasts.

Soon after passing the down-boat, we would be able to see to the northwest the long blue line of the Catskill Mountains, which would continue to hold our interest for many miles of the trip.

Our next landing, about fifteen miles above Poughkeepsie and on the same side, would be Rhinebeck landing. Rhinebeck village was inland and the settlement that had grown up around the landing had in 1861 taken the name of Rhinecliff. This the Day Line ignored, for it always called the landing Rhinebeck. Actually, Rhineback was not the primary reason it landed there at all, for most of the passengers who debarked or embarked were either going to or coming from the villages of Rondout and Kingston across the river.

Rondout Creek entered the Hudson opposite Rhinecliff and Rondout village was located a short distance up the creek. It was an important port on the river, since the Delaware & Hudson Canal from the Pennsylvania coal fields reached tidewater on Rondout Creek. On the high ground back of Rondout was the village of Kingston, which, along with Rondout, became part of the new City of Kingston in 1872.

It was far too time-consuming for the through day boats to go into the creek to make a landing. On the west bank of the river at that point, wharves were limited and inconveniently located as far as shore-side access was concerned. Therefore, the Day Line continued the policy adopted by its immediate predecessors and landed for Rondout and Kingston passengers at Rhinebeck landing where there was ferry service to Rondout. This was also an important gateway to the Catskill Mountain vacation region, particularly after the construction of a railroad from Rondout into the Catskills.

Ten miles up the river from Kingston lies the village of Saugerties. While Saugerties was sufficiently prosperous to support its own night line to New York, its importance to the Day Line was the fact that it, too, was an entryway to the Catskills. The difficulty in landing at Saugerties was the same as at Kingston, only more pronounced. Saugerties' waterfront was on Esopus Creek, the proper name, although this tidewater portion of it was known locally as Saugerties Creek. At first there was no suitable landing at all on the river. Consequently, the Day Line often landed either at Tivoli, across from Saugerties and connected with it by ferry, or at Bristol Landing, Malden. This was on the west bank of the river above Saugerties, but a stage line served to transport passengers. Finally the Saugerties Long Dock, a pier of permanent construction, was built out from the shore to deep water below the mouth of Esopus Creek and in 1877 and 1878 the Day Line used this as a landing.

About eleven miles above Saugerties, the village of Catskill had early established itself as an entry to the Catskill Mountains for the vacation traffic. The name of Catskill alone was a selling point and the Day Line never failed to land there. One of the early major resort hotels in the Catskills was the Catskill Mountain House, which had been built in the 1820s and which for decades was *the* "Mountain House." Located on the east wall of the Catskills, it afforded a breathtaking view of the Hudson Valley and was most easily reached via Catskill village. There was no finer way of summering in the mountains than to stay at the Catskill Mountain House.

Saugerties was proud of its Long Dock, and the landing of the Day Line there resulted in a sharp rivalry between Saugerties and Catskill. In 1877, a Saugerties newspaper carried this editorial:

Catskill carries off the palm for meanness!

Last Friday when the steamer *Moses Taylor* with Snyder Hose excursion party on board landed at Catskill Point they were presented with a bill for fifty cents for wharfage! This would not have been done were it not for the petty spite which all Catskill has held against Saugerties since our Long Dock was built. Never mind, it don't matter how much you sputter and fume gentlemen, Saugerties eventually is destined to become the great thoroughfare from the Hudson to the Catskills. This, Catskill people know, hence their petty spite and meanness which bubbles over upon every conceivable occasion. They know full well that Saugerties landing is twelve miles nearer the mountains, and that sooner or later Catskill is doomed to be the year round what she in reality is when city people no longer fill her streets, a dull, miserable country town, filled with Greene County flats; while Saugerties will receive the immense summer travel that annually passes through that obscure place.

Alas for Saugerties! After 1878 the Day Line never landed in that vicinity again and Catskill had the last chuckle. In later years, when vacation traffic to the Catskills changed from "immense" to "mammoth" proportions, the people of Saugerties made strenuous efforts to induce the Day Line to come back, but it never did.

Having discharged the last of our Catskill Mountain vacationists at Catskill, we would make a short run of about four miles to the city of Hudson, located on the east bank of the river some 115 miles from the mouth. In addition to ordinary trade, Hudson also drew passengers going to Lebanon Springs and other vacation spots in the nearby country.

Across the river from Hudson was Athens, where the *Swallow* had been wrecked in 1845. Athens never achieved any great prominence and one guidebook writer who ferried over from Hudson to visit it remarked that ". . . there is, of course, nothing but Hudson to see."

In any event, it briefly eclipsed Hudson as a Day Line landing through the completion of a railroad called the Saratoga & Hudson River, which the wily Daniel Drew elected to support in the 1860s. He even induced Cornelius Vanderbilt to invest in it, although Vanderbilt later wondered why he had. As built, the line ran from Athens cross-country about 37¾ miles to connect with the main line of the New York Central east of Schenectady. It was nothing more than a cut-off, whereby freight and passengers between western points and New York could be transferred to steamboats at Athens, or vice versa. Obviously, it took less time to get to New York from Athens than from Albany, and also Athens could be reached by steamboats during the cold-weather months for a longer period.

Seeing the Hudson by daylight in 1870.—*Harper's Weekly.*

This is the Catskill Mountain House about 1839, with the Hudson River in the distance. The hotel was altered over the years, and part of the structure survived until recently, long after the last guest had departed. In January 1963 the abandoned shell was finally burned down by the New York Conservation Department. The prominent jutting rock in front of the building remains like a monument to one of the great resort hotels of its day.

The Saratoga & Hudson River Railroad was leased by the New York Central and in 1867 absorbed by it. Relations between the New York Central running between Albany and Buffalo, and the Hudson River Railroad, controlled by Cornelius Vanderbilt, between Albany and New York were not always harmonious, to put it mildly. There were close ties between Daniel Drew's People's Line and the New York Central and a great deal of the New York-bound freight of the latter went to New York during the season of navigation via the People's Line. To further harass the Hudson River Railroad, arrangements were made whereby the People's Line steamers connected with the Saratoga & Hudson River to provide fast through freight and passenger service by way of Athens.

Since the Day Line also had friendly ties with the New York Central, it scheduled its steamers to land at Athens in the season of 1867 instead of Hudson, although connections to the latter place were available by ferry. The Saratoga & Hudson River Railroad proved a failure to the extent that it came to be known as the "White Elephant Railroad." Freight was handled over it for a number of years but the through-passenger idea was a short-lived experiment. In September of 1867 the Day Line was again advertising landings at Hudson. Except for this brief interruption, Day Line steamers always landed at Hudson.

But we must get under way once more, for about 28 miles of steaming still lie ahead. Above the city of Hudson, we would find that the river shoaled badly in spots and called for careful piloting. In some places the scenery would be restricted because of a marked rise in the elevation of the land just back from the narrow river, but there were a long succession of islands and more towns.

Of these several pleasant settlements between Hudson and Albany only one, New Baltimore, found its way on Day Line timetables, and then for less than a full season.

Finally, the end of the journey would bring us to Albany, from where railroad connections were available to the west, north or east. Since Albany was a large city in its own right and the capital of the State of New York, perhaps we would want to go no further. Like countless proper Day Line passengers, we would have an enjoyable overnight's stay and a safe return back down the river the following day.

But if we were to judge by one guidebook writer, we would start back with the least possible delay. Said he:

Albany . . . shows almost no traces of its antiquity, which, comparatively speaking is considerable. It was made the site of trading-houses, built by the Dutch for traffic with the Indians. . . . but the ambition of the people of Albany seems to have been to get rid, as far as possible, of every thing that can make their town venerable, or betray its connection with the past.

. . . Albany is a common-place city, with scarcely any interest for the visitor. No doubt the State House is a compensation to politicians, and the Dudley Observatory to astronomers, but these are meagre attractions.*

It is perhaps unnecessary to add that this particular guidebook was not recommended by the Day Line. The recognized guidebook writer of the Day Line was Wallace Bruce. Born in 1844, he published his first guide to the Hudson and adjacent regions about 1869 under the pen name of Thursty McQuill, but eventually brought out his works under his own name. Bruce's book was constantly revised to keep it current and continued to appear until into this century.

Bruce was also a poet, a fact that had some influence on a foreword that appeared in his later guides:

GREETING: The Hudson, more than any other river, has a distinct personality—an absolute soul-quality. With moods as various as the longings of human life she responds to our joys in sympathetic sweetness, and soothes our sorrows as by a gentle companionship. If the Mississippi is the King of Rivers the Hudson is, *par excellence*, the Queen, and continually charms by her "infinite variety." It often seems that there are in reality four separate Hudsons—the Hudson of Beauty, the Hudson of History, the Hudson of

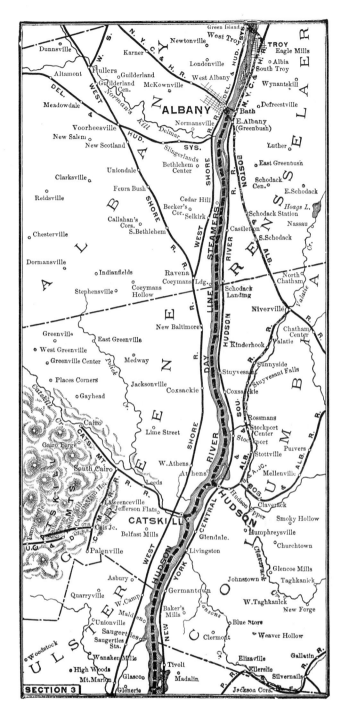

Literature, and the Hudson of Commerce. To blend them all into a loving cable reaching from heart to heart is the purpose of the writer. It has been his privilege to walk again and again every foot of its course from the wilderness to the sea, to linger beside her fountains and dream amid her historic shrines, and from many braided threads of memory it has been his hope to set forth with affectionate enthusiasm what the student or traveler wishes to see and know of her majesty and glory.

Miller's New Guide to the Hudson River, pp. 125-127.

Chapter 7

THE HAPPY 1860s AND 1870s

INASMUCH AS 1864 was the first full season for the new Day Line, let us cast a weather eye on steamboat operations of a century ago from the all-important viewpoint of money.

During the 1864 season, a total of 103,671 passengers were carried. The net operating earnings from the *Daniel Drew* and the *Chauncey Vibbard* together totaled a little over $38,000, with a loss of about $150 on the *Armenia*.

In terms of the present-day value of money, this appears insignificant until placed, for example, against 1864 wages. While these varied, a first-class steamboat pilot might receive $60 a month and his room and board; an engineer often considerably less; and deckhands and firemen about $25. Total wages for the *Daniel Drew* in 1864 were $9,010.43.

Bar supplies furnish another interesting comparison. In 1864 the Day Line bought bourbon at $2.00 a gallon; old rye at $3.00; common brandy at $3.00; gin at $3.50.

So, you see, $38,000 was not piddling.

Since freight was a source of income at this time, it is necessary to add a note of explanation. Tradition has it that the Day Line never carried freight and even relatively early accounts emphasize the point that it always transported only passengers. For most of its existence, of course, the Day Line was solely a passenger carrier. The category of freight persisted, however, and was probably used later to cover exclusively earnings realized by the fact that some passengers preferred to have their baggage handled by an express company via the steamers. Initially it would seem that at least at times the Day Line did carry some light freight and parcels. In 1866 it was advertising that it would receive neither freight nor horses, although this prohibition may have had its interruptions. Regardless of what was included as freight in 1864, receipts from that source were negligible.

For those who think of freight as heavy, bulky cargo, the Day Line literally had it in the form of baggage. In those days going away for the summer meant bringing trunkloads of apparel, and there is an actual case of a party of eight boarding one of the river boats with no less than forty trunks. During the busy season, the trunks were stacked on the main decks of the steamers in miniature mountains.

Alfred White served as passenger agent in the infant days of the Day Line. Friendly relations had to be maintained with the railroads, for a good part of the non-local business consisted of joint railroad-steamboat passengers. As we know, the New York Central was particularly important to the Day Line, since that railroad could steer passengers from the west down the Hudson on the steamboats instead of on the Hudson River Railroad and was usually happy to do it. Considerable of Alfred White's time was occupied in plodding through the labyrinth of the resultant ticket adjustments between carriers, but by 1865 he was able to write that they were "... progressing surely in the reforms needed."

Such letters as this, from a New York Central passenger agent in Toledo, Ohio, must have delighted Mr. White:

> Please find inclosed my voucher for posting Steamers for June July Aug. & Sept. . . . Hope it is satisfactory, we have sold a great many tickets to Albany. they prefer taking boat down the river. if satisfactory and I remain with N.Y.C. next season, would be glad to serve you again.

The opening of each Day Line season was always a joyous event along the river, since it marked the beginning of the vacation period and the dawn of prosperous days for those whose income was geared to the summer trade. Cannonading, flag-flying and cheering crowds were usually part of the festivities on the first day of the season. A saluting cannon at Albany, aptly known as the "Baby Waker," was employed on at least one occasion to give a resounding thirteen-blast welcome to both the *Chauncey Vibbard* and the

Daniel Drew upon the completion of their initial runs of the year.

Conversely, the last trip was tinged with melancholy. The final whistle and bell salutes to the steamers, and by them, as they made their closing passages of the season seemed to have a haunting funereal tone never otherwise heard.

As we have seen, considerable experimenting was made with the timetable with an eye to improvement. For the same reason, alterations were made to the steamboats. They were always completely refurbished during the long lay-up between the seasons and maintained to the peak of perfection. On the *Daniel Drew* and the *Chauncey Vibbard,* both the main saloon on the second deck and the ladies' saloon on the main deck aft were thickly carpeted, and the furniture colorfully upholstered. To many of the passengers, here was all the luxury of a Fifth Avenue home with transportation, fresh air and a view besides.

Between the seasons of 1867 and 1868 the *Daniel Drew* had her main saloon extended further aft. As part of this work, private drawing rooms or parlors were installed off the after end of the saloon on either side and were sumptuous with frescoed ceilings, Wilton carpets, and sofas and easy chairs covered with damask. Large bay windows of plate glass made them a splendid place from which to view the passing scene in quiet comfort. These rooms were intended to supplement or replace the original staterooms in the hold. In the same general period and for the same reason, the *Chauncey Vibbard* had private rooms added on her forward hurricane or top deck, on either side by the paddle boxes.

Said a Day Line advertisement:

These boats during the past winter, have been thoroughly overhauled and refurnished, and no pains or expense have been spared to render them equal if not to excel IN COMFORT, SAFETY, AND SPEED, any steamer in the World. LARGE AND ELEGANTLY FURNISHED ROOMS have been placed upon them, for the benefit of families traveling with invalids, who may desire the usual comfort and retirement of a home, and at the same time enjoy the beauties of the GRAND AND MAJESTIC SCENERY OF THE HUDSON By daylight and inhale the balmy air, usually so conducive to health.

The splendid maintenance practiced by the company is best shown by the fact that, while the *Armenia* was available for emergency use for seventeen years, she was rarely so employed. Nevertheless, the Day Line still had to keep her in

The *Chauncey Vibbard* at Poughkeepsie landing.—*New-York Historical Society.*

good order so that she would be ready for instant use. Naturally, it looked about for some way in which to employ her profitably, but never found it to any degree.

In 1866 she was placed on the Albany run on April 30 to afford early season service, and ran alone until late in May, when the *Chauncey Vibbard* and the *Daniel Drew* went into commission. On May 31 the *Armenia* was placed on the route between New York and Poughkeepsie, leaving New York at nine in the morning and Poughkeepsie on the return at two in the afternoon. She made practically all of the landings which the through boats did and some others in addition. This service, in which Van Santvoord had employed the *Alida* in 1860, catered principally to one-day excursionists and continued through September 29. It was not resumed in 1867, when the *Armenia's* activities were confined to the handling of a very few charters and an excursion to Newburgh on the Fourth of July.

In 1865 the net operating earnings of the three steamers increased by more than 50%, dropped sharply to slightly over $29,000 in 1866 and then soared to pass $70,000 in 1868. These figures are not indicative of the actual quantity of business, for the through fare between New York and Albany

The grace of the *Daniel Drew* is apparent in this photograph of her, taken when she was in lay-up. The name on the front of the pilothouse has been carefully covered and the ornaments have been removed from the tops of the spars.—*Elwin M. Eldredge coll.*

---

or vice versa does not seem to have been more or less stabilized at $2.00 until 1868. Thereafter it became what might be called a firm figure, for it was still in effect in 1917. Previously the rate might be as low as $1.00, as it was at least early in 1866.

In 1867 the Day Line carried 134,660 passengers and in 1868 only 106,234½ but in the latter year the steamers made almost nine thousand dollars more than in 1867. So far as the New York-Albany service was concerned, the number of passengers carried in 1867 and the net operating earnings of 1868 were peaks that were to stand until 1876.

In 1868 the *Chauncey Vibbard* netted earnings of $33,592.54 and carried 53,870 fares; the *Daniel Drew* netted $39,712.08 with 52,364½ fares. Of the total of 106,234½ passengers, 16,558½ had gone all the way from New York to Albany; 10,318½ from Albany to New York. The balance, 79,357½ had traveled either between New York or Albany and

way landings, or between way landings. The *Armenia*, which was almost exclusively "spare" that year, reduced the final earnings with a loss of about $3,000.

In the early years of the Day Line, Alfred Van Santvoord continued to occupy the position of general agent of the Hudson River Steamboat Co., the towing line in which he was a large stockholder and which was popularly known in Albany, at least, as Van Santvoord's line. It had been a lucrative investment and in the period 1846-1866 paid dividends of 366%. By the later 1860s, the Hudson River Steamboat Co. was interested in a proposition for three of its towing steamers. This matter was handled by Van Santvoord, who at the same time was contemplating an expansion of the Day Line.

That part of the plan involved the *Mary Powell*. Earlier, during the season of 1865, Captain Absalom L. Anderson, then in his fifty-third year, decided it would be pleasant to retire and spend the twilight of his life in his comfortable home by the Hudson. This meant that the *Mary Powell* would be sold, and in October of 1865, after the year's operations had ended, she was purchased by Thomas Cornell of Rondout. For a time Daniel Drew was his partner in the venture.

Cornell was an old hand at operating steamboats. He was already well versed in the intricacies of making money in water transportation when in 1848, at the age of thirty-four, he and an uncle purchased the steamboat *Norwich*, which was then running as a night boat for freight and passengers between Rondout and New York City. Cornell thought towing was a lusher field than the passenger business and after the season of 1851 devoted his time mainly to his towing fleet, of which the *Norwich* was by now a part. In 1854 he reentered the passenger and freight business between Rondout and New York, but was content to run only one steamboat, which, in conjunction with a steamboat owned by another firm, provided a regular night line between the two places. In the meantime his towing business grew steadily. Eventually incorporated as the Cornell Steamboat Co., it came to be the largest establishment of its kind.

Thomas Cornell was reported to have paid $180,000 for the *Mary Powell* and her well-developed and money-coining route, and ran her for three years, 1866-68. Now Van Santvoord and Davidson were interested in acquiring her, while Cornell was interested in participating advantageously in the partial dissolution of the fleet of the Hudson River Steamboat Co.

The negotiations finally bore fruit on February 18, 1869, when Cornell sold the *Mary Powell* and her route for $180,000 to Van Santvoord and Davidson as co-owners. Cornell, in turn, purchaesd three towing steamers to add to his fleet. This part of the transaction resulted in further trading of vessels between Cornell and the Schuyler Line Towboat Association.

The buying of the *Mary Powell* by Van Santvoord and Davidson was to result in no change as far as the operations of steamers was concerned. The *Mary Powell* would continue on the Rondout and New York day route, making a round trip daily except Sunday, and the *Chauncey Vibbard* and the *Daniel Drew* would run as usual between New York and Albany.

Aside from claims regarding the speed of the three steamboats, there had never been any competition between the two lines. The *Mary Powell*

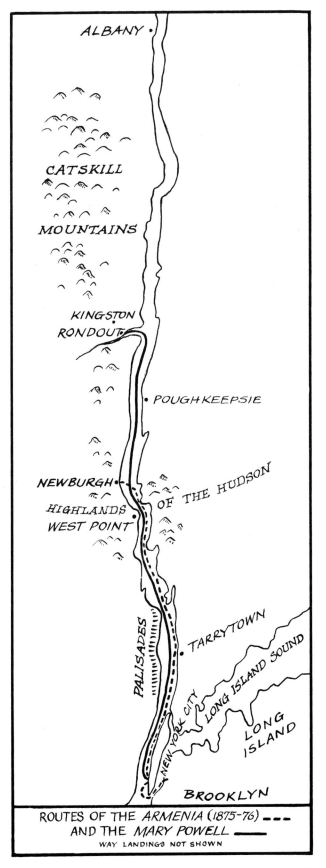

ROUTES OF THE *ARMENIA* (1875-76) - - -
AND THE *MARY POWELL* ——
WAY LANDINGS NOT SHOWN

usually left Rondout at 5:30 in the morning, while the southbound boat from Albany didn't pass down in that area until about noon. From New York the *Mary Powell* generally sailed on her return at 3:30 p.m., or about seven or eight hours after the departure of the northbound steamer for Albany.

On the other hand, the new owners were to make a considerable change in the appearance of the *Mary Powell*. Captain Anderson, as we have seen, had marked ideas about what a day boat should be like, and Cornell was content to leave the *Mary Powell* unaltered. But Captain Anderson's ideas were not at all in keeping with the ideas of Van Santvoord and Davidson, who planned to make the *Mary Powell* more like the *Chauncey Vibbard* and the *Daniel Drew*. Primarily, this called for a great extension in the size of the main saloon. King & Eells were hired for the job and when they were finished it had been carried far forward, to eliminate much of the open forward promenade deck that Captain Anderson always insisted his passengers wanted.

The wainscoating of this enlarged saloon was of solid walnut. Large mirrors were set about and the walnut furniture was upholstered in bright blue velvet. The steamboat was not readied for service until early June of 1869. In the meantime the *Armenia* had opened the New York-Rondout day route on May 1 and continued until replaced by the *Mary Powell*.

The *Armenia* apparently still had her shrill steam calliope, for a newspaper editor, perhaps with tongue in cheek, noted that it could be expected to play "A Life on the Raging Canal" at Rondout, "Beautiful City So Fair" at Poughkeepsie and "Isn't He a Darling, the Bould Soger Boy," at West Point. The calliope in military tradition might also have played "Taps" for itself, for it is said to have been removed soon after. The Day Line had passed the point where it would retain such a plebeian attraction even on its spare boat.

Figures, apparently furnished to Van Santvoord and Davidson by Cornell, showed the gross earnings of the *Mary Powell* to have averaged approximately $100,000 a year in 1866-68, during which period she carried a total of 341,592 passengers. On a route such as the *Mary Powell's*, one-day round trippers naturally were two passengers, one going down and one coming back. Her season had been somewhat longer than that of the Day Line, in that she commenced running in April.

The patrons of the route of the *Mary Powell* dropped off sharply in 1869 from the claimed average of about 114,000 per season in 1866-68. Passengers on the New York-Albany run also dropped off almost to 98,000 in 1869, but in 1870 rose to over 118,000. In 1870 passengers on the Rondout-New York route increased only slightly, to 92,990.

Although Van Santvoord and Davidson had initially gone all out in altering the *Mary Powell*, their interest in the Rondout day line seems to have paled rather rapidly. Admittedly the business may not have been as heavy as they anticipated, but for the first two years of their ownership the *Mary Powell* showed total net operating earnings of about $57,000. This left over $40,000 even after applying the entire net operating loss from the *Armenia* in 1869 and 1870. In that period, besides running between Rondout and New York in the spring of 1869, she was also in that service in the fall of 1870 after the *Mary Powell* had been withdrawn for the season.

In 1871 traffic dropped dismally on both the New York-Albany and the Rondout-New York lines. Van Santvoord and Davidson closed the latter route with the *Mary Powell's* down-trip on the early date of October 2, and the next day placed her on the New York-Albany run with the *Daniel Drew*. Even though 1871 was to prove a poor year, the Day Line had evidently made plans to have the *Chauncey Vibbard* lengthened as a result of consideration of traffic for 1870. It was announced that she was to be withdrawn so that an extensive rebuilding could commence.

Although the lengthening and rebuilding were to go forward, the *Chauncey Vibbard* seems to have been withdrawn early from the New York-Albany run only so that the Day Line could run the *Mary Powell* in her stead as an experiment. The *Mary Powell* was considerably longer than the *Daniel Drew* or the *Chauncey Vibbard*, and would still exceed the latter even after the lengthening. It appears that if the *Mary Powell* proved capable of maintaining the schedule in the New York-Albany service, the Day Line might then place her on that route permanently in place of the *Daniel Drew*. It would thus have for the 1872 season a pair of steamboats of about the same size. At least afterwards the Day Line maintained that that was its intent.

The *Mary Powell* made four trips between New York and Albany and was unable, according to marine historian John H. Morrison*, to make as

*History of American Steam Navigation, p. 155.

These two photographs spliced together show the *Chauncey Vibbard* at the Brooklyn shipyard where she was lengthened. A window of one of the private rooms on her hurricane deck may be seen by the top of the paddle box.—*Eldredge coll., Mariners Museum.*

good time as the *Daniel Drew*. No figures are given relative to this, though. Partisans of the *Mary Powell* had a strong point in their favor when they argued that the steamer was greatly weighted down by the enlarged saloon which had been added to her. In any event, in later years the Day Line made the most of the fact that the *Daniel Drew* had allegedly bested her.

Whether or not Van Santvoord and Davidson had already decided to dispose of the Rondout-New York route and devote themselves entirely to the New York-Albany service, it soon became evident that they would. In January of 1872 they sold the *Mary Powell* and her route for $150,000 to none other than Captain Absalom L. Anderson.

Why Captain Anderson returned to active steamboating we do not know. Perhaps he felt that the twilight of his life was going to extend much longer than he had anticipated and found retirement a tedious business for a man who knew that commanding a steamboat was the most pleasant of earthly occupations. We might not be far wrong if we assumed that he was becoming increasingly unhappy about the strange things that were happening to his *Mary Powell*, and decided to take the opportunity to do something about it.

Although it must have burdened his heart as much as it did the *Mary Powell*, Captain Anderson ran her in 1872 as he had acquired her. Then, after the season closed, he had the addition to the main saloon ripped out and let it be known that he ". . . wouldn't carry all that stuff if it were covered with pure gold." Once again his passengers were to enjoy plenty of pure air and good scenery on the wide-open spaces of the forward promen-

ade deck. They would go faster, too, for in 1873 the *Mary Powell* made one of her fastest runs between New York and Rondout.

Meanwhile, the *Chauncey Vibbard* had been lengthened as planned. James S. Dean did the work at his shipyard in Brooklyn, where the steamer was finally sawed in two aft of the paddle wheels on February 13, 1872. One section was then hauled 16 feet away from the other and the business of putting her back together was commenced.

She was relaunched late in March and fitted with new boilers by Fletcher, Harrison & Co., who at this time also placed in her a new and larger cylinder. With necessary joiner work done by Henry B. Eells of the old firm of King & Eells, the cost of the rejuvenation had come to almost $40,000.

The little illustrative matter available showing the *Chauncey Vibbard* after the lengthening leads us to believe that she lost a bit of her original grace and beauty in the process. More strengthening spars had to be added, and these were not an attractive feature. Together with the private rooms, they gave a somewhat helter-skelter air to the hurricane deck. But the main point was that she was now a more ample passenger carrier. The passengers enjoying the increased space would not be apt to be unduly concerned with her outward appearance, for of that they saw little.

The *Chauncey Vibbard* was given a rousing reception on her first trip up the Hudson in 1872, on May 28, and one reporter decided, "She is undoubtedly the finest craft on the river."

Captain David H. Hitchcock was still her commander, so we may be sure he concurred. He had been saying the same thing since 1864. His old friendly enemy Captain John F. Tallman, was no longer in the arena of the Day Line. A few years earlier he had married a "young Riverdale lady" and, following the 1870 season, left the Day Line and the *Daniel Drew*, his old Honey Cooler forever to try a new position.

After Captain Anderson reacquired the *Mary Powell*, her commander under Cornell and Van Santvoord, Captain Ferdinand Frost, remained with Van Santvoord and in 1872 was assigned to the *Daniel Drew*. Captain Frost was to go on commanding Day Line boats for many seasons.

On the *Daniel Drew*, according to a press account, he had an unhappy experience. On July 4, 1873, a day of peak northbound traffic, that steamer was the up-boat from New York. The passengers came in a steady stream, the paper said, until finally there were on board considerably more than the *Daniel Drew* could handle. The Day Line estimated there were 200 too many.

Naturally, no passenger was going to say, "Ah, yes! I am overloading the boat. I shall go ashore." Everyone took the very natural point of view that there he was, and there he would stay. When all other forms of persuasion failed, the line went so far as to call the police. The police were no more able than the Day Line to determine which two hundred should go ashore, and had no greater vocal powers to accomplish miracles. The next step would have been a rough-and-tumble, and that was the last thing the Day Line wanted.

Since nobody would leave her, the *Daniel Drew* sailed for Albany. She sailed slowly. In fact, she practically crept. Each time she exerted her cranky tendencies by listing, the water came over the guard; when she straightened up again, it flowed over her main deck. Such occurrences were not rare on heavily laden sidewheel steamers, but they were certainly not standard operating procedure. For the Day Line, it was an appalling state of affairs.

Again according to the newspaper, it was late afternoon before the *Daniel Drew* reached West Point. Here, we are told, the chief engineer decided he had had enough and went ashore. This is a little hard to believe, since the chief was likely Philip St. Pierre, who was on the vessel for many years. On the other hand, perhaps it was simply a demonstration of profound good sense on the part of Mr. St. Pierre.

The newspaper goes on to relate that, happily, the assistant engineer stuck by the steamer so that the *Daniel Drew* could continue on up the river.

The farther up she went, of course, the lighter she became, so that she was able to make Albany by 10:30 that night. If the story is not partially apocryphal, we prefer to assume that on this day the down-boat did not wait for the up-boat at Poughkeepsie!

Later in the same month Captain Hitchcock on the *Chauncey Vibbard* had a far happier day when he landed President U. S. Grant at Rhinecliff. The President had come up the river to spend a short holiday with his friend, General George H. Sharpe of Kingston. Grant spread his patronage out a bit by returning on the *Mary Powell*.

Between the seasons of 1873 and 1874, it was the *Daniel Drew's* turn to undergo a major overhaul. It was not considered feasible to lengthen her, since that had been done once, but it was thought desirable to widen her hull in an attempt to improve her stability and eliminate her crankiness. This was done by building onto part of her another hull, running to eighteen inches outside of the main hull.

A steamboat so treated was said to have been "hipped." The derivation of the word is obvious. She got wider in the middle. In the case of the *Daniel Drew*, the hipping seems not to have been completely successful.

Early in October of 1874, the *Chauncey Vibbard* and the *Daniel Drew* closed the two-boat service for that year and the ever-faithful *Armenia* was put on the run from October 7 for over three weeks, going up on Mondays, Wednesdays and Fridays and down on the following days. In 1875 the *Armenia* opened the Albany season on May 17 and continued on it alone until early June, when the *Chauncey Vibbard* and the *Daniel Drew* came out.

From June 23 through September 11, the *Armenia* was used in daily except Sunday round-trip service to Newburgh. This was a shortened version of her earlier Poughkeepsie run. The *Armenia* started from Fulton Street, Brooklyn, and after touching at the Day Line's New York landings, made such stops as Manhattanville, Dobbs Ferry and the amusement ground at Iona Island. As an added convenience, she left from Newburgh on her return following the arrival of the southbound steamer from Albany so that passengers bound for some of the lesser places could transfer to her. After finishing her Newburgh stint for the year, she went back on the Albany run on September 28 and ran with the *Daniel Drew* in place of the *Chauncey Vibbard* until October 11.

With some changes in landings, the *Armenia* again operated in the Newburgh trade in 1876, from June 26 through September 18.

The year of 1876 brought the Centennial Exhibition at Philadelphia, commemorating the 100th birthday of the nation. This was expected to be a banner year for Hudson River steamboating generally. Everyone who could beg, borrow or afford the necessary fare was bound for Philadelphia to see all of the latest wonders of the age, and it was hoped that a goodly percentage would include a trip on the Hudson River as part of the pilgrimage. The Day Line, anxious to get its share of the business, went into full two-boat operation on May 24 and its season did not close until November 11.

From September 27 through October 14, the *Armenia* was placed on the Albany run to serve as a second section to the *Daniel Drew*. The latter steamer was the express boat, while the *Armenia* took care of the way-landing business. In the closing period of the season, the Day Line advertised that its steamers would land en route only at Newburgh and Poughkeepsie. Thereby it operated primarily for the benefit of the through passengers, who were the only reason it was continuing so late in the year.

For the Day Line 1876 was indeed a banner year. Over 173,000 passengers were carried on the New York-Albany service as against approximately 133,000 in the best previous year of the 1870s, 1873. Not until 1890 would the 1876 record be topped.

And better than sheer numbers was the fact that in 1876 roughly half of the passengers made the complete trip, either from Albany to New York

or vice versa, as against only about 20% in 1873. The net operating earnings of the steamers for the year totalled approximately $138,000. This came entirely from the *Daniel Drew* and the *Chauncey Vibbard*, for the *Armenia* lost $16.03!

As usual, the Day Line soon turned some of the money back to the traveling public. Although the *Chauncey Vibbard* had been rejuvenated only six years before and the *Daniel Drew* four years previously, between the seasons of 1877 and 1878 both boats underwent extensive overhauling. As part of this work, the private rooms were removed from the hurricane deck of the *Chauncey Vibbard* and replaced by similar installations off the main saloon.

Service was begun on June 10, 1878, but the *Daniel Drew* was not ready until July 1. The *Armenia* ran with the *Chauncey Vibbard* during June. Oddly, this late appearance of the *Daniel Drew* brought some favorable publicity to the line, which was applauded for not permitting a boat to go in service until it was "perfect."

The 1870s were almost over. As perhaps its last operational innovation of the decade, the Day Line established no-fee parcel rooms on its steamers. This was a handy arrangement whereby one could check his packages and umbrella, and enjoy the trip unencumbered without extra cost. Although the check room was an obvious source of additional revenue, the Day Line chose to regard it as part of the service for the passengers. It accepted coats, light valises and the like for free checking until well into the twentieth century.

But bigger things than no-fee parcel rooms were soon to come.

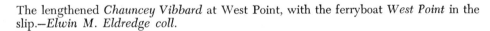

The lengthened *Chauncey Vibbard* at West Point, with the ferryboat *West Point* in the slip.—*Elwin M. Eldredge coll.*

Chapter 8

THE MEN WHO MANNED THE STEAMERS

B EFORE LEAVING the Day Line of the 1860s and the 1870s, it might be well to interject some comment on the manning of the steamers. Regardless of how much money the owners lavished on their steamboats, the steamboats by themselves were inanimate things. The continuing prosperity of the Day Line also stemmed in good measure from the performance of the officers and the crew. Since these were the people who could form the lasting impression of the Day Line in the eyes of the travelling public, the line made every effort to obtain the best available men to run its steamers.

The function of the officers on Hudson River passenger steamboats in the nineteenth century was generally the same as it is today, with the marked exception of the captain's. While the captain commanded the steamer in the present-day sense of the word, he was not required to have been first a pilot, or in fact originally to have any specific knowledge of piloting or navigation.

Some of the captains, of course, had been steamboat pilots in their day, others had navigated sailing vessels, and occasionally one was an engineer. But these men usually owed their more elevated station to having saved their money and invested it in steamboats.

The typical old-time captains either owned or were shareholders in their steamboats and, as such, did all of those things which any man would do in operating his own business. They might sell the tickets, collect the freight receipts, accept produce on consignment for resale in the New York markets, welcome the customers on board and make sure they were enjoying the trip, check on the quality of the meals being served, stop by the engine room to see that the engineer was not crowding on the steam unnecessarily and expensively, and keep a watchful eye on the way the steamer was being handled by the pilots. In cases where the captain was strictly an employee of the owner, he was required to do all of these things, too, as the manager on board.

Since captains were in constant contact with the public, they were expected to be genial men with pleasing personalities. They had to be if they were to be successful. Popular captains built up wide followings and in the days of intense competition, the disposition of the captain might be the difference between profit and loss.

During a good part of the nineteenth century, the name of the captain was often carried in advertising along with the name of the boat, so that passengers could plan to travel with their favorite captain. Of course their plans didn't always work out. Here a little ruse was sometimes practiced whereby the name of a well-known captain remained coupled with a steamboat months after he had left her for greener pastures.

One man who, as a boy, made a trip with his father on a Hudson River night boat, vividly recalled the captain coming to their stateroom to make sure they had enough blankets. This was the sort of attention that kept the customers coming back.

Although we might class the old-time captains as businessmen pure and simple, they had to be highly competent in the type of business they conducted and through years of experience had a broad general knowledge of steamboating. There was no more need for them to become specialists in, for example, piloting than there is today for a captain to learn how to operate the engine.

Pilots and engineers were required to be licensed by federal legislation of the early 1850s, and a couple of decades later the captains and chief mates of steam vessels came under similar legislation. Here the requirements for the Hudson River were based upon the position of captain as it then was.

It would seem that the Hudson River captains of those days, if they were properly efficient, could keep all departments under their thumbs more equitably than latter-day captains, after it became necessary for them first to have qualified as pilot. When this law was put into force, the captains of the old school came to be known as "deck captains." That carried with it something of the derogatory, which is unfortunate. The great days of Hudson River steamboating was the era of the deck captains, and there is no need to apologize for the way they ran their steamboats.

Since they had so many things to do, the captains could not be further burdened with the keeping of all the necessary records, nor could they give constant attention to their main-deck offices. Therefore, they had directly assisting them an officer who was originally known simply as "clerk." Hardly sufficient for a man engaged in such worldly work as clerk on a steamboat, this title gave way to "second captain" and eventually became "purser."

There was no prescribed rule. During the Civil War, when armed forces' titles were all the rage, the second captain was sometimes known as the "first lieutenant." Second captain best describes his position. He was the captain's right arm, familiar with all the duties of the master and ready to fill in during absences of his superior. He could be addressed as "captain."

We are reminded here of a Hudson River captain who, as he grew older, ceased to be either genial or accommodating. In fact, he became increasingly cantankerous. Since he was part-owner of his command, he obviously couldn't be replaced. This was where the second captain proved his worth. The second captain was one of those people whom everyone liked. So fond of him were the passengers that they were willing to overlook the shortcomings of the captain and continued to patronize the steamer.

As a result of the make-up of the captain's position, the navigation was usually entirely in the hands of the pilots. Piloting called for skill of a high order. The pilot had to be thoroughly familiar with every foot of the river and to be able to operate under extremely adverse conditions with few navigational aids to assist him. He studied the tides, he studied the winds and he knew what his steamboat would do under every conceivable condition.

Piloting was anything but a relaxing occupation. In addition to being mentally alert, the pilot had to be healthy and muscular. The steamers were "hand-geared." This meant that the pilot had to move the rudder by brute strength applied to the steering or pilot wheel, giving rise to the term "armstrong rig." The steering wheels themselves were of large diameter to provide maximum lev-

erage and in making a sharp change of course the pilot might "climb the wheel." In doing so, he would step on the lowest spoke on the proper side to add the weight of his body to the maneuver. As the wheel commenced to turn, he would step up to the next spoke and thus continue.

The use of the steam steering engine on later Day Line steamers did away with the physical labor and permitted the pilot to concentrate entirely on steering, which was enough. Here the turning of a small steering wheel actuated a steam-powered engine and this in turn applied the force to move the rudder. But the large steering wheel remained a prominent fixture in the pilothouse for hand-gear steering in case of a breakdown of the steering engine.

In the days before the engine-room telegraph, all signals from the pilothouse to the engine room were transmitted by pulling bell-pulls in the pilothouse. These bell-pulls were connected by wires to bells in the engine room, and usually three types of bells were employed — a large gong, a jingle bell and a cowbell.

The Day Line originally seems to have had only one pilot per steamer. He was likely assisted by a mate and later by a quartermaster or wheelsman. But before many years, two pilots were employed. Both men usually remained in the pilothouse all day long, except at mealtime, and had the titles of "first pilot" and "second pilot."

In the engine room, the titles at first were similar, with the ranking engineer being the "first engineer" and his assistant the "second engineer." These in time became respectively "chief engineer" and "assistant engineer." It was not uncommon for the chief to be known by the very descriptive nickname of "boss."

Engineering on beam-engined steamboats wasn't relaxing work. When the engine was started, the steam inlet and outlet valves in the steam chests at the top and bottom of the vertical cylinder had to be operated by manpower. This was accomplished by the use of a long starting bar which was moved up and down like the handle of a huge pump.

As the engineer pushed this bar up and pulled it down, he slowly increased its movement and thereby the movement of the engine until sufficient speed had been attained to permit "hooking up." This meant that the eccentric rods were dropped so that hooks on their ends engaged projecting pins on arms on the rockshafts, which now mech-

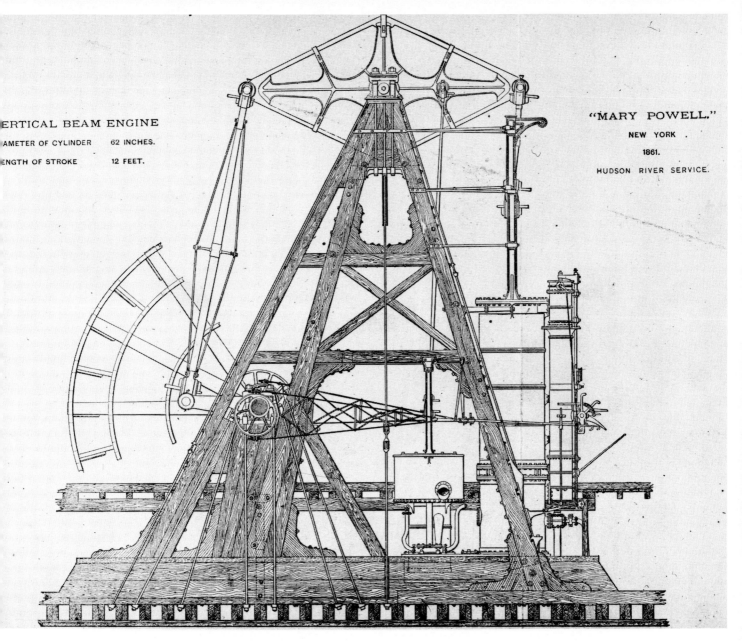

ERTICAL BEAM ENGINE

AMETER OF CYLINDER   62 INCHES.

ENGTH OF STROKE   12 FEET.

"MARY POWELL."

NEW YORK .

1861.

HUDSON RIVER SERVICE.

In the view of the vertical beam engine of the *Mary Powell*, the flow of power may be traced from the cylinder at the right via the piston rod and links to the walking beam, and from the other end of the walking beam down the connecting rod to the crank on the paddle-wheel shaft. The smaller connecting rod from the beam operated the air pump. Sticking out at an angle at the far right is the starting bar, and this may also be seen in the photograph opposite of the engine room of the twentieth-century *Robert Fulton*. Here the bar crosses in front of H. C. Magee, who was the first chief engineer of the vessel. The "duck-bill" affairs are the wipers on the rockshafts and toes on the vertical lifting rods.—*Opposite, Alexander P. Olcott coll.*

anically actuated the lifting rods that operated the valves. The engine then ran by itself and the throttle could be opened until full speed had been reached. Slowing down could be done with the throttle, but once the engine was stopped, reversing or going ahead meant further toil with the starting bar.

Needless to say, the engineers' labors were considerably less than those of their firemen. On boilers-on-the-guards steamboats, the firemen at least were able to see what was going on. But not even scenery made the work of shoveling coal into a firebox any less arduous.

Aside from those things which fell to the province of the engineers, the mate was responsible for the general up-keep of the steamer. In his department were the deckhands or sailors, who swept the deck, scrubbed the paint, handled the mooring lines at landings, carried the trunks on and off, and otherwise kept themselves busy.

Although taken in later years, this photograph shows the human-chain method of handling trunks on the Day Line.—*H.R.D.L. coll., Steamship Historical Society of America, Inc.*

Since everyone likes to watch someone else work, the carrying of trunks by the deckhands captured a large audience at landings. For fastest handling, the Day Line came to employ the human-chain method, whereby a deckhand grabbed the front end of a trunk, a second deckhand took the other end of it and the front of the next trunk, and so on.

Directing the activity of his cooks and waiters, the steward played a vital role in keeping the passengers happy. The food had to be good and well prepared, for the Day Line had established and maintained a fine reputation for the quality of its cuisine.

Another functionary who strove to keep the passengers happy was the baggagemaster. Anyone who has gotten off a steamer at a landing and realized a few minutes later that his baggage was going on up the river, can best appreciate the importance of the baggagemaster. His duties in the days of the great movement of trunks were complicated and involved, since it was important that the steamer not be delayed unduly at any landing.

Others on board included the ticket collector, the dining room cashier, the stewardess, and of course the bartender. The latter's name was always included boldly in early lists of the personnel of the steamers. We are sure that the bartenders, like the captains, had their own personal following.

Captain Hitchcock exemplified a pattern that was to be repeated by the Day Line through the years. He was often not the only Hitchcock aboard the *Chauncey Vibbard*. At one time his brother was second pilot; two of his sons were cashier and baggagemaster. Having several members of the same family on the payroll occurred often. Fathers brought their sons and brothers brought brothers so that the same names recur in the history of the line. It was to become a family affair in more ways than one.

Chapter 9

THE *Albany*

INTO THE 1870s the Day Line continued to style itself the "Day Line of Steamers on the Hudson River," but on timetables of the period used something more descriptive of the route, such as "New York, Albany & Troy Day Line" — Troy, of course, being reached by connecting steamers from Albany. Finally, for letterhead purposes, it abandoned "Day Line of Steamers" for "New York & Albany Day Line."

In 1879 Van Santvoord and Davidson decided that the time had come to incorporate their holdings, and the necessary certificate was filed on June 17. One would think that a likely name for the new corporation would be "New York & Albany Day Line" or something similar. But the name selected was "Hudson River Line," which was probably the choice of Van Santvoord. His ties with the early days of steam navigation on the Hudson were strong and one of the steamboat lines formed in the 1820s after breaking of the Fulton-Livingston monopoly had called itself the Hudson River Line.

Even the Day Line later admitted that the name was not a good one. Descriptively, it was even less satisfying than "Day Line of Steamers." To remedy this, the new Hudson River Line used as a second line on its letterhead, "New York & Albany Day Boats." But it did design a house flag with "H.R.L." in large letters for flying from the jackstaffs of its steamers and devised uniform buttons with an "HRL" monogram.

The Hudson River Line was capitalized at $125,000, which was the price for which it acquired the *Chauncey Vibbard, Daniel Drew* and *Armenia* from Van Santvoord and Davidson. Of the 1,250 hundred-dollar shares, Alfred Van Santvoord and John McB. Davidson held 600 each; Charles Townsend Van Santvoord, 40; Abraham Van Santvoord, 5; Clarence R. van Benthuysen, 5.

Charles T. Van Santvoord was the son of Alfred Van Santvoord. Born in Albany in 1854, he graduated from Rutgers in the class of 1873 and went to work for his father in the Day Line, of which he became the general manager. Young Van Santvoord was a well-proportioned six-footer who was strongly inclined toward athletics, hunting and yachting. There was another side to his nature for he was a gentleman with charming manners and was a lover of art. He attracted a wide range of friends.

Clarence R. van Benthuysen was also a native of Albany, having been born there in 1853. In 1870 he graduated from Andover Seminary, where he was particularly proficient in mathematics. He then worked in Albany at an ironworks and with his father, Charles van Benthuysen, proprietor of a well-known printing house of the period. Clarence later joined the Day Line and subsequently became its general ticket agent.

The fifth stockholder, Abraham Van Santvoord, was an admiralty lawyer in practice in New York with his father, Cornelius, who was a brother of Alfred Van Santvoord.

Alfred and Charles T. Van Santvoord and John McB. Davidson became the first directors, and of course Alfred Van Santvoord was elected president.

The Day Line was under no delusion as to the transitoriness of the great business of 1876. Passengers in 1877 dropped to 109,306 and in 1878 fell to 99,603. In the 1870s, the latter was the lowest mark on the New York-Albany route since 1871. But in 1879 business again commenced to swing upward, and the total for that year was to be 117,704.

The first major business undertaken by the directors was the construction of a new steamboat and, indeed, that may have been the reason for the formation of the corporation. Van Santvoord and Davidson had begun their operation of the Day Line with the intent of giving the travelling public the best possible facilities for day steamer travel that could be found in the country. That they succeeded is well shown by the fact that no one ever tried seriously to compete directly with them. To do so required what in those days would have

Charles Townsend Van Santvoord, son of Alfred Van Santvoord, became his father's right-hand man in the operation of the Day Line.—*Elmendorf coll., New York State Library, Albany, N. Y.*

been a fortune as an initial investment, and would have resulted in a knockdown, drag-out battle of lengthy proportions. Van Santvoord and Davidson had both capital and a going line.

Of course they did not have a true monopoly. Anyone could get to any of their landings by other means, and if he took the New York Central & Hudson River Railroad (the two roads had consolidated in 1869), he could get there in considerably less time. So, to hold and increase their business, they felt they must now improve their fleet.

The ideal would have been the construction of a pair of new steamers, but the Day Line did not believe it could afford such a large expenditure at one time. As steamboats went, neither the *Daniel Drew* nor the *Chauncey Vibbard* was old. The latter was the younger by four years and the longer by 21 feet, so the Day Line elected to build one new vessel of about the same length as the *Chauncey Vibbard* and to alter that vessel in keeping with the design of the new one. It further decided that the hull of the new vessel would be of iron. Iron-hulled vessels were no novelty, they had

been constructed in the United States for many years. They were most uncommon on such routes as those on the Hudson River, where wooden hulls had always been satisfactory.

Obviously, iron was sturdier, able to withstand more stress and strain than a staunchly braced wooden hull. Iron even had a passenger appeal, for it conveyed to the public the idea of greater safety. The Day Line believed that the wooden hull was the hull of the past and the iron hull, the hull of the future.

William Foulks of Lawrence & Foulks, builders of the *Chauncey Vibbard*, supplied a hull model which was accepted. For a time the Day Line seems to have considered having Lawrence & Foulks build the hull, with ironwork supplied by Thomas F. Rowland's Continental Works in Brooklyn. Iron shipbuilding was centering on the Delaware River and finally the Day Line decided to have the hull built by the Harlan & Hollingsworth Co., whose yard was located at Wilmington, Delaware. The specifications were approved early in September, 1879.

Besides having an iron hull, the new vessel was to present an exterior considerably different from her predecessors. The Day Line also believed that boilers on the guards were a thing of the past and planned for three boilers to be in the hold. In effect, this amounted to placing on either side of the hold the boilers that normally would be on the guards, and putting the third boiler between them. As a result there would be three smokestacks athwartship rising up above the hurricane deck.

The absence of the boilers on the guards made possible the utilization of more space in the area heretofore dominated by them; the fact that the boilers would take up a section of the hold didn't matter. There would be ample room for them, since a feature of the new vessel was the location of the dining room on the main deck aft so that the passengers could watch the scenery while at meals. This in turn meant the elimination of the large ladies' saloon which had occupied main decks aft for decades, but times were changing and the ladies no longer needed all that privacy. Similar though more limited facilities would be afforded them on the second deck.

Spars and tie rods, so necessary as part of the strengthening components for the larger wooden-hulled sidewheelers, could not be eliminated by either the iron hull or the design of the new vessel. While there was no need for them to help support the heavy boilers on the guards, and the weight of the overhanging paddle wheels was taken up as usual by the king posts, the standard radial paddle wheels and vertical beam engine would produce considerable vibration. The radial paddles struck directly into the water; the beam engine produced a thrust as the crank went upward or downward and a lag as it passed the center. Spars and rods were considered necessary, therefore, to sustain the hull fore and aft under the strain of this vibration.

Fletcher, Harrison & Co. were to construct the engine, while John E. Hoffmire was selected as the joiner contractor. Hoffmire was in the tradition of the man-who-made-good of the nineteenth century. He worked his way up from apprentice joiner to shop foreman with Hiram Perry, a ship and steamboat joiner, and after Perry's death took over the business. During his lifetime, Hoffmire erected the joiner work for a long list of celebrated American steam vessels, became a bank director and served as president of the Knickerbocker Steamboat Co. Like many leading figures in the steamboat business of that era, he came to be known as Commodore Hoffmire.

The Day Line seriously considered naming the new steamer the *Peter Cooper*, but afterwards changed its mind. Nevertheless, word of the proposed name leaked out and spread through the nautical fraternity. Captain Dave Hitchcock was to command the vessel and one day a reporter went to see him.

"How's the *Peter Cooper* getting on, Captain Dave?"

"The who?"

"The *Peter Cooper*, the new boat to run with the *Vibbard* next year?"

Captain Hitchcock laughed. "Why, bless your heart," he said, "the new boat will not be named the *Peter Cooper*. The name has not yet been agreed upon. But you may be sure of this: it will not be after any man or woman."

On another occasion, Captain Hitchcock let it be known that he wouldn't be surprised if the name were either *Capital City* or *Albany*. Albany loomed large in the background of all the important figures in the line.

The hull was launched from the Harlan & Hollingsworth yard on January 13, 1880. An early morning snowstorm had kept many potential spectators at home, but the white blanket on the ground set off the red bottom of the hull in startling fashion. At 1:28 p.m. the hull moved down

the ways into the waters of what is now called the Christina River, a tributary of the Delaware. Alfred Van Santvoord was watching, along with Andrew Fletcher and Joseph Belknap, who had superintended the construction.

A reporter for the *Nautical Gazette* was quite carried away and wrote that the hull was ". . . smooth as a kid glove, graceful . . . as a swan, and sits on the water like a cork. She's a beauty." He also added the information that the affair was strictly a business launching and that there was no christening. But some newspapers reported that Charles T. Van Santvoord, Alfred's son, had christened the vessel the *Albany*.

Although Alfred Van Santvoord promptly wrote a letter to Captain Hitchcock to tell him of the launching, he made no mention of the name. Hitchcock, who apparently was on tenterhooks as a result of the omission, replied under date of January 15, "has she a name as yet as the Albany papers has [sic] been so much exercised over a name for her that they have almost daily had her in the papers with a new name every time. . . . if the name is settled on it will relieve them of their anxiety in regard to what the name will be and and [sic] give them more space in their papers for other matters."

Anyway, she was definitely the *Albany*. And, after Harlan & Hollingsworth had completed their work, she was towed up to New York, arriving February 11. There Fletcher, Harrison & Co. would install the engine and boilers, and Hoffmire erect the joiner work. While the *Albany* was being built, the *Chauncey Vibbard* was being rebuilt into a reasonable facsimile.

On May 12, 1880, the *Albany* set out on a trial trip intended to test the engine and boilers. Her joiner work was far from complete, but from two to three hundred guests were invited for the occasion.

The *Daniel Drew* and the remodeled *Chauncey Vibbard* opened the season and ran together until July 3, when the *Albany* was pressed into service in place of the *Daniel Drew* in anticipation of heavy traffic. The *Albany* was still not finished, and Commodore Hoffmire's workmen sailed off on the maiden voyage to Albany with their saws and hammers adding unusual notes to the general festivities.

A peculiar thing about the *Albany* was that she had no open promenade deck forward, a feature or lack of one that must have horrified Captain Anderson of the *Mary Powell*. On the *Albany* one could go forward on the second deck only to the front of the enclosed saloon on the inside, and no farther. Presumably the steamer was so built to make it impossible for passengers to sit outside in front of the saloon windows and obstruct the view of those sitting within. For the fresh-air fan the third or hurricane deck was available. Her length was 284 feet and her total cost came to $187,318.58.

Captain Hitchcock and most of his crew moved from the *Chauncey Vibbard* to the *Albany*, while Captain Frost similarly took over the *Chauncey Vibbard*. Now the Day Line had a spare boat in the *Daniel Drew*, and the *Armenia* was offered for sale.

The old *Armenia* had been running for a short while in 1880 as, of all things, a milk boat. At that time much milk was shipped into Kingston via the Wallkill Valley and Ulster & Delaware railroads and forwarded on to New York on Thomas Cornell's steamboat *William Cook*, familiarly known as the "Milkmaid." In the spring of 1880 the *William Cook* needed a new shaft and the

Armenia, as probably the fastest steamboat available, was chartered to take her place.

In 1883 the Day Line finally found a buyer for the *Armenia* in Henry Brothers & Co. of Baltimore, Maryland, who wanted to use her as an excursion boat on the Potomac River between Washington, D. C., and Lower Cedar Point, where the Henrys operated a hotel and summer resort. After overhauling in Baltimore, the *Armenia* was scheduled to begin her new trade in June of 1883. It is said that following the summer season, she was sometimes used to carry freight between Baltimore, Potomac River landings and Washington. While in winter quarters at Alexandria, Virginia, she took fire on the morning of January 5, 1886, and was scuttled to extinguish the flames. That marked the end of the fine little steamer.

The coming of the *Albany* to the Hudson immediately gave rise to great speculation on the part of the high-speed debaters as to what she might be capable of on a long run. But this was not 1864 and the *Albany*, keeping to her schedule, was only able to show occasional bursts of speed between landings.

The *Armenia* at her Brooklyn pier in 1876, when she was running between there and Newburgh. In the background is a tower of the Brooklyn Bridge, then under construction.—*George W. Murdock coll., New-York Historical Society.*

These are the *Albany* when she was spanking new and the *Chauncey Vibbard* after she had been rebuilt into a suitable running mate. In a period when paddle boxes were conspicuously ornamented and when such artistry had reached a peak on the Hudson in the night boats of the People's Line, Alfred Van Santvoord apparently eschewed the prevailing style, for the boxes on the *Daniel Drew* and the *Chauncey Vibbard* were utterly plain. On the *Albany* the paddle boxes were unusual, since they curved all the way up from the main-deck rail. Perhaps because of this the Day Line decorated the rims of the boxes on the *Albany*, set off the name with a mildly elaborate border and placed a design above this.—*Above: William H. Ewen coll.; below: R. Loren Graham coll.*

Boatmen were fascinated by her and all who could find an excuse to be at one of her landings dashed aboard for a hurried survey. Engineers in particular were interested and one day there were reported to have been over a dozen disciples of the grease cups aboard, with Andrew Fletcher holding the center of the stage.

After the close of the 1880 season, the *Albany* was to go to Albany to lay up for a time. The Day Line accordingly decided to take advantage of this chance to test her. Alfred and Charles T. Van Santvoord, John McB. Davidson and Clarence R. van Benthuysen were to go along and invited a small number of guests, including the Messrs. Fletcher and Harrison.

Twenty-four tons of coal sweepings were put aboard and on the morning of October 22, 1880, the *Albany* set forth. She made no landings until Rhinecliff, where the guests disembarked. Some of the important facts about this trip are as obscure as usual. For record purposes the running time was taken apparently from the vicinity of West 22d Street to Poughkeepsie, and one is evidently free to apply anything from 3 hours 8 minutes to 3 hours 13 minutes for the distance. The *Albany* had the last of the flood tide underfoot and started out with a southeast or favoring wind of eight miles per hour. This later shifted to a northeast or head wind of double that velocity.

On August 6, 1874, the *Mary Powell* had sailed from Vestry Street to Poughkeepsie in 3 hours 39½ minutes elapsed time, from which an allowance of 20½ minutes for time lost at six landings was deducted. The running time of 3 hours 19 minutes resulted in an average speed of about 22.3 miles per hour. Although this 1874 passage was not quite her best time to Poughkeepsie, it was one of those sacrosanct trips in that Andrew Fletcher had been aboard for at least part of the way.

The *Mary Powell*, which did not hold to a schedule on northbound runs, had been carrying passengers in her regular business and her starting time was taken from a point almost two miles south of West 22d Street, so the *Albany's* showing was not as superior as it might appear at first. All things considered, her average speed to Poughkeepsie may have been higher than the *Mary Powell's* on August 6, 1874, by only a hair.

At least the *Albany* had given Captain A. L. Anderson a mark at which to shoot and the season of 1881 had not long commenced when on June 7 his *Mary Powell* ran from Vestry Street to Pough-

keepsie in 3 hours 47 minutes elapsed time, having made seven landings for which a low allowance of two minutes each was claimed. This was not nearly as good as her 1874 time, but it was sufficient to send the high-speed boys scurrying to their press clippings.

A reporter for the New York *Sun* interviewed Captain Anderson, who opened with his standard remark on such occasions, "Now, I want to tell you, in the first place, that we don't try to make fast time. This is a family boat. . . ." Having relieved himself of this observation, he went on to discuss fast trips and then sent the reporter to see Andrew Fletcher.

Mr. Fletcher naturally could not be pinned down. Since one of the latest products of his engine works was the engine of the *Albany*, he did say that from her build and machinery she ought to be a little faster than the *Mary Powell*. After all, he couldn't be expected to say less than that. But he took the slight sting out of it by adding that the *Albany*, the *Mary Powell* and the *Chauncey Vibbard* were all very fast. Also, without naming the point of departure, he set the *Albany's* running time as far as Poughkeepsie on her 1880 trip at 3 hours 13 minutes and made the point that the run had been a straight one — that is, there had been no added distance through making landings.

On June 20, 1881, the *Mary Powell* made another fast passage. If high-speed talk had been boiling before, now it was fairly bursting the pot. Most of the newspapers in the Hudson Valley seem to have decided that they had a holy mission to force a match race between the *Albany* and the *Mary Powell* before the season was over. They commenced to carry columns of material to keep the subject uppermost in the minds of the public.

By July it was darkly hinted that the race would certainly come to pass. The *Mary Powell* adherents claimed that a passenger on the *Albany* had talked with her chief engineer about such a contest, and that the chief had told him to bet on the *Mary Powell*. One of the engineers on the *Mary Powell* was said to have observed that there would certainly be no race, because the *Albany's* owners knew she would be defeated and couldn't stand to lose prestige.

A reporter thought to ask Captain Hitchcock of the *Albany* about the matter. "We're ready for 'em!" responded Captain Dave in his best mariner's voice.

This placid photograph of the *Chauncey Vibbard* seems to typify the lost luxury of leisurely steamboat travel.—*Roger W. Mabie coll.*

Queried the reporter, "I'm told your model has been tried and failed?"

"Why, I know they told you that on the *Mary Powell*," Hitchcock instantly came back, "and of course they did. They think there never was a model like hers."

After the *Mary Powell* had ended her season and there appeared to be no prospect of her doing any further running, it commenced to dawn even on the newspapers that "the greatest race the Hudson River will ever see" was not to be.

Just before this became apparent, a reporter from the *Newburgh Daily Journal* had approached Captain Hitchcock. "Well, Captain, what are the prospects of a race with the *Powell*?"

Said Hitchcock, "The *Albany* is ready for them at any time. We told them that we would be ready for them as soon as we laid up for the season."

"Did you challenge the *Powell* to race?"

"Yes, we extended to them a formal challenge. We are ready to match this boat against the *Powell* for fun or for $5,000. But I never expected that there would be a race. Captain Anderson says his boat is a family boat, and he doesn't want to risk his reputation. We are prepared to risk ours; but I am pretty certain that if the *Powell* goes fooling with this boat she will lose her reputation. Now, the *Albany* is never behind time whether the wind and tide are against her or not. In fact, she has to wait for her time at almost every landing place. You never heard of the *Powell* waiting for her time, for it is seldom she is on time. There is no reason why the *Albany* should not beat the *Powell*. She ought to do it. She was built for speed. We owned the *Powell* three years, and knew all about her. . . . Talking about a family boat, I'll bet a copper that the *Albany* carries ten times more babies than the *Powell* does."

"How fast can the *Albany* go, Captain?"

"Well, she can make at least 28 miles an hour. I know that for one this boat is ready for a race any day."

While the *Mary Powell* was lying at the shops of the Cornell Steamboat Co. on Rondout Creek in Kingston, a reporter for the *Kingston Daily Freeman* went aboard to interview Captain Anderson, who was engaged in supervising the removal of the piston. He took time out to read the *Newburgh Daily Journal's* account of the interview with Captain Hitchcock, ". . . with an alternating smile of amusement and contempt." Finishing, he removed his glasses and launched a counterattack.

"I do not want to get my name into the papers, and so do not like this continual bantering between the *Albany's* commander and myself; but as to the above there is not a bit of truth in anything Captain Hitchcock is reported to have said. I have never received any challenge either formal or informal from the *Albany's* people and have never sent any. I am satisfied with the speed of the *Powell.* I know she can beat the *Albany.* Therefore of what benefit can it possibly be to me or to my boat to race? I am now in the confidence of the public as being a cautious commander, and running a safe boat. Every one knows we run on less than 30 pounds of steam, for they can see it on the steam gauge there in plain view."

When opportunity presented itself, the reporter asked, "Well, how about this talk of Captain Hitchcock that the Day Line people had once owned the *Powell,* and had found her unfit and incapable of doing their work?"

In this instance Captain Anderson failed to dwell on the increased weight of the enlarged saloon. Instead he recited the many changes made in the steamer since he reacquired her — the installation of a larger cylinder between the seasons of 1874 and 1875, the fitting of larger boilers and the rebuilding of the hull between the seasons of 1880 and 1881.

Came the next leading remark by the reporter, "Captain, the *Albany* is claimed to have never been behind time, and that she has been obliged to wait at almost every station to prevent being so much in advance of the schedule time, and they also aver that such a thing cannot be said about the 'Queen.'" ("Queen of the Hudson" was the proud title of the *Mary Powell.*)

Said Captain Anderson, "I don't know anything about the *Albany's* being on time at her landings, except what people tell me. . . . They must not say that the *Powell* is seldom on time, for such is untrue. On our down trip we run on schedule time, and I can honestly say that we have never been more than a minute or two behind, and to more than offset that we have often waited from eight

---

The *Mary Powell,* showing the main saloon extended far forward. This was done when Van Santvoord and Davidson acquired her, and she carried it from 1869 through 1872.

to ten minutes at landings and then ran 'shut off' to keep from getting ahead. On our up trip of course we come like a race horse. There are not so many passengers to be taken on at way landings, and we always have a large load of people who wish to get home as soon as possible. Therefore it is not necessary to run on schedule time on that trip, and we never did."

In summation, Captain Anderson said he felt that there would never be a race between the *Albany* and the *Mary Powell*, and believed that Captain Hitchcock would lose his appetite for such a contest if he thought that it would really come to pass.

The reporter, in his ultimate paragraph, added some opinions of his own.

". . . We know that the *Albany*, notwithstanding Captain Hitchcock's assertion, has been behind time, and that often. We know positively that she was twenty minutes late at Rhinecliff one day and as much as fifteen another. These two instances we know of from personal observation, and we have been told of many others. We have no partial feeling towards either boat, but it does look as though Captain Hitchcock spoke too much as though he knew Captain Anderson would not race with him. There is now no doubt that there will never be a race between these two fleet-winged craft, more's the pity. Whoop! what a time there would be if there was a race. Wouldn't it be a harvest for scribes?"

Well, Captain Hitchcock had had his say and Captain Anderson had had his. They ran their race verbally and each felt that he had convinced his adherents that his steamer was the winner. At this distance it seems safe to state that there never was any intention on either side to have an actual race. They were quite content to reap loads of good newspaper publicity with no risks. For each there was nothing to gain and everything to lose. The Day Line in particular would have suffered considerable embarrassment if its newest steamer had been bested by a vessel nineteen years her senior. But this should not be taken as an opinion that the *Mary Powell* would have won. As to that, no man can ever say.

The following spring, on May 26, 1882, the *Mary Powell* made another fast run on which she was said to have covered the distance from West 22d Street to Poughkeepsie on a regular trip in

3 hours 13 minutes maximum running time. This was exactly the time given by Andrew Fletcher for the *Albany* on her straight-line run of 1880. The heat of the *Albany-Mary Powell* controversy may have had some slight bearing on this figure, but perhaps not. The *Mary Powell* had a favoring tide and wind and a light load of passengers. At the close of the trip, Captain Anderson was described as being in an "unexpectedly" good mood and waxed enthusiastic about better things to come.

Actually, as it turned out, this was about the last shot of the Anderson-Hitchcock duel. Early in the morning of June 16, 1882, Captain Dave Hitchcock died at his residence in Albany, where he had been confined for only a short time. All of the vessels in Albany harbor ran up their colors to half-staff and throughout the city many buildings likewise displayed this token of mourning for one of the most popular and widely known Hudson River steamboat captains of his era.

Captain Dave of the genial disposition, the sunny smile and the sometimes rash statements, had left the river forever. The passengers would miss him as an entertaining commander in the best Hudson River tradition. He loved to talk and his store of anecdotes went back to the greatest years of steamboating. The management of the Day Line would miss him, too. He had been a close associate of Alfred Van Santvoord for decades and was a good businessman.

That year of 1882 also marked the end of Captain Absalom L. Anderson's career on the Hudson River, although he departed under happier circumstances. Once again the captain retired and did it completely by moving to California, where he died in 1895. Once again the *Mary Powell* was sold to Thomas Cornell. This time Cornell operated the steamer for only one season, 1883, and then resold her.

That sale shortly resulted in the formation of the Mary Powell Steamboat Co., in which Captain A. L. Anderson's son, A. Eltinge Anderson, was a stockholder. He served as purser on the *Mary Powell* through the season of 1885 and then became captain, to carry on in the manner of his famous father. A. E. Anderson remained captain of the *Mary Powell* until his death in 1914, so that between them Captains Absalom L. and A. Eltinge Anderson put in over forty years commanding that noted steamboat.

By a happy accident the *Daniel Drew* was in the background when someone unlimbered his camera to concentrate on another subject at Kingston Point. Cropped and enlarged, his picture has provided us with a poor but at least photographic record of what the *Daniel Drew* looked like after her boilers had been placed in the hold. Her two stacks almost appear as one. By a less happy accident, the steamboat was subsequently destroyed by fire at Kingston Point. Notice the starboard paddle-wheel shaft, with the crank on the inner end of it.—*Above, Elwin M. Eldredge coll.*

Chapter 10

THE *New York*

As EARLY as 1881 the Day Line had gotten an estimate on two new boilers for the *Daniel Drew,* even though that steamer had now become the spare boat. Eventually they were ordered from W. & A. Fletcher Co. — successor to Fletcher, Harrison & Co. — completed in 1885 and installed in the hold in place of the two boilers on the guards. This modernized her appearance and made her more nearly similar to the *Chauncey Vibbard* and the *Albany.* It was also hoped that the change in the position of the boilers would give the *Daniel Drew* greater stability — something that the hipping of the hull had not completely acomplished.

Her second or promenade deck was extended out to the stem, making her the first Day Line steamer to have a second deck running the full length of the vessel. That represented a complete reversal of the thinking that had prevailed when the *Albany* was built.

Entirely refurbished, the *Daniel Drew* sailed from New York on June 3 on the opening trip to Albany of the Day Line's 1885 season. Alfred Van Santvoord was on board and evinced pleasure as he divided his attention between his watch and a timetable. For the present the *Daniel Drew* was to run with the *Albany* and it was like old times to have her up and going again after her long retirement.

The *Daniel Drew* was not to go for long. On her third down-trip of the year she smashed into the landing at Hudson, tearing away her guard and joiner work on the port side aft of the paddle box and doing estimated damage of almost $2,000 to herself. Two landings down, at Rhinecliff, she gave a minor repeat performance to add to the injury. When she got to New York, she was withdrawn and the *Chauncey Vibbard* hastily put in commission.

After the heavy traffic was over, the *Daniel Drew* went back in service in place of the *Chauncey Vibbard* and continued until the close of the season in mid-October. Again in 1886 she ran in place of the *Chauncey Vibbard* from May 31 through June 26. The next day she went to Kingston Point to be berthed there as the spare boat.

During this period the Delaware & Hudson Canal Co. maintained an island wharf at Kingston Point, almost opposite the Day Line landing at Rhinecliff. It had been constructed expressly for loading coal into large schooners. Although the Canal Co. had extensive works up Rondout Creek, it was not possible to fully load deep-draft schooners and get them out of the creek. The Kingston Point wharf had been designed so the canal boats could unload along the inner side while schooners took on cargo on the outer.

This wharf was well suited for the mooring of the Day Line's spare boat since there was ample room available and it was reasonably equidistant from either Albany or New York. Theoretically the *Daniel Drew* was in an ideal spot to hasten off to replace either of the other boats in case of an emergency. Engineer Isaac R. Jackson and Captain A. Foster lived aboard, keeping water in the boilers and fuel in the furnaces to be ready for quick action.

Sunday, August 29, 1886, proved to be an exciting day in the Kingston Point area. First a sea serpent was sighted by a great many people, all of whom were "perfectly sober." A few minutes later, shortly after 3 p.m., an engine house on the Delaware & Hudson wharf took fire from undetermined causes — probably spontaneous combustion in waste rags. The sea serpent at least was absolved from all blame.

The fire burned briskly and was shortly carried by an easterly or southeast wind to the *Daniel Drew.* Almost immediately it ate its way into the steamer's storeroom. Captain Foster attempted to fight the fire with buckets, but had to jump for his life with badly burned hands and face. Within ten minutes the steamboat was all ablaze.

A small passenger vessel, the *Charles A. Shultz,* coming down from Glasco for Kingston, made an attempt to pull the *Daniel Drew* from her berth, but the fire was so hot she quickly gave up the effort. The United States vessel *Tallapoosa,* lying nearby, stretched two lines of hose, but the streams of water were as nothing against the growing headway of the blaze. Soon the *Tallapoosa* was forced to retreat into the river for her own safety. When the fire companies arrived, they saw that the *Daniel Drew* was doomed and went back to their fire houses.

Crowds of people were attracted to the scene of the fire and to many vantage points in the area, while all sorts of small craft flitted about on the river. The *Daniel Drew* at least had the satisfaction of dying before an audience reminiscent of the throngs that watched her when she was the talk of the Hudson Valley. She finally settled to the bottom in the shoal water. When the flames at last burned out, little remained above the surface but the boilers, the engine, the toppled walking beam, and odds and ends of metal.

Off and on the Day Line had done exploratory work on a mate for the *Albany.* In 1883 they had the W. & A. Fletcher Co. prepare estimates for both a compound beam engine and a simple, or one-cylinder, beam engine. Perhaps one reason for their procrastination in constructing another new steamboat was the state of their passenger traffic. From 136,135 passengers in 1880, the number went to over 149,000 in 1881 and 1882, but then fell for three successive years to reach a low of 112,434 in 1885. In 1886 business grew more brisk and total passengers for the season were to be 136,010.

The loss of the *Daniel Drew* seems to have pushed the Day Line to a decision, for the fire both deprived it of a spare boat and gave it a sizeable amount of available funds from insurance. The hulk had scarcely cooled before the Day Line had an estimate under date of September 3, 1886, from the Harlan & Hollingsworth Co. for a new hull. It was to be built from the same model that had served for the *Albany,* with necessary modifications to take care of what was to be an added length of seventeen feet.

The Day Line replied the next day and on the sixth the Harlan & Hollingsworth Co. sent an additional estimate for increasing the depth of hold to accommodate boilers that would be larger than those in the *Albany.* On September 8, Van Santvoord wrote, ". . . Referring to your proposition of the 3rd inst. I conclude to accept, and go on at once with the construction."

In those days when a man's word was his bond and major business arrangements were consummated that simply, Van Santvoord added a little additional information. The engine would be 75 inches in diameter of cylinder and 12 feet in stroke, the feathering paddle wheels would be 28½ (*sic*) feet in diameter, and "Boilers to go forward of Engine." Presumably this was to give Harlan & Hollingsworth a rough idea of what the steamer for which they were to build the hull, would look like.

As can be seen from this, the Day Line had decided to have a one-cylinder vertical beam engine, two inches larger in diameter of cylinder than the *Albany's.* Although like the *Albany* the new vessel was to have three decks and would have the same general accommodations, her motive power was to be installed in reverse order. Hudson River style, as previously mentioned, was to have the paddle-wheel shaft ahead of the engine and the boilers. The practice had been followed in the *Daniel Drew, Chauncey Vibbard* and *Albany.* In the new vessel the three boilers would be forward, followed by the engine and then the shaft. This meant that, for a Hudson River steamboat, the paddle wheels would be far aft and that the main gangway would be forward of the wheels, rather than aft as in the *Albany* and the *Chauncey Vibbard*

As Van Santvoord had written, the paddle wheels were to be of the feathering type, which was then so little used in the United States as to be considered novel. While the idea was not new, it was said at the time that the only steamboat running regularly out of New York with such wheels was the freight steamer *City of Fall River* of the Fall River Line. Designed by George Peirce, the Supervisor of Steamers for that line, she had been engined by the Fletcher works and entered service in 1883. It is likely that the efficiency of the feathering wheels as demonstrated on the *City of Fall River* induced Van Santvoord to adopt them. A second freight steamer for the Fall River Line to have feathering wheels, the *City of Brockton,* entered service in October, 1886.

In the radial paddle wheel, the paddles were in a fixed position and banged their way into the water. In the feathering wheel, driving and radius bars operated by a center-placed eccentric to the shaft, changed the angle of the paddles as the wheel revolved. The result was that each paddle sliced into the water, straightened to present a full surface for the catch, and then sliced out of the water. Besides the obvious increase in efficiency, the feathering paddle wheel largely eliminated the constant jarring produced by the radial wheel. The principle and the name sprang from the humble

This is a feathering paddle wheel on the present-day *Alexander Hamilton*. The picture was taken when the vessel was on dry dock.—*Photograph by Conrad Milster, Jr.*

rowboat. Ages before rowers had discovered the advantage of feathering their oars.

Harlan & Hollingsworth felt that with the great reduction of vibration from the use of feathering wheels, it was not really necessary to place spars in the vessel to provide support for the hull, as in the *Albany*, but the Day Line decided to have them.

The new steamer was to be named the *New York* in honor of the southern terminus and in keeping with the *Albany*, which carried the name of the northern terminus. The launching took place at the Harlan & Hollingsworth Co.'s yard at Wilmington on February 5, 1887. As far as the high command of the Day Line was concerned, it was a subdued one, for only six days before John McB. Davidson had died.

Davidson had been in failing health for over a year and his physicians had demanded that he remain in Saratoga Springs instead of returning to his winter residence in New York. His passing in his 63d year was ascribed to cerebral apoplexy and came on Sunday, January 30, 1887.

The finished hull of the *New York* left Wilmington under tow on February 24 and arrived at New York the following day. There was a slight mystery as to what kind of a hull it was. The specifications had originally called for iron, but by a subsequent decision steel was substituted. Consequently, the United States Government had no qualms about classifying the hull as a steel one. That material was named in the application for an official number for the vessel, the Inspector's Certificate stated the hull was of steel, and in Government records the *New York* was always carried as a steel steamer.

Nonetheless, the Day Line, in all of its releases for public consumption, consistently referred to the *New York's* hull as being of iron. This is understandable, for at the time the use of the stronger

The *New York* was a sleek and graceful greyhound. She was the last Day Line vessel to appear with the traditional mark of steamboat punctuation, the period after the name on the paddle boxes. Her boxes, like those on the *Albany*, curved upward from the main-deck rail and had decorative rims. Originally and briefly, the *New York* also had a decorative design above the name, but that had been eliminated by the time this early view was made.—*P. L. Sperr photograph, Mariners Museum.*

and lighter steel in hull construction was comparatively new in this country. Iron would be expected to carry greater connotations of durability and sturdiness to the public mind, than the less familiar steel.

In any event, the hull was now at New York. The W. & A. Fletcher Co., of course, was to supply the engine and boilers, and John E. Hoffmire & Son were to erect the joiner work. Throughout the spring and into the summer of 1887, the construction of the *New York* continued.

Although she had been in operation previously for testing, the official trial trip on July 13 was a never-to-be-forgotten occasion in the New York steamboat fraternity. All sorts of perspiring steamboatmen and representatives of the press, shipyards and engine works made their way to the foot of West 22d Street early on the warm afternoon of that memorable day. Aside from the fact that the *New York* was bedecked with flags and bunting, it seemed at first glance that she was not going anywhere. Commodore Hoffmire's joiner workers were toiling away like mad, filling the air and littering the decks with sawdust and shavings.

Between five and six hundred guests came aboard and one of these, United States Inspector Marsland, remarked: "There's the largest gathering of steamboatmen on this boat that has been seen since the world began. There are steamboatmen here that I haven't seen in forty years. Some of them have been resurrected."

The promising young second pilot of the *Albany*, David H. Deming, had been assigned to the *New York* as pilot for the day. Shortly after 2 p.m. he signalled to the engineer and the *New York* was off. As Deming finished blowing one long blast on the whistle, vessels in the vicinity burst forth in loud salutes.

The instant the first signal sounded in the engine room, all of the steamboatmen on board were galvanized into action. Shifting their champagne glasses to their left hands, they drew forth their ponderous pocket watches and commenced to make mental notes. With so many steamboatmen aboard, it was perfectly obvious that there would be no complete accord as to how much time it would take the *New York* to cover any particular distance or how far that distance would be. There wasn't.

The official timekeeper was Stephen G. Taylor, a draftsman for the W. & A. Fletcher Co. He reported: "She made from Thirty-fourth street to Yonkers in just thirty-three minutes. That is twenty-four and one-half miles an hour, and is the best time ever made with the same steam and tide."

Nobody could corner a man with a qualified conclusion like that!

The *New York* then turned around and sailed down to the Statue of Liberty before returning to West 22d Street. That afforded the guests plenty of time to discuss the trip over a few more friendly glasses of champagne.

One steamboatman set down the leaving time from 22d Street at 2:05 p.m. and the time of reaching Yonkers at 2:42 p.m., making 37 minutes for the whole distance. This, he said, was 14 miles. He added that the *New York* had made from 28 to 29 revolutions with 40 pounds of steam and had bettered the best time of the *Mary Powell*. Others said she had gone 15 miles in 35 minutes; 15 miles in 33 minutes; 14½ miles in 35 minutes; 14½ miles in 33 minutes; and so on.

Finally, apparently after a canvass at the champagne dispensary, all decided to agree — for the moment, at least — that the *New York* had run from 22d Street to Yonkers in 36 minutes. In the proper spirit of good-fellowship, they all further agreed that she had not been pushed.

Said the engineer, "The *New York* had ten pounds of steam to spare. That's equal to two revolutions. The old man's aboard, too; that's equal to two more revolutions. He won't let us let her out."

Said Andrew Fletcher, the engine builder, "We have several links to let out yet."

Said Alfred Van Santvoord, "We have calculated this for a long while. She has done just what we figured."

The *Nautical Gazette* reported that the trip had been thoroughly enjoyed by all.

Presumably throughout the big event Commodore Hoffmire's men had gone right on producing more and more sawdust and shavings. And they continued to toil like beavers to have the steamer ready for her first trip to Albany on July 18.

The day should have been a festive one for the high command of the Day Line, but was saddened, as had been the *New York's* launching the previous February, by the death of one of the five men who had incorporated the company as the Hudson River Line. The first victim had been John McB. Davidson; now, early on the day set for the new steamer's initial voyage to Albany, death was to strike Clarence R. van Benthuysen, the general ticket agent, who was only in his mid-thirties.

To the residents of the Hudson Valley, the first up-trip of the *New York* on Monday, July 18, remained a triumphal event. She was greeted continuously with whistles, bell-ringing, cannonading, fireworks, cheering, and even women waving table-cloths from a housetop. The crowd which jammed the landing at Albany put its opinion in the form of a question — "Ain't she a beauty?"

The *New York* was 301 feet in length; her exterior woodwork was of the usual pine, with the interior finished in hardwood. On the main deck, mahogany was used in the dining room at the after end and up to the shaft. Forward on the main deck, and in the saloon on the second deck, ash was employed. Because the *New York's* engine and boilers were "turned around" as compared with the *Albany's*, so was her saloon arranged differently. Her private parlors were located off the saloon forward rather than aft. Incidentally, private parlors were no longer intended principally as an attraction for invalids or the fatigued. They were popular with those who could afford to pay an additional charge for seclusion. In their parlors they were in a world apart from their fellow travellers, free to relax in quiet comfort with no possibility of distraction or disturbance from the busy flow of life on the steamer.

The *New York's* second or promenade deck ran the full length of the vessel from stem to stern. Later the *Albany's* second deck was extended all the way forward to make her the same in this respect as her running mate. W. & J. Sloane furnished carpeting made expressly for the *New York;* D. S. Hess & Co., along with two other firms, supplied the furniture. For the comfort of the pilots rather than the passengers, a Williamson Steam Steerer was installed.

A member of the staff of the Norwalk, Connecticut, *Gazette* traveled on the *New York* shortly after she appeared and reported, ". . . even imperial Caesar, never rode in such luxurious state. Reader, don't miss this trip."

The total cost of the *New York* was almost a quarter of a million dollars. Since the *Albany* had cost over $187,000, the Day Line in about eight years had spent almost $430,000 for the two new steamers which produced earnings for less than five months of the year.

The Day Line had no reason to be disappointed in its newest steamboat, for in performance she lived up to the expectations aroused by her official trial trip. Regardless of her greater size, she consumed less fuel than the *Albany.*

In 1890 the smokestacks of the Day Line steamers were repainted in a color described at the time as being either cream or yellow. Whatever it was then, buff eventually became the line's official stack

color. Black had always been standard for steamboats on the Hudson. Obviously, it was most practical. Now through the use of light paint, the Day Line gave to its steamers a more pleasing aspect and eliminated the stark contrast of three tall black stacks towering above the gleaming, over-all white. Light stacks were then popular on steam yachts and so were particularly appropriate for the Day Line. It liked to say that its steamboats were really large yachts.

In the fall of 1889 the Day Line had received an estimate for feathering paddle wheels for the *Albany* and had also been in correspondence relative to lengthening the vessel. Nothing happened immediately. In 1890 the Day Line carried 173,358 passengers to break the New York-Albany service record total of 173,242 in 1876. These figures of course included both through passengers and way-landing passengers. In 1891 the total rose to 176,-917½ and in 1892 soared almost to 192,000. Finally, in the fall of 1892 the *Albany* went off to the Harlan & Hollingsworth yard to be lengthened thirty feet.

This was done to increase the capaciousness of the vessel and would also offset the great additional weight of the feathering paddle wheels with which she was to be equipped. In the course of the alterations, the old rounded paddle boxes were removed, panelled woodwork was built across the wheel area on the second deck, and small houses constructed on the hurricane deck to cover the tops of the wheels. The era of the huge, rounded paddle boxes was fading. Later, in keeping with the new school of thought that the paddle housing should be disguised as completely as possible, dummy windows were fitted into the woodwork on the second deck.

When the *Albany* went into service in 1893, she was able for the first time to lord it over the *New York,* for she was thirteen feet longer than that vessel. She enjoyed the distinction for only five seasons. In the fall of 1897 the *New York* was cut in two and lengthened thirty-four feet. She became 335 feet in length as against 314 for the *Albany.* Since the *New York* had been built with feathering wheels, the paddle boxes were not changed.

Between the seasons of 1899 and 1900, the *Albany* had her main saloon considerably enlarged forward. This was another of the successive changes that combined to make her appearance markedly different from what it had been in earlier years.

The Day Line had come to point out in its advertising that the number of passengers which

The *Albany* is shown above with her promenade deck extended to the bow. The awning forward, which in this case is protecting the passengers on the main deck from the sun, was rolled up when not in use. Next in her career the *Albany* was lengthened and fitted with feathering paddle wheels. Here the female passengers are warding off the rays of Sol with an impressive array of umbrellas.—*Above: A. Loeffler photograph, Mariners Museum; below: George W. Murdock coll., New-York Historical Society.*

The *New York* during the course of her lengthening at the John N. Robins Co. yard, Erie Basin, Brooklyn, and as she appeared afterwards.—*H.R.D.L. coll., Steamship Historical Society of America, Inc.*

Compared with the illustration at the bottom of page 73, this picture of the *Albany* at Newburgh about 1907 shows additional changes made to her over the years: the saloon has been extended well forward; dummy windows have been placed across the paddle house; the stacks are closer together; there are two spars forward and two aft; the pilothouse has been altered and there is a bridge abaft it. In the deck view taken on the *Albany* in the 1890s, the passengers on the promenade deck display the then prevailing preference for shade rather than sun. The two ladies in the foreground dared to advance beyond the shadow of the saloon only because they had come completely equipped with umbrellas. Sometimes the dainty parasol was used, but the more utilitarian umbrella made a better traveling companion. Running down to the right-hand corner of the picture is a tie rod from the forward spar.—*Above: Detroit Publishing Co. photograph, Library of Congress; below: H.R.D.L. coll., Steamship Historical Society of America, Inc.*

its steamers would carry, was well below the legal limits that could have been set on vessels of the size of the *New York* and the *Albany*, ". . . thus guaranteeing ample room for all and the absence from crowding which is so essential to comfort" or ". . . in order that there may be no disagreeable crowding." As intended, this presented to potential passengers the restful picture of large areas of vacant deck space from which to enjoy the beauties of the Hudson. But sometimes the picture was better than the reality.

About 1890, the *New York* and the *Albany* apparently held regular licenses for 1,800 passengers, and later in the decade they were licensed for 2,500, or well below the maximum.

As the number of passengers mounted, the room on board the steamers that was taken up by trunks, increased proportionately. To avoid some of the resultant decrease in deck space for passengers on days of peak traffic, the Day Line eventually resorted to a baggage boat. This was a steamboat chartered by the line to handle baggage from New York to those landings which received it in greatest volume, or from those landings to New York, depending on the direction of the flow of vacationists. That relieved the Day Line steamer of a considerable burden. Baggage boats continued to be employed on those days when, from experience, the need for them could be foreseen in advance, and until vacationing with trunkloads of apparel became passé.

Upon the advent of the *New York*, the line continued to retain the *Chauncey Vibbard* as a spare boat, but not for long. The splendid performance of the *New York* and the *Albany* convinced the Day Line that it no longer needed to bear the expense of maintaining a spare boat. In the summer of 1890 the *Chauncey Vibbard* was sold. For 16 years thereafter the entire Day Line fleet comprised the *Albany* and the *New York*.

The *Chauncey Vibbard's* new assignment was as an excursion boat on the Delaware River, principally between Philadelphia and Lincoln Park, an amusement resort on the New Jersey shore of the river. Late in October of 1898, while en route to a naval parade to celebrate the ending of hostilities of the Spanish-American War, she sprang a leak and had to be beached. About 2,000 passengers were said to have been aboard her at the time. She was reported to have operated to Lincoln Park in 1899 and thereafter evidently was laid up. In November, 1900, it was rumored that she had been sold to Peter Hagen for $15,000 for scrapping and in August, 1901, her hulk was said to be lying at Hagen's East Camden yard, near Cooper's Point.

Presumably only her engine, boilers and other metal parts had been removed. A newspaper item of January, 1903, deals with further dismantling. It is particularly interesting when one considers that the *Chauncey Vibbard* had spent most of her life catering to the whims of the cream of the traveling public on the Hudson. "The timbers of the famous old river steamboat, the *Chauncey Vibbard* are being carried away daily by scores of men and boys, to be used as fuel in the homes of the Camden [New Jersey] poor. The old boat is being dismantled to bring heat and fuel to those who cannot purchase coal. The *Vibbard* is imbedded deep in the mud flats off Cooper's Point, hardly a semblance of her former magnificence remaining. . . . The fuel-seekers are working assiduously and unless someone appears to stop the daily raids nothing but a skeleton of the famous old steamer will be left."

The *Chauncey Vibbard* on the Delaware.—*Edward O. Clark coll.*

Chapter 11

GLAMOUR AND CHANGE IN THE 1880s AND 1890s

OVER AND OVER in the 1880s and 1890s, the point was underscored in the press that the Day Line was "strictly first-class—no freight."

In an unidentified clipping of the period, we are told: "With rare exceptions, the passengers are nice people. The peanut and sausage eaters; the beer drinkers; the pipe smokers; the expectorators; the loud talkers; the life long enemies of soap and water, are never seen there."

The Newburgh *Daily Journal* reported: "The Albany day boats are doing an unusually large business. . . . The excursionists are of the better class — people who take more interest in the beauties of nature than they do in whisky."

"A sail on the river gives renewed vigor to the children and enables them to withstand the trying heat of the season," said the New York *World*, which urged, "Give them a trip up the Hudson on the Albany day boat steamers. . . ."

We cannot resist including a Day Line tribute which involves the Fall River Line, the celebrated night line from New York through Long Island Sound to Newport, Rhode Island, and Fall River, Massachusetts. Its magnificent sidewheelers wrote a bold page in the history of American steam navigation, and its passing in 1937 was lamented to a degree that few expired transportation lines ever approached. For many it was the *ne plus ultra* of steamboating. In 1883 a Day Line passenger wrote:

We had an idea drilled into us by oft recurring praises of the "Fall River Line," that the boats of that company were as far ahead of all others in the world as they are in the gilt-edge cheekiness of their three dollar fares. But the Albany day boats *Albany* and *C. Vibbard* discount them entirely for their elegance, comfort and appointments, and are far ahead of them in furnishing, finish and convenience. They are peculiarly day boats for the accommodation of day passengers, but, with this distinction well borne in mind, there can be no questions as to their being unapproachable for luxurious and easy travel.

And where in all the world was this piece of Fall River Line heresy published? It was published as editorial correspondence in the Fall River, Massachusetts, *Weekly Advance!*

An additional observation of this writing gentleman is also of interest:

One of the peculiarities of summer travel on the Hudson is the number of straw hats which are to be seen floating down stream. Every tourist wears a straw hat, as a matter of course, and ten per cent. of them have them blown overboard, as a matter of fact.

"Do you use much wood for fires in these parts?" said I, to a native who had got on the boat far down the stream.

"Oh, dear no. We fish up as many straw hats in the tourist season as supplies us with fuel in the winter. They burn well and they come cheap."

That reminds us of a Day Line pilot of comparatively recent years who one night found a blown-off straw hat in a life boat of his steamer. Being an enterprising man by nature, he recovered it and sold it to his brother pilot, who got considerable good usage from it. Maybe he finally burned it up. We don't know.

The Day Line felt that it received pleasant acclaim in the press only because it was doing what it strove to do — give the public the best. By 1886 it decided that its passengers needed music for at least part of the trip and hired an ". . . excellent brass and string band." That summer the orchestra played on the northbound steamer as far as Poughkeepsie and there went ashore to transfer to the southbound steamer, on which it provided further music on the way to New York. The following year an Albany orchestra was employed to play between Albany and Rhinecliff, and Rhinecliff and Albany. The orchestras did not play continuously, of course, but offered frequent concerts of varied music, ranging from classical selections to popular songs of the times.

For many years this feature was maintained by the orchestra of Colonel Sinn's Park Theatre and

An artist for *Harper's Weekly* sketched passengers on the hurricane deck of the *Albany* in 1890, while passengers on the *New York* were captured photographically a number of years later. The young gentleman in the foreground on the *New York* seems to have considered the danger to headgear on a steamboat and brought along both a cap and a straw hat. Opposite is the cover page for an 1899 number of *Hudson River by Daylight*. "Brooklyn by Annex" in the timetable refers to a ferry connection between Desbrosses Street and Brooklyn. Appropriate to the times was the opening musical selection of the day, "Admiral Dewey's March."—*Above: Lucius Beebe; below: H.R.D.L. coll., Steamship Historical Society of America, Inc.*

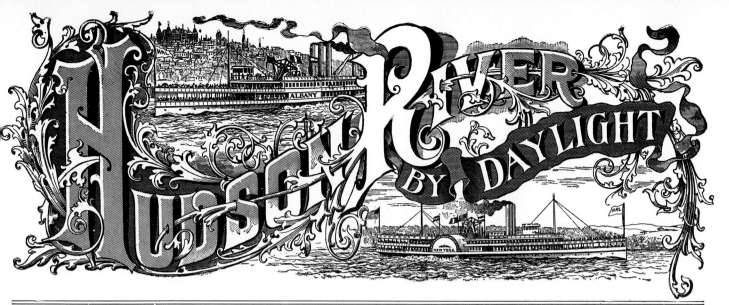

HUDSON RIVER BY DAYLIGHT

VOL. XII. NEW YORK AND ALBANY, OCTOBER 9, 1899. No. 20

GENERAL OFFICERS

Hudson River Day Line,

NEW YORK & ALBANY DAY BOATS.

A. VAN SANTVOORD, President.
E. E. OLCOTT, Gen'l Manager and Treas.
F. B. HIBBARD, General Passenger Agent.
W. B. ELMENDORF, Agent, Albany.

General Offices, Desbrosses St. Pier, New York.

DIMENSIONS OF STEAMERS.

	"New York."	"Albany."
Length over all	341 feet.	325 feet.
Breadth " "	74 "	75 "
Breadth of Hull	40 "	40 "
Tonnage	1,850 tons.	1,415 tons.
Horse Power	3,850	3,200
Stroke of Piston	12 feet.	12 feet.
Diameter of Cylinder	75 in.	73 in.

OFFICERS OF STEAMERS.

	"New York."	"Albany."
Captain	J. B. Briggs	Geo. A. White.
Purser	A. H. Harcourt	C. B. Orcutt.
First Pilot	P. Magee	D. H. Deming.
Second Pilot	Louis Briggs	Staats Winnie.
Chief Engineer	H. C. Magee	S. C. Midlam.
Asst. Engineer	Oliver Brodt	Warren Welsh
Mate	E. Magee	Chas. Griffin.
Baggage Master	E. J. Bailey	E. E. Wygant.
Clerk, Coat Room	E. M. Wygant	A. F. Holding.
Ticket Collectors	C. W. Skelton	J. P. Carter.
	E. H. Rodgers	Floyd Decker.
Steward	H. Boteler	James Ashe.
Cashier, Dining-room	A. J. Meyer	C. N. Wright.
Cashier, Lunch Counter	W. M. Swann	E. A. Sweet.

DAY LINE TIME TABLE, 1899.

DAILY EXCEPT SUNDAY.

GOING NORTH.	A. M.	GOING SOUTH.	A. M.
Brooklyn by Annex,	8.00	Albany,	8.30
New York :		Hudson,	10.40
Desbrosses St.,	8.40	Catskill,	11.00
22d St., N. R.,	9.00		P. M.
Yonkers,	9.45	Kingston Point,	12.25
West Point,	11.50	Poughkeepsie,	1.20
	P. M.	Newburgh,	2.15
Newburgh,	12.25	West Point,	2.50
Poughkeepsie,	1.15	Yonkers,	4.30
Kingston Point,	2.10	New York :	
Catskill,	3.25	22d St., N. R.,	5.30
Hudson,	3.40	Desbrosses St.,	6.00
Albany,	6.10	Brooklyn by Annex,	6.20

PROGRAMME

OF

CONCERTS

WEEK ENDING OCT. 14, 1899.

FROM

NEW YORK TO POUGHKEEPSIE

MORNING CONCERT.

BY THE ORCHESTRA OF
COL. SINN'S MONTAUK THEATRE,
OF BROOKLYN.

F. W. PETERSCHEN, DIRECTOR.

PART I.

FROM 9 TO 10 O'CLOCK.

1. ADMIRAL DEWEY'S MARCH..................CARY
2. OVERTURE, "Raymond"................THOMAS
3. CAVATINA, "Autumn"...............DAMARE
4. CAPRICE, "The Jolly Cadet"............GILDER

PART II.

FROM 10:15 TO 11:20.

5. SELECTION, "Martha"..............FLOTOW
6. BALLAD, "Because"..................BOWERS
7. MORCEAU, "Wizard of the Nile"....HERBERT
8. INTERMEZZO, "Cocoanut Dance"......HERMAN
9. EXCERPTS, from the "Fortune Teller"...HERBERT

later his Montauk Theatre in Brooklyn, between New York and Poughkeepsie; and by Holding's Orchestra of Albany between Albany and Rhinecliff. F. W. Peterschen directed the theatre orchestra and afterwards had an orchestra under his own name, Peterschen's Orchestra and Military Band. The Albany orchestra was directed by W. J. Holding.

In 1888 the Day Line commenced to provide for free distribution to its passengers a journal called *Hudson River by Daylight*. This phrase was a favorite with the line in advertising, and was also the title of other material it disseminated.

The size, the number of pages and the periods of issue of the Day Line journal changed with the years. For a few years it appeared in weekly numbers of 32 pages throughout the season. The name changed to *Hudson River Day Line Souvenir Magazine* and finally to *Hudson River Day Line Magazine*. The publication contained the schedule of the line, a list of the officers of the steamers, programs for the musical concerts and general information for passengers, such as this from an 1890 number,

> Restaurant and Lunch-Room. Meals are served *a la carte* at all hours in the Restaurant on the Main deck aft. Sandwiches, fruits, pastry, soda water, etc., can be obtained during the day at the Lunch-room, entrance by stairway from the Main deck forward.

Significantly absent was the fact that the stairway from the main deck forward also led to the bar. The Day Line was slowly coming to regard it as something that was there, but wasn't to be boasted about. In the early 1890s the bartenders on the steamers suffered the mortification of having their names deleted from the list of "Officers of Steamers."

In the early 1890s the line added *table d'hote* dinners in its dining rooms.

Here are a couple of more "Information for Passengers" items:

> SMOKING IS NOT PERMITTED on Promenade (second) deck, either in the saloons, or on deck, but it is allowed on the Hurricane deck, and on the Main deck, except near the Dining Saloon.

> Views, papers, periodicals, etc., can be purchased at the news stands in the after saloon on the Promenade deck.

Also in the journal was a good deal of advertising, particularly of hotels, and naturally jokes, like this one, season of 1899,

Tommy Wagg — Pa, what does "M.D." after a doctor's name mean?

Mr. Wagg—Perhaps it refers to his patients, my boy, and stands for "many dead."

Or this one,

"They seem to be havin' a powerful lot o' accidents on these ocean steamers nowadays," said old Mrs. Spriggins, putting down the evening paper.

"What's happened now?" asked Spriggins.

"One of 'em's just broke her record."

Then there were articles about points of interest along the route, biographies of the steamers and news of the Day Line itself.

One item which found its way into the Day Line journal dealt with the problem of left-behind passengers and had appeared in the old humor magazine *Life* in 1886. Passengers from time immemorial have occasionally been late. Once the steamboat was under way, it was quite impossible to back into the landing and too time-consuming to circle around in the river to reland. The late passenger lost considerable time and money in trying to get to where he was going by some other means. The company lost a fare.

Life's suggestion was that the Day Line install a "steamboat battery" at the end of its New York pier. This battery would consist either of guns of the type used by circus acrobats or field pieces of various calibres. The passenger who arrived an instant too late simply climbed into a gun of the right size, a dock hand lighted the fuse and with a boom the passenger was off on his way to the deck of the departing steamer. Said *Life,* "Time, Tide, Steamboats and Soda Water wait for no Man."

Perhaps the classic story of the left-behind passenger appeared in Wallace Bruce's guidebook, which appeared with such titles as: *Hudson River by Daylight* and *The Hudson by Daylight*. Writing of the *New York* and the *Albany,* Bruce said:

> . . . Probably no train on the best equipped railroad in our country reaches its stations with greater regularity than these boats make their various landings. It astonishes a Mississippi or Missouri traveler to see the captain standing like a train-conductor, with watch in hand, to let off the gank-plank and pull the bell, at the very moment of the advertised schedule.

> . . . a western man . . . got off at West Point a few years ago. It was at that time the first landing of the steamer after leaving New York.

> As he was accustomed to the Mississippi style of waiting at the various towns he thought he would go up and take a look at the "hill." The boat was off and "so was he;" with wife and chil-

The dining room of the *Albany*. When she was built, the windows were separated, but in the *New York* and later vessels they were fitted as a continuous series to provide the passengers with an even better view of the passing scenery. Eventually the dining room of the *Albany* was similarly rewindowed.—*Elwin M. Eldredge coll.*

dren shaking their hands and handkerchiefs in an excited manner from the gang-plank. Some one at the stern of the steamer shouted to him to cross the river and take the train to Poughkeepsie.

Everyone was on the lookout for him at the Poughkeepsie landing, and, just as the steamer was leaving the dock, he came dashing down Main street from the railroad station, but too late. Then not only wife and children but the entire boat saluted him and the crowded deck blossomed with handkerchiefs. Someone shouted "catch us at Rhinebeck." After leaving Rhinebeck the train appeared, and on passing the steamer, a lone handkerchief waved from the rear of the platform. At Hudson an excited but slightly disorganized gentleman appeared to the great delight of his family, and everyone else, for the passengers had all taken a lively interest in the chase. "Well," he says, "I declare, the way this boat lands, and gets off again, beats anything I ever see, and I have lived on the Mississippi nigh onto a quarter of a century."

In 1888, with two practically new steamers of the latest type, with orchestral concerts and with a free journal, the trip the full length of the river —

if you didn't miss the boat! — was a better value than it had ever been before. Now came the spectre of water competition. But it was a rather ridiculous spectre, in the person of Walter H. Shupe.

Shupe, who preferred to be known as Father Columbia, claimed to be backed by the secret Order of Sons and Daughters of Columbia. He was a thin, pale man, with hollow cheeks and chin whiskers, and was obsessed by a desire to break up the great "steamboat monopolies" on the Hudson by charging a ten-cent fare. This, he claimed, when added to the profit from freight and meals, could enable him to operate without losing money. He had earlier tried to prove his theory, but his attempt in 1888 is of some interest since he decided to oppose the Day Line with, of all steamers, the *City of Albany*, which Van Santvoord and his associates had had built during the Civil War.

After her wartime service, she returned to civilian life in 1866 and in 1867 was documented under the name *Adelphi*. She had a number of owners and ran both on the Hudson River and Long Island Sound. While on the latter waters, in 1878, she suffered a boiler explosion with loss

The *City of Albany* plows along in her latter years, with a small boat snugged securely beneath her stern. During this period when she again carried her original name, her connection with Albany was of the slightest. Alfred Van Santvoord's sleek beam-engined steam yacht *Clermont,* shown in the spectator fleet at a sailing race, was subsequently lengthened. Directly off her starboard side is the excursion boat *Cygnus* of the Iron Steamboat Co.'s Coney Island route.—*Above: F. Van Loon Ryder coll.; below: Melancthon W. Jacobus coll.*

of life. In 1885 she was rebuilt and her original name of *City of Albany* was again given to her.

Shupe chartered her from the New York & Norwalk Steamboat Co. for his 1888 experiment, which commenced on September 17. The day was wet, with some fog, and the initial crowd was slim. The *City of Albany*, which had not been in a class with the *Daniel Drew* in 1863, was certainly far from being comparable to the *New York* and the *Albany* in 1888. She did offer music, in the form of a German band which specialized in "Der Fraulein Waltz." There is no record of the reaction of band members to the German orthography of the title of this selection, as it was noted in newspapers. A printer was on board with a small press and during the day struck off a report of the trip called *Boat Bulletin No. 1,* Shupe's challenge to the Day Line journal.

The haughty *Albany* passed the *City of Albany* before the latter had gotten very far and ignored her as though she hadn't been there. But a few steamers did salute the new enterprise and some people on shore bade her welcome.

The ten-cent fare proved to be a second-class fare, entitling the holder only to the forward portion of the steamer. To use the after portion of the cabins he had to pay an extra dollar, but that was also good for as much food as he cared to eat. Dinner was served all day long and a hungry man, if he wanted to, could spend the entire trip in doing nothing but eating. The high point of the meal was the pies. Holding a piece in his fingers, Shupe said: "There are three grades of these delicacies sold at 3, 4 and 7 cents per pie. The three-cent brand contains 70 per cent. of crust and 30 per cent. of filling. The four-cent variety contains crust and filling in equal proportions, and the seven-cent kind has but 30 per cent. of crust and 70 per cent. of delicious filling. These are the seven-cent kind, but I can make money on them, though, for no one person on board could eat a dollar's worth of pies, and they are the most expensive of all the eatables."

For the return trip from Albany the next day, the weather was better, but not the number of passengers. The *City of Albany* was considerably late getting into New York. Some who had gone to the pier to watch her arrival were moved to remark that they feared the expedition had "fallen in the shupe!"

During the course of the trip Shupe had lectured on more plans for the future, including the establishment of a Turkish bath and a corn-cutting enterprise to run at one-tenth of the prevailing

Alfred Van Santvoord was a Hudson River steamboat operator of the first order.—*Hudson River Day Line coll., New-York Historical Society.*

rates. The Columbians, he said, numbered 600,000 and all had given him a dollar apiece to support his ventures. After the first round trip, however, he was unable to produce sufficient cash to continue the charter of the *City of Albany.*

Incidentally, the *City of Albany* ended her career only a few years later. In early fall of 1894 she was laid up in the Harlem River and shortly afterwards, on Saturday evening, October 6, was destroyed by fire. Allegedly an oiler, who was shipkeeper, invited a party of friends aboard for dinner. This would seem to have been a success, since the fire is said to have started when one of them knocked over a lamp, which exploded.

As previously mentioned, John McB. Davidson had died in January 1887. The Van Santvoords quickly acquired his holdings in the Day Line and were now completely in control of the company which was to remain a family business. Its policy stemmed from family consultations and in later years the family would on occasion gather aboard one of the steamers to study and discuss proposed alterations.

Alfred Van Santvoord had business interests aside from steamboats. To provide passengers easy

access from Catskill landing to resorts in the Catskills, including the famous Catskill Mountain
House and its rival Hotel Kaaterskill, the Day Line
had invested in the Catskill Mountain and the Otis
Elevating Railways. He was also connected with
other railroads, was a founder of Lincoln National
Bank and Lincoln Safe Deposit Co. in New York,
and belonged to several noted social and yacht
clubs. Primarily his life had been devoted to steamboating and, like other prominent steamboat owners, he came to be referred to as Commodore Van
Santvoord.

He had a rather novel yacht built in 1892, a
sizeable craft with a wooden hull, originally 148.4
feet in length. For her name he went back to the
beginning of Hudson River steamboating and decided to call her the *Clermont*. The novel thing
about her was that she was a sidewheeler with a
beam engine built by the W. & A. Fletcher Co. To
anyone who expressed surprise at the idea of a
sidewheel yacht being built in the 1890s, the Commodore was apt to reply, "I made all of my money
out of sidewheelers, and I'll stick to 'em as long as
I live." The *Clermont* was described as a roomy
boat with elaborate and tasteful interior fittings
and a speed of 18 miles an hour.

Life was to deal the Commodore a sharp blow.
In July 1895 his only son, Charles Townsend Van

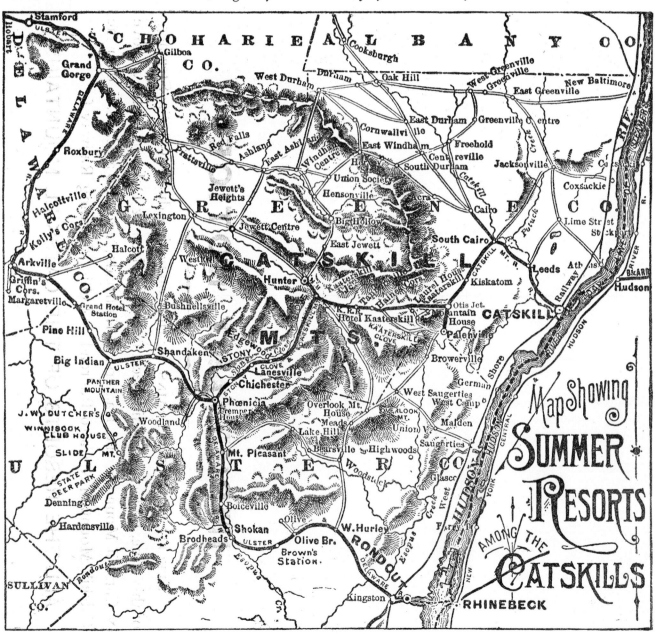

The mammoth Hotel Kaaterskill was built by a wealthy and real Philadelphia lawyer, George Harding, and might rightly be called a thorn in the side of the old Catskill Mountain House, since it loomed up nearby both in size and altitude. Allegedly Harding built it as a "spite" hotel and there are stories that he did so because he had not received the service to which he thought he was entitled at the Mountain House. The Kaaterskill opened in 1881 and called itself "The largest mountain hotel in the world." That year the Catskill Mountain House, which earlier had been advertising as the ". . . only first-class House on the Mountains," was saying, "Reduced rates." The Hotel Kaaterskill and the Catskill Mountain House were not of course the only hotels of size in the Catskills, but the latter had early gained international fame because it afforded such a magnificent view of the Hudson Valley; the Kaaterskill offered a similar view in more splendid and modern surroundings. The Otis Elevating Railway, a cable line which commenced operations in August 1892, provided a rail link from the Catskill Mountain Railway into the mountains. The locomotive at Otis Junction station is said to be the ALFRED VAN SANTVOORD. Well to the left of the top of the Otis Railway, some distance before the mountain on the horizon commences to rise noticeably, the Catskill Mountain House is dimly visible. In the map opposite, from 1894 Day Line literature, the rail routes into the Catskills may be traced. The Stony Clove & Catskill Mountain Railroad and the Kaaterskill Railroad (K.R.R. on the map) were part of the Ulster & Delaware system.

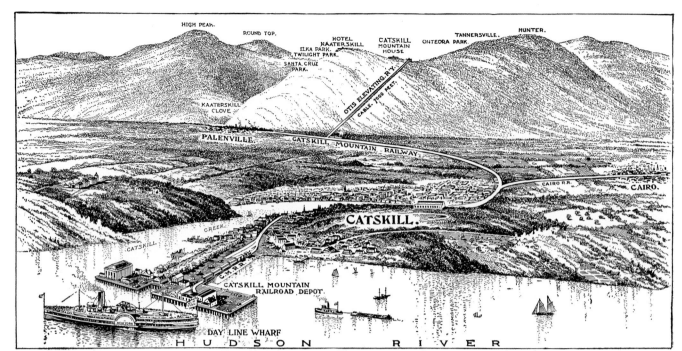

THE APPROACH TO THE MOUNTAINS, VIA CATSKILL.

A simplified drawing, with the *New York* in the foreground, shows the rail route to the mountains from the Day Line landing at Catskill. Another short segment in this system, the Catskill & Tannersville Railway, continued on from Otis Summit station at the head of the Otis Elevating Railway.—*Below: post card, Herman F. Boyle coll.*

Kaaterskill-in-the-Catskills, N. Y. Otis Summit R. R. Station and Power House.

Santvoord, died following an operation for that "dread disease appendicitis." About 41 years old at the time, he had never married and made his home with his father; his mother had died some time before.

To succeed his son as general manager of the Day Line, the Commodore chose the husband of his daughter Kate, Eben Erskine Olcott. Born in New York City on March 11, 1854, Olcott was almost the same age as Charles T. Van Santvoord, but his background was unusual for a man about to enter full tilt into the steamboat business.

He had attended the College of the City of New York and then the School of Mines of Columbia University, from which he graduated in 1874. After first working as a chemist in North Carolina, he became associated for a time with the Pennsylvania Lead Co. and later went to Venezuela as superintendent of a gold mine. Thereafter his profession took him to western United States, Mexico and many parts of South America. As a consulting engineer he went on expeditions in that continent to investigate gold, silver and copper deposits. He was highly regarded in his field and even after joining the Day Line continued to practice as a consulting engineer for a number of years.

Actually, his transition to a steamboatman was not too great for a man interested in mining gold. The Day Line was a gold field to be mined under the most civilized circumstances, in contrast to the primitive conditions to which he had been accustomed. When Olcott gained both experience and a free hand, he made the most of it and built the line into something that was probably far beyond the wildest dreams of old Commodore Van Santvoord.

Olcott was an extremely energetic man and a very democratic one. By the end of his first season as general manager, his popularity with the employees was established and continued as long as he lived.

Once he was aboard the *Albany* at New York when a new fire pump was being installed. The engineers of the steamer were shorthanded, so Olcott donned a pair of overalls and set to work. During the course of his activities, he had occasion to go ashore and accidentally stepped overboard. He was rescued with some difficulty, but was completely equal to the occasion. Said he, "Just went down to see if the bottom [of the steamer] was clean. There's nothing like having things tidy and shipshape. Come on and have one on me."

For a man who had spent so many years in far-off and isolated places, Olcott was extremely publicity conscious and was a fine Day Line pub-

Eben E. Olcott (left) and William B. Elmendorf are bound for a naval ceremony. Elmendorf was the son of John Elmendorf, Jr., who served as Albany agent for the Day Line through the season of 1884, after which William B. succeeded him and continued into the 1930s. The position came to be titled general agent and was broad in scope. —*Elmendorf coll., New York State Library.*

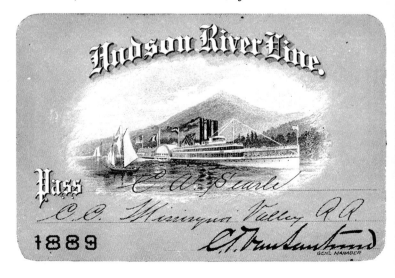

licity agent long before such a title had been invented. Probably it was he who convinced the Commodore that the line should change its formal name to one that it was frequently using. In August of 1899 the legal requirements were completed, whereupon the official announcement was prepared. It read:

The name Hudson River Day Line has been granted by an order of the Supreme Court [New York] to take effect on October 1st, 1899. The Corporate title of this popular Line of Steamers has been for years the Hudson River Line. This name was not considered sufficiently distinctive of the service, and resulted in the use of many and conflicting titles, such as Albany Day Line, New York and Albany Day Line, and the more popular and shorter appellative, Day Line. Of course this last name is in a manner distinctive and will always be understood.

The official title, however, of the famous Line which has no equal in this Country or any other and whose fine and splendid Steamers, the *Albany* and *New York*, are the pride and boast of all Americans who know them, will be the Hudson River Day Line.

Since the Day Line throughout its existence had been varying its name, it was obvious that the patrons were not going to be quite convinced by that. Over a decade later the Hudson River Day Line was still getting letters calling it such things as the "Hudson River Daylight Steamboat Co."

By the 1880s the schedule of the Day Line had settled into a more or less stable pattern, and in 1885 an elapsed time of 9 hours 30 minutes was allowed for the run between New York and Albany in either direction.

On May 21, 1887, the Tarrytown-Nyack ferryboat *Tappan Zee* took fire while laid up for the night at Nyack, and was destroyed. The vessel secured to fill in until a new ferry could be built, apparently was not suitable for connection with the day boats, for the "meet" was discontinued. If this was a temporary change, it became permanent, for the arrangement was never resumed. Because of the size of the *New York*, which appeared in 1887, the Day Line may have decided that the handling of such a large vessel in unfavorable weather conditions with a ferryboat alongside, interjected an element of risk that should be avoided. Perhaps it decided that, having been forced out of the Tarrytown-Nyack area by circumstances beyond its control, it would take advantage of the opportunity to stay out with a minimum of to-do from civic-minded local citizens.

The new name of Hudson River Day Line has been entered on this stock certificate of the Hudson River Line. Apparently the American Bank Note Co., which printed it, had available as a suitable cut only that of a Mississippi River steamboat.—*H.R.D.L. coll., Steamship Historical Society of America, Inc.*

The northbound *Albany* (left) and the southbound *New York* pass just above the Day
Line landing at Poughkeepsie. The Poughkeepsie railroad bridge was the first span to
be built across the Hudson south of Albany.

After all, in 1887, without whatever patronage had
come to it from Tarrytown and Nyack, the Day
Line carried over 150,000 passengers to mark the
heaviest traffic since "Centennial Year," 1876.

Tarrytown in particular felt badly, because at
that time both Captain Frost of the *New York* and
Captail Odell of the *Albany* lived there. Tarry-
towners were prevented from going out to take a
sail with their fellow citizens.

In 1890 the New York terminus once again became Desbrosses Street. At this time the landings
between there and Albany were 22d Street (which
had replaced 24th Street in 1881), Yonkers, West
Point, Newburgh, Poughkeepsie, Rhinecliff (Rhinebeck landing), Catskill and Hudson.

The only landing change thereafter in the 1890s
was the simple one of moving back across the river.
Day boats, before the time of the Van Santvoord-
Davidson Day Line, had abandoned Kingston
Point on the west shore as a landing in favor of
Rhinebeck landing opposite. This was due both to
the limited wharfage at the Point and to the fact
that the approach road to the isolated spot ran
across a swamp and was then generally in a deplor-
able condition. Ferry service was maintained to
Rhinebeck landing and it was less difficult to get
to or from the day boats by this means, for on the
west side the ferryboat landed in the heart of

Rondout, which in 1872 became part of the City
of Kingston.

In the 1890s there was some new thinking
about Kingston Point, and the thinking was probably done by Samuel Decker Coykendall. Upon the
death of his father-in-law, Thomas Cornell, who
had once sold the *Mary Powell* to Van Santvoord
and Davidson, Coykendall succeeded to the control of the varied Cornell investments. While these
were centered in the large towing fleet of the Cornell Steamboat Co., they also included the Ulster
& Delaware Railroad, which ran from Kingston
into the Catskill Mountains and so was heavily
patronized by summering Day Line passengers.

The plan was to make the old Delaware & Hudson Canal Co. wharf at Kingston Point, at which
the *Daniel Drew* had burned, into a suitable landing for the Day Line steamers and extend the
tracks of the Ulster & Delaware out across a trestle
to the landing. This would add to the attraction of
that railroad, for passengers would now be able
to walk off the steamers and into the railroad cars
without the ferryboat transfer. Loss of business by
the ferry was a negligible consideration, for Coykendall controlled the ferry company, too.

The plan, of course, may have stemmed from
Alfred Van Santvoord, but that seems unlikely.
The resultant advantage to the Ulster & Delaware

Vacationists who disembarked at Catskill would be carried on their way either by the horse-drawn stages in the foreground or the cars of the Catskill Mountain Railway.— *H.R.D.L. coll., Steamship Historical Society of America, Inc.*

would doubtless lure some potential customers away from the Catskill Mountain and the Otis Elevating Railways in which the Day Line was interested. On the other hand, passengers would appreciate the dock-side connection with the Ulster & Delaware and some might be drawn who heretofore had been going to and from the mountains via the West Shore and the Ulster & Delaware railroads. The West Shore had been built as the New York, West Shore & Buffalo and ran through the west side of the Hudson Valley. For about forty miles its tracks were along the bank of the river. Conceived to compete with the New York Central & Hudson River Railroad, it was running passenger trains over its Hudson Valley trackage to Albany in July, 1883. In 1885 it went under the hammer, and after being reorganized as the West Shore Railroad Co., was leased to the New York Central & Hudson River for 475 years from January 1, 1886.

Aside from railroad connections, there was another point to be considered by the Day Line. Whether or not they were Catskill vacationists, most of the passengers handled at Rhinecliff either were bound to or came from the west shore of the river. With other improvements in access to Kingston Point, the change to that place would make for greater convenience for the large majority of patrons concerned. Accordingly, in 1896 Kingston Point became a Day Line landing.

The adjacent wasteland was before long transformed into an attractive park. By intent it was

bucolic, with charming summerhouses set about and meandering paths and walks through the woods. For these Downing Vaux, the landscape artist who designed it, chose such nostalgic names as Under Ledge Path, Over-Knoll Walk, Briarwood Path, Mulberry Path, Shadow Walk to Shadow Bay, and Piney Ridge Walk. They were also plebeian attractions through the years, including a merry-go-round, a dance hall and a shooting gallery. In the evening there were often fireworks and band concerts from a bandstand on a man-made island in the lagoon behind the steamboat landing. Kingston Point Park was a mecca for pleasure-seeking Kingstonians, who came and left by trolley.

Kingston Point Park was splendid for the Day Line, too. For many years it had featured reduced-rate one-day sails from Albany, on which previously passengers had left the down-boat at Rhinecliff to wait there for the up-boat. This wait was of almost two hours duration and at Rhinecliff there had been little to help the passengers while away the time. Now Kingston Point Park made the destination as attractive as a sail on the river and aided the excursion business from Albany. If all the members of the Sunday Schools and graduating classes from the Albany area who made the pilgrimage to Kingston Point on the Day Line were gathered in one spot, they would form an army of formidable proportions. Even today in Albany the mention of Kingston inevitably kindles happy recollections of Kingston Point.

P. O. & U. & D. Railroad Station, Haines Falls, Catskill Mts.

Of these two Ulster & Delaware Railroad trains, one is at Haines Falls on the Kaaterskill branch; the other is at Kingston Point awaiting an influx of arriving Day Line passengers. A corner of the Day Line ticket office and waiting room may be seen at the extreme left; the large structure to the right is a public pavilion. Towering over the passenger cars is a bandstand, with the trolley car station in the background beyond it. Dockside railroad connections at Kingston Point lasted through the season of 1932.— *Above: Herman F. Boyle coll.; below: H.R.D.L. coll., Steamship Historical Society of America, Inc.*

GLAMOUR AND CHANGE IN THE 1880s AND 1890s

Chapter 12

TURN OF THE CENTURY

BESIDES THE MANY other changes within the Day Line during the 1880s and 1890s, there were also changes in the men who manned the steamers. Mortality, resignations, promotions and the coming of the *Albany* and the *New York* brought much shifting of the officer staff of the vessels. Some of this is dealt with in Appendix B.

The Day Line came eventually to retain its officers on a seasonal basis. Of these the mates and engineers usually worked long before the season began and after it closed. Deckhands, oilers and firemen could expect to be employed far beyond the period of actual operation for there was never-ending maintenance work to be done. The lot of these latter people therefore was about the same as that of others who followed steamboating on the Hudson.

One personnel problem was retaining in the purser's department the men who had close contact with the passengers. For that reason and by the nature of their work, they had to be possessed of some intelligence. If they made the Day Line a career, they might·well be out of work for half of each year. The Day Line solved this problem about 1890 by commencing to employ for these positions college men on summer vacations. The plan worked so well that it was continued thereafter. Not all of the men in the purser's department were college students, but it became common for the majority of them to be.

Dishonest employees are not unique in any form of business. Transportation lines, because of their type of operations, have always had their share. A vulnerable point was tickets, since tickets represented cash and, if discreet methods were used, could be turned back into cash.

The Day Line was no more immune to internal thievery than any other transportation line. One such case was uncovered in 1888 when it was found that on both the *New York* and the *Albany*, the baggagemaster, who also served as an assistant ticket collector, was withholding tickets and turning them over to a porter of an Albany hotel for resale at cut prices. There were other cases — some discovered, others never detected. In over-all steamboat history there have been many employees who built up small fortunes on modest salaries. But it should not be assumed that this sort of thing was widespread. On the whole, Day Line employees were on the same high plane as its passengers.

Commodore Alfred Van Santvoord customarily went aboard his yacht *Clermont* in June and remained for the summer. Except for cruises up Long Island Sound or the Hudson, he generally didn't go far from the New York area. But old steamboatman that he was, he preferred being afloat rather than ashore during the warm months.

Although he was 82 and in failing health, he was on his yacht as usual in the summer of 1901. In July while the *Clermont* was lying at anchor at Sea Gate, the Commodore was seized with a stroke and Saturday evening, July 20, he died on his yacht. He had literally stayed with sidewheelers as long as he lived.

Sunday night Captain White and four of his officers from the *Albany* stood watch by the casket following special services for the *Albany's* crew. After the *New York* arrived in New York Monday, similar services were held at the pier for her people. Following obsequies at the Van Santvoord home in New York, July 23, the Commodore's body was placed on the *Clermont* for a last trip up the Hudson for burial at Albany Rural Cemetery. Steamers along the river mournfully saluted the memory of the Commodore as the yacht passed. When the *Clermont* passed the *Albany*, crew and passengers on that steamer bared their heads in silent tribute. Below Albany a similar display of respect was met from the southbound *Adirondack* of the People's Line. At Albany the *New York's* crew was lined up on deck and sang a requiem as the yacht passed by in the darkness, a solemn, impressive tribute in the still summer evening.

Graveside services were conducted the next morning by Van Santvoord's son-in-law, the Reverend Wilton Merle-Smith. Now the old Commo-

The night boat *Adirondack,* with her huge hogframes, was built in 1896.—*Elwin M. Eldredge coll.*

dore was gone to join John McB. Davidson, Captain Dave Hitchcock, and most of the others who had populated the river in the days when the Day Line was born.

Van Santvoord and Davidson had formed their Day Line to provide service between New York and Albany and there had been little deviation. Except for those few seasons in which the *Armenia* ran between New York and either Poughkeepsie or Newburgh, and the three-year operation of the *Mary Powell,* they had never tried to branch out. Van Santvoord had been content to have the New York-Albany route remain his principal interest.

At the time of his death, the several night lines on the Hudson were still doing a thriving business in freight and passengers. The most important continued to be the People's Line — the New York-Albany night line — operated by the New Jersey Steamboat Co. The largest steamboat on the river was their new *Adirondack,* built in 1896 with a wooden hull 388.2 feet in length. She had three

tiers of staterooms above the main deck, two smokestacks set fore and aft, enormous hogframes and six spars. The *Adirondack* was not quite as long as the earlier *St. John,* the career of which had been ended by a fire while she was in winter quarters in 1885.

Between Troy and New York there was the Citizens' Line of the Citizens' Steamboat Co.; between Coxsackie-Hudson-Catskill region and New York, the Catskill Evening Line; between Saugerties and New York, the Saugerties & New York Steamboat Co.

In 1899 a new and important company had come into being with the formation of the Central-Hudson Steamboat Co., which effected a consolidation of three old-established night-line operators. These were the Poughkeepsie Transportation Co., running between Poughkeepsie and New York; the Homer Ramsdell Transportation Co. between Newburgh and New York; and the Romer & Tremper Steamboat Co. between Kingston and New York.

Romer & Tremper also owned the Newburgh & Albany Day Line, which was included in the consolidation. This latter was the route on which Van Santvoord and his associates had placed the *Jesse Hoyt* in 1862.

In addition to these lines, there were other shorter ones, such as the day line for freight and passengers between Haverstraw and Newburgh, and between Peekskill and New York, and the "yachts." The latter were little steamboats plying on short routes all along the river after the manner of buses of the later years. There was still the Mary Powell Steamboat Co., running the *Mary Powell* as she had always run, on the day route between Kingston and New York.

In 1902 a heavy shadow fell over Hudson River steamboating. It was cast by Charles Wyman Morse, the "Ice King," promoter and speculator extraordinary. Morse was a Downeaster, born in Bath, Maine, on October 21, 1856. His father, Benjamin Wyman Morse, was a large investor in the towing business on the Kennebec River and sent his son to Bowdoin College. Scholastic endeavors were not enough for Morse. With his cousin, Harry F. Morse, he went into business at the same time, buying ice that was harvested on the Kennebec River and selling it in New York. To transport it, the Morses had their own vessels built.

In those days before mechanical refrigeration, ice from the Kennebec and the Penobscot Rivers in Maine helped fill the insatiable need for nature's product in New York City during the hot months. Naturally, the greatest source of ice was nearer to home, on the Hudson River. Its upper reaches were lined with enormous icehouses for the storage of the ice which was harvested during the winter season.

Morse did well with his Kennebec ice. It has been said that when he stepped up at Bowdoin for his diploma, he was worth half a million dollars. Whether he was or not, he was a wealthy man and his career had barely begun. His father entered into business with him and his cousin. They added southern lumber to their line. Buying timber stands or the cuttings of others, they moved it to market in their own sizeable fleet of sailing vessels.

C. W. Morse eventually moved to New York City to guide the destiny of the firm and in 1897 formed the aptly named Consolidated Ice Co. into which to consolidate, by fair means or otherwise, less financially firm ice dealers. The other major operator in the field, the Knickerbocker Ice Co., was merged with the Consolidated in 1899 into the American Ice Co., which was greatly overcapitalized. In 1900, as the weather commenced to warm, Morse's ice trust doubled or more than doubled the market price of ice in New York City.

In the hue and cry and investigation which followed this move, it was found that Mayor Robert A. Van Wyck of New York had holdings of American Ice Co. stock which Morse had sold to him at half of par value and to pay for which Morse had loaned him money. To reciprocate this "favor," Van Wyck had arranged for Morse to have docking facilities to the extent that it became almost impossible for the independent ice companies to operate. Along with Van Wyck, other Tammany politicians were involved.

Morse had made an estimated 12 million dollars in the ice business. Now he devoted most of his attention to expanding his interests in banking and shipping, interknitting them in his own complex fashion and building by his usual method of rapid consolidation. He made himself felt in the Hudson River passenger business in 1902 when he effected a merger of the Albany and Troy night lines — the People's Line and the Citizens' Line — by acquiring control of the New Jersey Steamboat Co. and the Citizens' Steamboat Co. Then, in the same year, he formed the Hudson Navigation Co., which in 1905 formally absorbed the New Jersey Steamboat Co. and assumed control of the Citizens' Steamboat Co.

There were rumors that he would not be content until he had gained complete domination of Hudson River steamboating and that the Hudson River Day Line was high on the list of companies that he planned to grasp. Anyone with the slightest knowledge of Morse's methods had no reason to doubt such rumors.

Chapter 13

A NEW PRESIDENT TAKES CHARGE

COMMODORE VAN SANTVOORD was succeeded as president of the Hudson River Day Line by his son-in-law, Eben Erskine Olcott, who also continued his previous duties as general manager.

It was no secret that the control of the Mary Powell Steamboat Co. could be purchased from A. Eltinge Anderson and I. C. Wickes, who together held a majority interest. Although the *Mary Powell* was getting old in years, she was still in fine condition and a likely acquisition for Morse or anyone else who wanted to compete with the Day Line. By placing her on the New York-Albany run or in New York-Poughkeepsie round-trip service at cut-rate fares, an interloper could make himself extremely annoying.

To forestall such a possibility may have been the primary intent of E. E. Olcott when he opened negotiations to acquire a majority of the stock of the Mary Powell Steamboat Co. On the other hand, he may simply have been repeating the actions of his late father-in-law, who long before had joined in buying the *Mary Powell* to add to his steamboat holdings. In any event on October 6, 1902, about 52 per cent of the stock of the Mary Powell Steamboat Co. was quietly transferred to the Hudson River Day Line, which thereby gained control of the *Mary Powell*. Her management had returned to the Day Line at the end of a second full circle.

Although there were many rumors that something had happened, it was a month later before the news was confirmed in the press. At the annual meeting of the Mary Powell Steamboat Co. on December 31, 1902, Eben E. Olcott was elected president of that company. Captain A. E. Anderson, who retained one share of stock, continued as captain of the *Mary Powell* and manager of the company. His salary, which just previously had been $6,500 per annum, now became $2,500. Mr. Olcott, it might be added, cut the salary of the president of the Mary Powell Steamboat Co. in half and paid himself $2,000 per year.

As far as the operation of the Mary Powell Steamboat Co. was concerned, its acquisition by the Hudson River Day Line resulted in no immediate change. But just as Alfred Van Santvoord had made alterations in the *Mary Powell* to make her more like the New York and Albany day boats, so did Eben E. Olcott. Between the seasons of 1902 and 1903 her promenade deck was extended to the bow as it was on the *New York* and the *Albany*. This, of course, increased the available deck space and thus added to the capaciousness of the vessel.

In May of 1903 she ran for a short time between New York and Poughkeepsie, making a round trip a day until the *New York* and the *Albany* went into service on the through run to Albany. Then the *Mary Powell* was placed on her own route between Kingston and New York.

When the season was over, she went to the Townsend & Downey Shipbuilding & Repair Co.'s yard at Shooters Island for a thorough overhauling. She was fitted with new boilers, smokestacks and paddle wheels, and parts of her engine were renewed. On the main deck, portholes were placed in her deckhouse from forward of the paddle boxes to aft of the boilers in an effort to modernize her appearance. Another modernizing change was the painting of her new smokestacks in the Day Line color instead of the familiar black which she had worn all her life.

In 1904, her sailing hour from Kingston was changed. During most of her period of operation, throughout the major portion of the season, she had departed punctually at 5:30 a.m. Today this seems like an unholy hour to set out on a trip and even by 1904 it was becoming a shade too early, hence it was changed to 6:00 a.m.

Another change in schedules, affecting the Day Line as a whole, had occurred a bit earlier, in 1902, when the company offered its patrons another New York landing by calling at the 129th Street pier in uptown Manhattan, just south of the terminus of the ferry to Fort Lee, New Jersey. Due to a later renaming of streets and parts of streets in the area, the ferry came to be at the foot of 125th Street,

The *Mary Powell* about 1906 displays changes which had been made to her by the Day Line. These included the extending of the promenade deck to the bow and the placing of portholes along the outer housing on the main deck. The early rendering of the *Hendrick Hudson* was intended to give an interested public a general idea of how she would look when completed.—*Above: Detroit Publishing Co. photograph, Library of Congress; below: Elwin M. Eldredge coll.*

which was understandable to New Yorkers who knew that 125th Street now turned towards the northwest before it reached the Hudson and crossed the line of 129th Street. But it was puzzling to the uninitiated who took the trouble to think about it. In 1938 the Day Line made it all simpler by calling its uptown landing 125th Street.

In 1905 it changed its midtown landing from West 22d Street to the West 42d Street pier. The West 42d Street pier was actually at the foot of West 41st Street, for at the foot of West 42d Street was the terminus of the New York Central's West Shore Railroad ferry to Weehawken, New Jersey. Since 42d Street was a principal east-west artery, the name of that street was given to the pier. This apparently puzzled no one.

Meantime, Olcott was going along with plans that would develop into something greater than ownership of the Mary Powell Steamboat Co. or changes in landings. He felt that the time had come to build another steamboat. Total passengers carried by the *New York* and *Albany* had in 1899 passed the 200,000 mark to reach 232,805, and in 1902 were up to 266,504. Hints of a new vessel appeared in the press years before she came to be. During the winter of 1902-03 it was reported that the Day Line would soon construct her and probably have her in commission by 1904. It did not come about as quickly as that.

The proposed steamer would be considerably larger than the *New York* and it was intended that she would in every way be the finest day passenger vessel in the country. Much time was spent in assembling data on outstanding American and European steamers in search of improvements that could be incorporated in her. Captain White of the *Albany* went abroad to inspect steamers in England and Scotland and with Mr. Olcott went to the Great Lakes to examine new vessels in those waters.

To supervise her design and construction, the Day Line secured the services of Frank E. Kirby of Detroit, a naval architect who was to leave an indelible impression on American steamboating. Associated with him in the work was J. W. Millard of New York. To plan the interior, Louis O. Keil of Detroit was selected.

There was no question but that she would be a sidewheeler. The nature of the route, with the shallow reaches in the upper Hudson calling for a light draft; the great maneuverability of a side-wheeler in getting into and out of landings in a minimum of time; and the added breadth attainable through the wide, overhanding guards, all

made a sidewheeler most desirable. But in machinery she was to be markedly different from her predecessors.

Up to this time, the vertical beam engine had been almost universally used on the larger Hudson River passenger steamers ever since the development of that type of engine for marine purposes. Since most of the Hudson River steamers were sidewheelers, for them the most practical engine had been the tried and true vertical beam. It was economical to construct, to operate and to maintain. And it had powered the fastest steamboats the Hudson had ever seen.

A vertical beam engine had been selected for a new steamer which the People's Line put into commission in 1904. This vessel, named naturally the *C. W. Morse*, was 411.1 feet long. She took from the *Adirondack* the glory of being the largest steamboat on the river, and was also the longest yet to be constructed for the Hudson, for she exceeded the *St. John* of 1864 by over eighteen feet.

In planning its newest vessel, the Day Line decided to depart from the old tradition. All things considered, it felt that the performance it needed could best be obtained by using the more modern inclined engine, with cylinders set in the hold at an angle and connected directly to the cranks on the paddle-wheel shaft. For the Day Line, speed was more essential than it was to the night lines. The Day Line had many landings and a tight schedule to maintain, whereas the Albany and Troy night boats ran through without landings and had no need to get their passengers anywhere until the following morning. The night boats were not slow vessels, but by the nature of their trade did not need to have as much available speed as the day boats.

In June of 1905, the Day Line contracted with the W. & A. Fletcher Co. to build the engine and serve as prime contractor for the vessel. The hull was to be built by the T. S. Marvel Shipbuilding Co. of Newburgh, New York; the boilers by the New York Shipbuilding Co. of Camden, New Jersey; the joiner work by John Englis & Son of New York.

There had originally been considerable speculation as to what name the Day Line might select for the new vessel. Intimates of Mr. Olcott had suggested that he call her after himself and there were doubtless others who would have liked her named for Alfred Van Santvoord. But Mr. Olcott is credited with having had his own ideas on the subject and early selected the Dutch version of

When she entered service in 1904, the *C. W. Morse* was the largest steamboat ever built for the Hudson and was to be exceeded in size by only one other. She is shown at Albany, with the New York State capitol visible over her stern. A part of the large crowd on the *New York*, speeding up the river, makes good use of the abbreviated fourth deck she acquired with the addition of her "new bonnet" or observation room on the hurricane deck.—*Both: Elwin M. Eldredge coll.*

Snow covered the ground when the *Hendrick Hudson* was photographed on the stocks at the T. S. Marvel Shipbuilding Co. in Newburgh on March 16, 1906.—*H.R.D.L. coll., Steamship Historical Society of America, Inc.*

the name of the explorer of the river. Thus was established the line's policy of naming all future vessels after noted men whose lives had at some time been connected with the Hudson River.

In this case there was indecision as to spelling. It will be remembered that an earlier steamboat of 1845 had been enrolled as the *Hendrick Hudson* but had appeared with the first name spelled Hendrik. In a drawing of the new steamer published in 1905 the latter spelling was used before giving way to Hendrick. Although Hudson had sailed up the river in the employ of the Dutch East India Co., he was by birth an Englishman and his given name was accepted to have been Henry. Since the Dutch had settled the Hudson Valley and the Hendrick form was in common use there, that choice did not seem unreasonable to the Day Line. Nevertheless, there followed a great deal of controversy. Aside from purists, there were some boatmen and others who for mysterious reasons of their own always referred to the steamer as the *Henry Hudson*.

The *Hendrick Hudson* was to be launched at Newburgh on March 31, 1906. In honor of the great event President Olcott decided to place the *New York* in commission to take invited guests up to the ceremony. These passengers were presented with a little printed apology which well indicates the feeling of the Day Line for its steamers:

The bon mot relative to beauty unadorned was not coined for marine use. Few things are more forlorn looking than a steamboat out of commis-

sion or in deshabille, as is the case of the *New York* today. She is really in winter quarters until May 15, when the season opens, but the temptation to go up and see her little sister launched was too great and she had to go, and she hopes her guests will pardon her disarray. During the winter she has been given a new set of boilers which will considerably increase her power, and a commodious and comfortable observation room has been placed upon her hurricane deck — she calls it her new bonnet. With these, and a few other important changes which will have been added to her regular make-up, she hopes, when she makes her prettiest bow to you in the spring, that you will not remember her unkindly for this madcap prank of a trip, but will come to see her again adorned in her best ever.

Now who could resist that? And as part of her "madcap prank" she carried on board the saluting cannon borrowed from the yacht *Charmary*, formerly Alfred Van Santvoord's *Clermont.**

The *New York* set forth for Newburgh late on the morning of March 31, in the face of a strong north wind that snapped and cracked the colors with which she was bedecked. An orchestra was on board to enliven the trip for the guests of the Day Line, the number of which has been placed at from 800 to 1,000. Mr. and Mrs. Olcott played

---

*The *Clermont* had been sold in 1903 to Charles G. Gates who renamed her *Charmary*. Later she was converted to an excursion boat and still later resumed her original name. Eventually she went to Tampa, Florida, was renamed *Bay Queen*, and in July 1921 burned in the Hillsboro River.

A great crowd at the shipyard awaited the launching of the *Hendrick Hudson* at Newburgh; others watched from floating vantage points as she drifted well out into the river, with the *Commodore* saluting loud and long. The ferryboat is the *Fishkill-on-Hudson*, serving as an excursion boat for the occasion. The *Atlantic* is to the left.—*Both: Elwin M. Eldredge coll.*

the roles of host and hostess at an oversized party. With them were their children, Alfred Van Santvoord, Mason, Charles T. and nine-year-old Katharine, who was to act as sponsor, and Mr. Olcott's 87-year-old mother.

On the way up the river a landing was made at West Point to take aboard more guests — dignitaries of the Army from the Academy. Then at Newburgh the *New York* put in at Marvel's shipyard so that the launching party and anyone else who wished, could go ashore.

On hand to witness the event were the architects; members of the Fletcher family from the W. & A. Fletcher Co.; and those chroniclers of the story of American steamboating in words and pictures, John H. Morrison, the Reverend C. Seymour Bullock, F. J. Sedgwick, Fletcher Du Bois, and undoubtedly Samuel Ward Stanton.

The chief guest was the venerable Charles H. Haswell. In his 97th year, he was so proud of his age that he entered his date of birth — May 22, 1809 — as part of his return address on the envelope when he accepted the invitation. He had either been aboard or remembered Robert Fulton's *North River Steam Boat*, held the distinction of having been the first person to hold the position of engineer in the United States Navy, and later served as engineer-in-chief of the Navy. After leaving the Navy, he had a long and varied career as a civil and mechanical engineer. Attending launchings and similar events seems to have been an avocation with him. As practically a youth in his late seventies, he had been on the official champagne trial trip of the *New York* in 1887.

The launching was scheduled for 3:00 p.m. The Day Line took such pride in doing things on time that someone made it a point to hold his watch in hand and found that the hull commenced to slide down the ways almost on the dot — four seconds early! Practically simultaneously Katharine Olcott smashed a bottle of Catskill Mountain water on the bow with the words, "I christen thee *Hendrick Hudson!*" while her father removed his hat and exclaimed, "She moves!" Then, after the Japanese custom, white carrier pigeons were released from a basket on the bow.

There is little reason to doubt that the decision to use Catskill Mountain water stemmed from Eben E. Olcott's wife, Kate Van Santvoord Olcott. She was a strong advocate of temperance and to her has been attributed the fact that, while the *Hendrick Hudson* was planned to have a bar, there was no bar at the completion. The season of 1905 was the last in which the happy bartenders of the Day Line dispensed their stimulants. In 1906, if you wanted alcoholic beverages, you had to partake of them in the dining room with your meal. Should you need more than that, you had to carry your own bottle. But, as someone observed, you had to be careful not to get tight, for nothing offensive to sight or smell was allowed on the Day Line's model steamers.

When the plan to use Catskill Mountain water for the launching reached Captain Thomas S. Marvel at his shipyard, he was alarmed. So far as we know, he bore no grudge against the Catskill Mountains, but he was sure that no good would ever come from christening a vessel with water. Accordingly, he purchased a bottle of champagne. As the launching party ascended the platform at the bow, he descended to a position along the ways. Then, as Miss Olcott broke the bottle of water, he broke his bottle of champagne on the hull and performed his own private christening.

As the hull began to move, the sun broke through a cloudy sky, the steam vessels in Newburgh Bay gave out loud blasts on their whistles and old Commodore Van Santvoord's saluting cannon boomed forth from the *New York*. This had an unexpected effect on one guest on that steamboat. Being of the "they don't build good boilers any more" school, he was convinced that one of the new boilers of the *New York* had exploded and it took some little time to soothe him.

The tug *Hercules* of the Cornell Steamboat Co. served as the attending vessel and brought the hull back to the Marvel yard. Then the launching party and those guests who had gone ashore, returned to the *New York*. With a few final salutes on the cannon, she cast off to go back down the river and the guests were treated to tea, chocolate and George Junior Republic wafers. It had been a great day for the Day Line.

As the *Hendrick Hudson* lies in dry dock, the work of completing her goes forward. From Newburgh the hull was towed to the W. & A. Fletcher Co., which by this time was located in Hoboken, New Jersey. There the machinery and boilers were installed. Finally the upper works were constructed. The *Hendrick Hudson* was to be licensed for 5000 passengers, but that figure was afterwards increased.—*All: Elwin M. Eldredge coll.*

Chapter 14

THE *Hendrick Hudson* ENTERS SERVICE

THE DAY LINE intended to place the *Hendrick Hudson* in service on Monday, August 20, 1906, so that she could help handle the heavy traffic that came between then and early September. On August 18 she made a trial trip up the Hudson as far as Tarrytown and achieved the eminently satisfactory speed of over 23 statute miles per hour. In fact, her maximum speed on the run has been placed at 23⅞ miles per hour. The steamer was not yet finished, for considerable work remained to be done on the fittings and the interior, but the Day Line had already decided that she would go into service as she was. Another apology was printed for distribution to the passengers:

The "Day Line" trusts that what you see done in this steamer will warrant pardon for the things undone.

The home rush of travel compelled her being taken from her builders before the completion of her decorations, although every requirement for safety and stability is more than filled.

The maiden voyage was practically a holiday in the Hudson Valley. Everyone who could get within sight of the river turned out to greet the *Hendrick Hudson* on August 20. At Newburgh, where the hull had been built, the crowd was enormous, and at Poughkeepsie it seemed as if the whole city had stopped work for the occasion. Kingston Point was jammed and at Albany a crowd estimated at at least 4,000 waved torches, fired skyrockets and even built bonfires — an old Albany custom which still persists at election time.

The *Hendrick Hudson* was a brave sight, with a huge name-flag flying from the pole abaft the pilothouse, with a line of flags running down on either side of this pole and with flags strung between the side poles — in all about fifty.

Many of the guests at the launching were aboard, including old Mr. Haswell, now in his 98th year. The excitement apparently was too much for Wallace Bruce of the guidebooks. He was overcome with what was described as a slight paralytic shock and so became the first person to use the emergency first-aid room with which the steamer was equipped. At Poughkeepsie he was carried ashore and the vessel proceeded without him. Also amongst the guests was a man who was practically a must. He was the mayor of Hudson, New York, the Honorable Henry Hudson.

Maiden voyages are often imperfect and this one was no exception. There was considerable delay apparently caused by a journal running hot at least once and the *Hendrick Hudson* arrived very late at Albany. Probably time was also lost at the landings, not only because of the nature of the trip but because each presented a new problem in handling for the pilots.

Everything on the river saluted the *Hendrick Hudson* that day, including the sidewheel towboat *Norwich*, built in 1836 and the oldest steamboat running on the Hudson. Maybe Mr. Haswell had been along the waterfront when she made her maiden voyage. One of the final salutes of the day came from another old vessel, the sidewheel towboat *Oswego* which had been built for the Van Santvoords' towing line in 1848. The next morning when the *Hendrick Hudson* started back for New York the yacht *Charmary* boomed a salute with the cannon that had been returned to her after the launching.

Far and wide, word had spread that the total cost of the *Hendrick Hudson* would be about a million dollars. The Hudson Valley press heralded the arrival of the "million dollar steamer" and at least one paper spread the cost in banner headlines. There was no particular reason to question the figure, for there seems little doubt but that the information came from the Day Line. It was accepted by marine journals and was to be quoted thereafter. Actually, the total cost of the *Hendrick Hudson* didn't come anywhere near a million dollars — in cold cash, anyway. The outlay for equipping was $47,130.62 which, when added to the amount expended otherwise, resulted in a figure in the Day Line ledger discreetly captioned "Total Cost" and reading, "$621,336.84."

First Pilot Staats Winne looks formidable enough to steer anything afloat as he stands at the wheel of the *Hendrick Hudson*. Behind him are the massive pair of "hand-gear" steering wheels for use in case of an accident to the steam steering engine. Far below in the engine room are Chief Engineer Thomas Hall, First Assistant Engineer D. S. Brown and Second Assistant Engineer E. S. Welch. Hall was chief engineer of the vessel, 1907-12. When the *Hendrick Hudson* made her maiden trip to Albany, such things as windows above the name were unfinished (above). The view in the saloon (lower middle) looks aft and shows the ports on the inner side of the paddle-wheel housing, around which runs the balustrade. One could look over the balustrade through the visible steel deck beams to the main deck. In the recess at the extreme right in this picture is a drinking-water faucet, with communal cups securely chained beneath it. The Stairway of the Dragon (lower right) led from the main deck to the after end of the saloon.—*Below opposite: Elwin M. Eldredge coll.; above: Roger W. Mabie coll.; others: H.R.D.L. coll., Steamship Historical Society of America, Inc.*

The after observation room or "convention hall" of the *Hendrick Hudson* (above) was crowned by a dome of Tiffany glass; its forward bulkhead was decorated with a mural of Henry Hudson's *Halve Maene* (*Half Moon*) in Haverstraw Bay. In the saloon the mirror on the front of the housing around the engine-room ventilator, was flanked by paintings of the Senate House on the right and of Idlewild. In the sides of the ventilator housing were windows, seen above the near chair, through which passengers could look down on the engine. Ports in the paddle-wheel housing are at the left in the picture.—*Both: H.R.D.L. coll., Steamship Historical Society of America, Inc.*

If the Day Line was responsible for the million dollar figure, its motive was not an attempt to disguise a cheaply built steamboat. At 1906 prices, the *Hendrick Hudson* certainly had not been cheaply built and for a vessel of her type, little more could have been spent with any purpose. The intent of the million dollars was likely nothing more sinister than a desire to keep up with Mr. Morse. When the *C. W. Morse* appeared in 1904, her cost had been given as a million dollars. What she really cost we don't know and, considering Morse's well-known flair for delusion, perhaps nobody else knew either.

In any event, a cost comparison between a night boat and a day boat would be misleading to the general public. Possibly the Day Line had a very good idea as to the total expenditure for the *C. W. Morse* and found that the People's Line had taken considerable liberty with the million dollar figure, too. It was all good clean fun. The *Hendrick Hudson* had scarcely gotten into commission before the People's Line announced that it would build another new night boat to cost $1,500,000.

The *Hendrick Hudson's* length was 379.1 feet; the company gave her overall length as 400 feet. This last figure was intended again to counteract the *C. W. Morse*, which was 411.1 feet in statutory length. It looked better to have the *Hendrick Hudson* in the rare 400-foot class. Decades later, when she had survived to become the largest steamboat running on the Hudson, Day Line literature listed the overall length as 390 feet.

With her steel hull, steel deck beams and trusses, inclined engine and feathering paddle wheels, the *Hendrick Hudson* had no need of spars and rods for strengthening the hull and was the first Day Line steamer to be built without them. Because of her large engine and six boilers, she was also the first Day Line steamer to carry two assistant engineers.

As in the *New York* and the *Albany*, the dining room was on the main deck aft, the lunchroom in the hold forward, and the main saloon on the second deck, here designated as the saloon deck. The saloon was finished in mahogany, carpeted in Wilton in two shades of green, and adorned with ferns, palms and plants. The third deck was now the promenade deck, but the crew called it the boat deck, since the lifeboats sat on it. Two large observation rooms were located forward and aft and finished in green-stained cypress. The after observation room was known as the "convention hall" and was planned for use by organizations or large groups. On such occasions it was closed off to afford privacy for those who had engaged it.

The main top or hurricane deck was officially the shade deck, but the passenger who went there seeking shade was fated to find little of it. Forward on this fourth deck were two private parlors and, aft of them, staterooms for officers. The pilothouse was on the fifth or bridge deck which ran over these rooms. Initially, the portion of the bridge deck abaft the pilothouse seems to have been open at times to the passengers, but the practice was not continued.

Except for the two parlors on the hurricane deck, the rest were located off the main saloon and all were tastefully furnished. Styles included Louis XV, Louis XVI, Art Nouveau, Dutch, Colonial and Empire, with finishing of poplar, oak and mahogany. Altogether the *Hendrick Hudson* was planned to have 23 parlors, which became 24 when the captain's quarters were relocated on the hurricane deck. No other Day Line steamer was ever to have so many.

Also located off the main saloon was the Persian writing room, done in teakwood. Here were available writing paper and souvenir postals at no charge. Amongst the other facilities elsewhere for the passengers were a barber shop with a bath attached and a photographic darkroom.

The bandstand was suspended between the main deck and the saloon forward. Since it was over the entrance to the lunchroom and had wells above it opening into the saloon and the forward observation room, the orchestral concerts could be heard all the way from the hold to the third deck.

A novelty conceived by Captain George A. White was the placing of plate-glass ports in the bulkhead on the inner side of the paddle-wheel housings. The constant splashing of water against these ports when the steamer was under way never failed to attract passengers and temporarily deluded some of them into believing that the vessel was sinking. The arrangement also had a practical value. Engines were always warmed up in the morning before sailing and heretofore it had been necessary for one of the engineers to go out on the catwalk on the outer side of the paddle wheels to make sure there were no logs or timbers floating in such a way that they might be picked up with damaging effect. With the ports, the engineer had only to step out of the engine room and peek through to see that all was clear. Too, in the case of maintenance work on paddle-wheel buckets, it was now possible to bring the buckets in the proper position without a chain of shouted commands. All of the sidewheelers later built by the line had these ports.

Early in the *Hendrick Hudson's* career, the vertical ends of the woodwork on either side of the paddle-house name were altered into curves. This little change improved the appearance of the vessel (above). Her great room for passengers is startlingly evident in the bird's-eye view (oppo-site) taken many years later. Here her bridge deck is longer than it was originally, as a result of the addition of four more rooms for crew members on the hurricane deck ahead of the forward smokestack.—*Above: Elwin M. Eldredge coll.; opposite: Alexander P. Olcott coll.*

Both the *Albany* and the *New York* carried a number of paintings for decorative purposes. On the *Albany,* by the Day Line's description, "A life-sized marble bust of a young girl ornaments the head of the grand staircase. It is Palmer's ideal conception of 'June.' The walls are adorned with oil paintings by Emile Princhart of Paris, F. D. Briscoe of Philadelphia and Yzquierdo of Madrid, Spain." On the *New York* were paintings by Albert Bierstadt, J. F. Cropsey, Walter Satterlee and David Johnson. This liberal display of art may have been due to a combination of the fact that Charles Townsend Van Santvoord had been interested in the subject and that his father, Commodore Van Santvoord, had a high regard for the traditions of steamboating. The interior of the first Hudson River steamboat named *Albany,* built in the 1820s, had been embellished with paintings by well-known artists of that period.

In the case of the *Hendrick Hudson,* the artistic decorations were in keeping with the steamer and her route. Robert Fulton Ludlow executed a painting of her namesake, while Vernon Howe Bailey was commissioned to do a number of murals, including depictions of Hudson's *Halve Maene* in Haverstraw Bay, Washington Irving's home, Sunnyside; Nathaniel P. Willis's home, Idlewild; the Senate House at Kingston, Washington's headquarters at Newburgh, Philipse Manor at Yonkers and the New York State capitol at Albany.

The *Hendrick Hudson* ran for about a month in 1906 in place of the *Albany,* which was temporarily withdrawn. That vessel was now a spare boat, but the Day Line had gotten along very well without a spare boat since 1890. Accordingly, it decided to revive the New York-Poughkeepsie round-trip service in 1907. The *Albany* was put on the run as the "special" or "extra boat" — to differentiate her from the through boat — on the Special Poughkeepsie Service. She was also known as the "hour-later" boat, since she left Desbrosses Street at 9:40 a.m., one hour after the departure of the through boat for Albany. In 1907 the *Albany* landed en route at West 42d Street, 129th Street, Yonkers, West Point, Cornwall and Newburgh, and lay at Poughkeepsie for an hour and a half to give her passengers ample time for sightseeing, which might include a ride to Vassar College. At 4:10 p.m. she started back for New York.

The use of the *Albany* in this service did not mean that she never again saw the city for which she had been named. At first the Poughkeepsie run did not commence until weeks after the opening of the through service and closed well before it did. The *Albany* could still be used on the New York-Albany route in spring and fall when traffic was lighter.

In the years ahead the Poughkeepsie special was to grow steadily in favor. Besides affording a pleasant one-day excursion from New York, it offered additional service for regular passengers traveling on the lower river.

Already the Day Line was considering the building of an even larger vessel than the *Hendrick Hudson* to run with her in order to have a balanced pair of steamers on the Albany route. The *Hendrick Hudson* was licensed for far more passengers than the *New York* and outshone her generally.

Again the name was selected well in advance. This time it was to be *Robert Fulton* and there would be no dissidence about how to spell it. Hudson and Fulton were the two men most deeply entwined historically with the Hudson River and to name a companion for the *Hendrick Hudson* after anyone else just wouldn't do. Further, the groundwork was already laid for the Hudson-Fulton Celebration to be held in 1909 in joint commemoration of the tercentenary of Hudson's exploration of the river and the 1907 centennial of Fulton's introduction of steam to the Hudson. The new *Robert Fulton* was intended to be ready for service in 1909.

On April 12, 1907, the Day Line set up an equipping account for the vessel to record the payment of $200 to Robert Fulton Ludlow for a painting of his grandfather, Robert Fulton. What better way was there to commence a steamboat than to acquire a painting of the man for whom she was to be named? A drawing of the proposed vessel was published, showing her as somewhat similar to the *Hendrick Hudson,* but with one stack ahead of the paddle wheels and the other aft. The Day Line, however, seems to have decided that it could not yet afford a second "million dollar" steamer. By the fall of 1908 no positive steps toward construction had been taken. It will be recalled that the contract for the *Hendrick Hudson* had been signed in June of 1905 and that she was not ready until August of 1906.

Now fate proceeded to change the situation completely.

Here is a *Robert Fulton* that never came to be.—*Elwin M. Eldredge coll.*

Chapter 15

HUDSON-FULTON YEAR

On October 16, 1908, as the *New York* was going from 42d Street to Desbrosses Street at the end of her down-trip from Albany, she was rammed off West 34th Street by the tugboat *W. H. Flannery.* When the tug was sighted, a signal for a port-to-port passing had been sounded by the *New York,* but the tug veered and headed directly for the day boat, which backed her engine hard. The subsequent collision resulted in some slight damage to the *New York's* guard and considerable damage to the *W. H. Flannery's* pilot-house. The captain of the tug summed up the cause of the accident succinctly when he remarked that he ". . . had been on a bat for four days."

The next day, Saturday, the *New York* sailed for Albany and on Monday, October 19, made the closing trip of the Albany service for the year. Tuesday morning she went up to the Marvel shipyard at Newburgh, where she arrived at 11:55 a.m. Here she was to undergo a routine overhaul of her guards and on Wednesday was to be visited by the steamboat inspectors, who presumably were to lay out such work as they might deem necessary. In preparation for this inspection, her fires were killed and her boilers cleaned, and the crew set to work cleaning up generally.

At the end of the day the crew was free to go ashore. In the best nautical tradition, some of them had a few friendly glasses during the course of the evening.

As was customary on Day Line steamers, the male personnel in the steward's department were quartered in rooms in the hold aft of the kitchen, beneath the dining room on the main deck. Some time before midnight fire broke out in this area. It seems likely that one of the men, under the influence of stimulants, violated the no-smoking rule. Perhaps he dropped a match or a cigarette on bedding or on some other inflammable material. Perhaps he dropped off to sleep while smoking in his berth. Apparently some of his fellows attempted to extinguish the fire and then one of them went to get the watchman.

The vessel was in a most vulnerable condition, for there was no steam to operate the pumps. Water from the kitchen was carried to the blaze and next some of the crew manned a hand pump on the main deck, aft. One account has it that, in order to get at the fire, they cut a hole in the deck, but not in a spot where they could get the water directly on the flames. This was the beginning of a series of events which might well have been conceived by Mack Sennett.

A fire alarm was at last turned in at 12:02 a.m., October 21, from a box near the Marvel shipyard and the response was commendably prompt. A steamer company, a hose company, a hook and ladder company and a chemical engine company rolled to the scene, but they saw no sign of a fire and there was no one to tell them where it was. The blaze was still confined to the after hold of the *New York* and between them and the *New York* loomed an obstruction to their vision — the hull of the new steamboat *Trojan,* being built for the Hudson Navigation Co.'s Citizens' Line and almost ready for launching.

At last the firemen got the word and were satisfied that it wasn't a false alarm. But no company by itself had enough hose to reach from the hydrant through the shipyard to the *New York.* Although contemporary accounts vary slightly, it seems that the companies got down to business by engaging in a hassle as to which should man the hydrant and which should lead out. This was settled when the Washington Steamer Co. took the hydrant and the Columbian Hose Co. moved to another one in the area.

The Columbians had great difficulty in getting their hydrant open, but at last success crowned their efforts. Then they found the hydrant was dead. There was no water!

Back at the other hydrant, the Washington Heights Chemical Engine Co. was now allegedly refusing to let the Washington Steamer Co. use any of its hose. Accordingly, the waterless Columbians went to the aid of the Washington Steamer Co.

The last master of the *New York* was Captain Alfred H. Harcourt, center. Pictured with him are Pilot J. R. Magee, left, and Mate Claude Benedict. The *New York* herself is at Kingston Point.— *Above: Edward O. Clark coll.; below: George W. Murdock coll., New-York Historical Society.*

and there was put together hose enough to reach the fire. At least the firemen thought it was enough. They rushed forward with the nozzle end amongst the timber and other obstructions that lay about in the shipyard. At the same time some well-meaning spectators — characterized by a reporter as "blockheads" — grabbed the other end of the hose and also rushed forward. This mistake was shortly discovered and rectified in reverse. Amidst general confusion, the wrong end of the hose was carried back to the hydrant.

Finally the hose was attached to the hydrant, but it was still too short. Now the Chemical Engine Co. came through at last and supplied added lengths. When the Columbians, who were manning the nozzle, went aboard the *New York* only about twenty minutes had elapsed since the alarm sounded. All things considered, that was nothing short of amazing!

Meantime on the dignified *New York*, the sergeant in charge of the police detail at the scene had recruited volunteers to man a hand pump located forward. The efforts here were as ineffectual as the initial activities of the firemen. The pump was not connected and no one knew how to perform that feat. A member of the crew was found who had the knowledge, but no wrench. When this lack was remedied, it brought about no great change in the steady burning of the fire. While the volunteers pumped like mad, the stream of water produced was not powerful enough to break the plate-glass windows in the dining room. And the clouds of smoke rolling out made it impossible for the men to approach close enough to smash them. The after hold had become an inferno, but aside from the smoke, the only other outward sign of the fire was the glare from the portholes in the hull.

Although the Columbians were now on board and in action, it was readily apparent that at best they were only holding the fire. Nevertheless, no call for additional apparatus was made. Then, at 12:47 a.m. a second alarm went in, and for good reason. Two minutes earlier, in the words of the Newburgh *Daily News*:

> . . . the flames burst above the hull for the first time and a bright glare on deck betokened the doom of the beautiful vessel. Almost immediately after, a tiny fork of flame shot through the upper deck between the wheelhouses. . . . From the shore there came the cry to the men on board to get ashore. . . .
>
> . . . It was not more than three minutes after the first flash of flame appeared above the deck

that the whole boat was a mass of writhing flame. No one not present can conceive of the speed with which the flames traveled once they appeared. Fanned by a gentle breeze from the southwest they swept the boat from stern to bow. The position was most unfavorable for the conditions, for the fire had started in the stern and was rushed forward to the forward part of the boat like a fiery cloud of dust before a wind. Had the boat been fired by a powder train it could not have been more quickly done.

Then was unfolded the most terrible spectacle Newburghers have ever seen. With a roar like a cyclone the fire advanced, devouring everything before it. Flames mounted high in the air, there often being a most peculiar spiral effect. The whole sky was illumined and the river was as bright as day. At 1 o'clock the fire was at its zenith and was such as no one ever saw here before.

It now became necessary for the firemen to direct their activities toward protecting the Marvel shipyard. In particular danger was the new *Trojan*. Although her hull was of steel, the wooden cradle in which it sat was vulnerable and the burning of part of it might have resulted in the falling over of the hull. Incidentally, once the firemen had gotten into action, they seem to have performed their work efficiently and bravely. When conditions were most desperate, the wind fortunately shifted around to the north and blew the flames in a direction in which they could do little further harm. A check of the crew showed that four men were missing. They had been trapped in the after hold and were burned to death. All Negroes, they were the second porter, the butcher, and the first and second pantrymen.

Eben E. Olcott had been notified of the fire by telephone and proceeded promptly to the Marvel yard. Early in the morning, after the fire had burned out sufficiently, he was the first to go aboard the *New York*, leading a party to search for the bodies, all of which were found.

Little remained of the vessel but the hull, the engine, boilers, smokestacks and the paddle wheels. Like the *Daniel Drew*, the *New York* had died in a hurry.

Her loss came at the worst possible time and was a severe blow to the Day Line. Only seven months remained before the start of the 1909 season. Even though the Hudson-Fulton Celebration proper was not to take place until early fall, the impetus of the coming event, with the focusing of the interest of the nation on the Hudson River, was expected to make 1909 a great year generally for Hudson River steamboating. Here was the Day

After the fire the *New York* sank to the bottom and was a sad sight to behold.—*Elwin M. Eldredge coll.*

Line with only the *Hendrick Hudson,* the *Albany,* and the *Mary Powell* of its Mary Powell Steamboat Co., and neither of the latter two was roomy enough for the peak demands of the Albany run. A new steamer had to be built and it had to be built fast.

The Day Line naturally solicited bids on a proposed large *Robert Fulton* of the same general size as the *Hendrick Hudson,* but it was soon found that no yard could make delivery of such a vessel in time for the 1909 season. The engine of the *New York* and her three practically new boilers were inspected and found serviceable. By reducing the dimensions of the new steamer to approximately those of the *New York* and by utilizing the *New York's* engine and boilers, it seemed that valuable time could be saved. Not only could a smaller steamer be built faster than a larger one, but the problem of machinery would be taken care of even before construction was commenced.

Frank E. Kirby designed the smaller steamer and again J. W. Millard worked with him. On November 24, 1908, Mr. Olcott went to Camden, New

Jersey, to sign a contract with the New York Shipbuilding Co. for the vessel. Since that organization had covered ways, prolonged delays because of adverse weather would be obviated.

There was no question as to what the name would be, for the Day Line had been practically committed to *Robert Fulton* since 1907. Her keel was laid on "K" ways at the New York Shipbuilding Co.'s yard on January 11, 1909, and building went on at a rapid pace. No difficulty seems to have been experienced with the boilers of the *New York*. On the other hand, the engine proved troublesome. As the parts were removed at Newburgh, they were first sent to Hoboken, New Jersey, for examination at the Fletcher works. Normal wear-and-tear or damage by the heat of the fire made necessary the replacement of some parts, and others had to be discarded because the breadth of hull of the *Robert Fulton* would be slightly greater than that of the *New York*. All in all, the cost of this major renewal of the old engine was far in excess of what had been anticipated, and higher than the estimated cost of a new engine.

114

In the *Robert Fulton,* the engine was to be placed ahead of the paddle-wheel shaft as it had been in the *New York,* but the boilers were to be abaft the shaft. This meant that the *Robert Fulton's* three stacks would be aft like the *Albany's.*

The launch of the *Robert Fulton* took place on March 20, 1909. Since Mr. Olcott's daughter Katharine had officiated at the launching of the *Hendrick Hudson,* the honor this time went to his niece, Anita Merle-Smith, a daughter of the Reverend Wilton Merle-Smith. Water was again used, from a well on the old Livingston estate of Clermont, on the Hudson River. Amongst those present were Robert Fulton Ludlow; Captain David H. Deming of the *Hendrick Hudson;* Captain Alfred H. Harcourt, who was to command the new vessel; and the designers.

The *Robert Fulton* made her first trial trip on the Delaware River on May 8 and was delivered to the Day Line on May 18, when she sailed away from Camden for New York. She was the first Day Line steamer to be completed at the shipyard where the building had commenced. At New York the work of putting aboard her furnishings was

begun and on the night of May 25 the line held a dinner on the vessel to honor the presidents of the New York Shipbuilding Co. and the W. & A. Fletcher Co.

On May 29, 1909, about four-and-a-half months after the laying of the keel, the *Robert Fulton* sailed for Albany in regular service. The Day Line breathed a sigh of relief and didn't particularly care that the trip wasn't the spectacular affair that the *Hendrick Hudson's* first trip to Albany had been.

The *Robert Fulton* was not a forward step, but that was no fault of the Day Line's. Necessity had dictated the building of a steamer which in outward appearance was more reminiscent of the 1880s than of 1909. To the general public, of course, the *Robert Fulton's* exterior was not necessarily old-fashioned. For almost thirty years the three stacks athwartship on the *Chauncey Vibbard,* the *Albany* and the *New York* had been familiar sights on the Hudson. And there was certainly nothing strange about building a beam-engined Hudson River steamboat even in 1909. That very year the Hudson Navigation Co. placed in service

All ready for the launching of the *Robert Fulton* are, left to right, Miss Anita Merle-Smith, the sponsor; Eben E. Olcott, Mrs. George A. White, Miss Anna Olcott and Miss Katharine Olcott, sponsor of the *Hendrick Hudson.* The latter holds in her right hand a dinner bell allegedly from Robert Fulton's *North River Steam Boat.—H.R.D.L. coll., Steamship Historical Society of America, Inc.*

Above, right, oiler Conrad Milster, Jr., turns down a grease cup on the connecting-rod end of the walking beam of the *Robert Fulton* in 1954; above, another oiler tends to the crosshead. Right looks aft on the main deck in 1939, with the engine room at the left and showing the paddle-wheel shaft, which was well above deck level. Below, the piston with a new rod attached, is replaced in the cylinder, March 1954. Lower right is the steam steering engine. In a windowed case on the main deck forward, this was an intriguing but incomprehensible attraction for most passengers. The near side of the case has been lifted for this picture.— *All but middle right: Conrad Milster, Jr.*

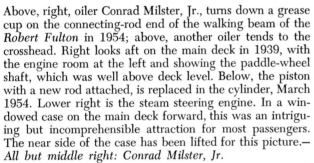

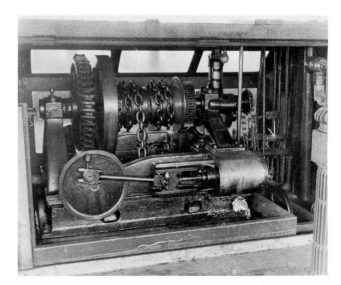

The *Robert Fulton* was built entirely at one yard and was well on the way to completion when she was launched. After being finished she is pictured off the covered ways of the New York Shipbuilding Co.—*Both: H.R.D.L. coll., Steamship Historical Society of America, Inc.*

two new steel-hulled beam-engined vessels, the *Trojan* and the *Rensselaer*, for its New York-Troy night line.

The Day Line's difficulty in presenting the *Robert Fulton* to the travelling public on a par with the *Hendrick Hudson* was due to the fact that only three years before it had unveiled the latter vessel as the most modern of her type. All comparisons were in her favor. But the Day Line had the maritime press on its side and had also built into the *Robert Fulton* a particularly charming interior, designed by Louis O. Keil. This feature the company stressed and to many the *Robert Fulton's* was the most restful and satisfying interior of any of the Day Line steamers. Unlike the massive and sombre mahogany of the *Hendrick Hudson*, the *Robert Fulton* had in her saloon the light treatment of the motif of a formal Italian garden. The colorings were largely white, gold and green, with the effect of a sky overhead between the deck beams. Besides vines, palms and plants, there were also caged birds.

The garden theme was continued in the private parlors ranging the saloon, but here the treatment was domestic. Each parlor was frescoed with such flowers of the Hudson Valley as mountain laurel, pinxter, dogwood and goldenrod.

The lunchroom was finished in ship's-cabin style; delft blue was chosen as decorative color for the dining room; a floral design was worked into the ceiling of the forward observation room on the third deck, with a miniature garden growing over the entrance stairway; and a dome, decorated with entwined roses and fitted with clerestory windows of rich yellow and golden-brown stained glass, enlivened the after observation room or convention hall.

Although the *Robert Fulton* had four decks, her hurricane or top deck originally was railed off so that passengers could use only the forward area between the pilothouse and the walking beam, and the after section abaft the smokestacks. Subsequently the intervening portion between these two areas was also made available to the passengers.

Robert Fulton Ludlow did for the steamer six portraits of noted Americans, including the one of Robert Fulton which had opened the equipping account in 1907. Besides the portraits, there were fourteen paintings of Hudson Valley scenes, ranging from an early view of Rondout to historic buildings, and executed by Vernon Howe Bailey, Frederick W. Glover, Raphael A. Weed and Samuel Ward Stanton. Stanton, the marine artist, historian and editor, did five murals illustrating the development of steam navigation on the Hudson — paintings which never failed to fascinate all lovers of steamboats.

With a length of 337 feet, the *Robert Fulton* was two feet longer than the *New York*, and cost the Day Line about $500,000. Included as part of her engine-room equipment was a steam ram. These had come into use with some of the larger beam engines and were to the engineer what the steam-steering engine was to the pilot. Instead of going through the manual labor of pushing and pulling the starting bar up and down to start the beam engine, the engineer had only to move forward and backward a vertical handle. He thus controlled the flow of steam to the small cylinder of the ram, which in turn controlled the flow of steam into and out of the main cylinder. Whether or not it operated efficiently originally, the steam ram of the *Robert Fulton* did not do so in later years and came to be used only when warming up the engine before sailing. In the 1930s it was removed.

The introduction of the *Robert Fulton* wrought no change in the general pattern of the Day Line. She was licensed for 4,000 passengers, which was her maximum and a third more than the *Albany* could carry. That steamer had been licensed to her maximum of 3,000 several years before. With an eye toward heavy traffic in 1909, the Day Line had the *Hendrick Hudson's* capacity raised to the maximum of 5,500 to bring to an end its old limited-capacity policy.

The year was to be as successful as expected. Gross earnings passed $600,000 for the first time, total passengers carried, excluding those of the *Mary Powell*, exceeded half a million — also for the first time.

Aside from the advent of the *Robert Fulton* and the excellent business conditions, another noteworthy mark was made in Day Line annals in 1909 when, on June 15, Alfred Van Santvoord Olcott assumed the duties of treasurer. A son of Eben E. Olcott and just out of Princeton, he was following in the footsteps of the grandfather for whom he had been named and was particularly fitted to do so because within him he had a natural love for both steamboats and the Hudson River. In the years ahead his position was to become a dominant one on the stream.

In the early fall of 1909 the eagerly-awaited Hudson-Fulton Celebration got under way with a great Inaugural Naval Parade at New York on Saturday, September 25. Actively participating were almost 750 vessels, including over 100 steamboats and ferryboats, about 270 yachts and motor-

Though a walking beam was always a fascinating and mysterious thing to ordinary passengers, few were so completely captivated as is this boy on the *Robert Fulton*. Oblivious of all else, he probably dreams of the day when he will be a chief engineer. In earlier years, clearly evident in the picture below, the hurricane deck from ahead of the beam to aft of the smokestacks, was not open to passengers.—*Both: H.R.D.L. coll., Steamship Historical Society of America, Inc.*

The *Norwich*, renowned both for her longevity and her ability as an icebreaker, was a prime attraction during the Hudson-Fulton Celebration. Built to run as a passenger and freight boat between New York City and Norwich, Connecticut, she came to the Hudson in 1842 and after being outmoded as a passenger carrier, served as a towing steamer. She was not sold for scrap until 1923. Her early engine was of the crosshead type, with the crosshead moving up and down within the gallows frame and connected to the cranks on the paddle-wheel shaft. Normally the gallows frame was closed, but was left open for the Celebration so the moving parts within would be clearly visible. Abreast of the *Norwich* in the background is the crowded *Hendrick Hudson.—Elwin M. Eldredge coll.*

boats, and more than 300 tugs and lighters. Along the line lay even more vessels and small craft at anchor. The U.S.S. *Gloucester* headed the procession as flagship of the parade's commanding officer, Captain J. W. Miller. Three torpedo boats in the escort squadron were commanded by young lieutenants whose names were to become most familiar decades later: J. O. Richardson, H. R. Stark, and W. F. Halsey.

The Day Line's assistant general manager, Captain George A. White, was flag officer of the first squadron, comprised of 12 divisions of steamboats and ferries. The first division included the *Hendrick Hudson, Robert Fulton* and *Albany*; the Long Island Sound steamers *Providence, Puritan* and *City of Lowell*; the new *Rensselaer* of the Troy night line; and the venerable towboat *Norwich*, built in 1836, and bearing on her paddle boxes the inscription, "Oldest Steamboat in the World."

The centerpieces of the Hudson-Fulton Celebration and cynosure of all eyes were the replicas of Henry Hudson's ship, the *Half Moon*, a gift of the people of Holland, and of Robert Fulton's first Hudson River steamer, the *North River Steam Boat*. This latter replica had been built at Staten Island for the celebration and was christened the *Clermont* for this had become the name of Fulton's famous craft for all time.

During the course of the festivities these replicas made a lengthy passage up the Hudson to the head of river navigation at Troy, greeted with a succession of elaborate civic ceremonies en route.

The working plans for the *Clermont* had been drawn by Frank E. Kirby and J. W. Millard after extensive research. She was launched on July 10, 1909, at the yard of the Staten Island Shipbuilding Co., Mariners Harbor, New York. Here again water from the well of the old Livingston estate at Clermont was used for the christening as ". . . a delicate tribute to Fulton's well-known temperance principles. . . ." After her construction was completed, she was entrusted to the Clermont Committee, of which Eben E. Olcott was chairman and which was empowered to make recommendations as to the final disposition of the replica.

What to do with the *Clermont* and the *Half Moon* when the celebration was over presented a problem. Although the Hudson-Fulton Celebration Commission had presented one of the great events in Hudson Valley history, it ended with a deficit of over $50,000 and little in the way of assets to meet its unpaid bills. As a gift of the people of a

120

friendly foreign land, the *Half Moon* had to be treated with care, and was placed in the Brooklyn Navy Yard during the winter of 1909-1910. Then, in June of 1910, the Executive Committee of the Hudson-Fulton Celebration Commission decided to turn her over to the Commissioners of the Palisades Interstate Park, New York Commission, which had "ample financial resources" and had requested the little ship. The *Half Moon* was accordingly delivered on July 15, 1910, ". . . in perpetual trust for the people of the State of New York."

Meanwhile, the *Clermont* was laid up at the shipyard where she had been built. With no money available to keep her in repair, her condition apparently deteriorated rapidly. Mr. Olcott offered to buy her for the Hudson River Day Line and on September 13, 1910, the Executive Committee voted to sell her ". . . in consideration of a cash payment and repairs to the vessel equivalent to $2,361.85, and in further consideration of that company's [the Day Line's] agreement to maintain,

care for, exhibit, and, when practicable, operate the *Clermont* as an object lesson in the science of steam navigation."

It was fitting that she should become the property of the Day Line, which had always evinced a strong interest in the early history of steam navigation. Actually, there is no indication that she would ever have been disposed of otherwise. She probably would have been left to rot away on the Staten Island shore.

The Day Line immediately had the *Clermont* overhauled and on October 10 she was towed from Staten Island to the 129th Street pier at New York to commence a career as a floating museum, with appropriate exhibits on board. Later in the month she was placed at the Day Line's Desbrosses Street pier and remained open to the public, with an admission fee of twenty-five cents.

Early on the afternoon of May 24, 1911, the *Hendrick Hudson* took the *Clermont* in tow for

Flying the Hudson-Fulton flag from her foremast, the *Clermont* steams along in a smart breeze. In the background to the left is the replica *Half Moon.—Edwin Levick coll., Mariners Museum.*

Poughkeepsie, where she was to remain for some time. Captain George A. White, Samuel Ward Stanton and the Reverend C. Seymour Bullock, along with a number of newspaper reporters, were aboard the *Clermont*. The towing hawser broke early in the trip, perhaps because the *Hendrick Hudson* was going too fast, but aside from that the passage seems to have been uneventful — except that here was one of the most unusual tows ever to go up the Hudson.

Now that it owned the *Clermont*, the Day Line went back further with its own historical antecedents. Its *Souvenir Magazine* in 1911 said, "Through officials whose fathers and grandfathers were connected with steam transportation on the Hudson since the time of the first company, the Day Line is the logical successor to the Fulton-Livingston Line of early days. . . . During the present season, the *Clermont* will be stationed at Poughkeepsie, and excursionists to that city on the Day Line . . . will have an opportunity of boarding and thoroughly inspecting this most interesting vessel for a moderate fee."

In September of that year the *Clermont* had a narrow escape from destruction when the Day Line's pier and buildings at Poughkeepsie burned. Although the little steamer caught fire she was towed out in the river and the flames extinguished.

Eventually interest in such a floating museum paled. It was inevitable that the *Clermont* could not continue indefinitely as an attraction, and hence the Day Line lost interest in maintaining her as one. In the fall of 1914, she was placed in a tidal lagoon on the inner side of the Day Line landing at Kingston Point and was sufficiently offshore so that she could not be boarded. For many years the company kept her in a presentable condition, but eventually considerable deterioration set in. During the depressed business conditions of the 1930s it was decided to break her up rather than leave her to rot away, and this was done in 1936.

Actually, the *Clermont* survived longer than the *Half Moon*, which ended her days in a park in Cohoes, New York. Here she became the center of a controversy as to whether she should be kept in repair or disposed of. The problem was solved when the replica burned in 1931.

This is a portion of the saloon of the *Robert Fulton*, showing the bell reputedly from Robert Fulton's *North River Steam Boat.—H.R.D.L. coll., Steamship Historical Society of America, Inc.*

Chapter 16

THE LARGEST DAY LINER

AFTER THE ADVENT of the *Robert Fulton,* the Day Line advertised its "palace steel steamers" or "palatial steel steamers" *Hendrick Hudson, Robert Fulton, Albany* and *Mary Powell.* Those whose memories harked back to the days of the "palace iron steamers" *Albany* and *New York* must have felt that steel had won an overwhelming victory. We wonder what Captain A. L. Anderson would have thought had he returned to find that through some twentieth-century wizardry his *Mary Powell* had had her hull changed from wood to steel by a dash of printers' ink! The greatest of the "palace steel steamers" was yet to come. There was still to be the suitable companion steamer for the *Hendrick Hudson* which had been on the verge since 1907.

Total passengers carried continued to rise in 1910, and by 1911 the Day Line was well enough along on the plans for the new steamer to devote over a full page to her in the *Hudson River Day Line Souvenir Magazine.* The vessel, somewhat changed from the original concept, was to have a capacity of 6,000 passengers, 500 more than the *Hendrick Hudson.* Since the Day Line had already used the name of *Robert Fulton,* it decided to honor Washington Irving, saying:

> As Washington Irving was one of the most refined and illustrious Americans known to our history and especially as he did so much in his own delightful way to acquaint the world with the glories of the Hudson River, it is purposed to have this epoch-maker, which will bear his name, in every way the most refined of floating structures. It will likewise be her privilege to acquaint the world with the still unclouded, scenic, romantic, and historical glories of the Hudson.

Irving, who had once written his thanks to God that his youth had been spent on the banks of the Hudson, would probably have been pleased.

Frank E. Kirby and J. W. Millard & Brother were the designers of the *Washington Irving,* with Louis O. Keil handling the interior architecture. The New York Shipbuilding Corp. — it had changed its name from "company" — was to build the steamer at its Camden, New Jersey, yard and the engine was to be a product of the W. & A. Fletcher Co.

The launching was set for December 7, 1912. Captain George A. White was acquainted with William McAndrew, principal of the Washington Irving High School for girls in New York City, and the two men thought it would be a fine idea and a publicity attraction to have a delegation of the girls from the school attend the launching. For this purpose some of the members of the school's Mascot Club — or Mascot's Club — were most suitable, for they were redheads.

The background of the club was that, years before, the school had been promised a new building. Nothing happened. Then a redheaded student read that good fortune followed the head of a red-haired maiden. Taking her cue from this, she organized all the redheads and near redheads in the school into a club, which went in for all sorts of incantations. Chiefly, though, they relied on the old crossed-fingers. At the next meeting of the Board of Estimate, the Mascot Club attended in a body and sat throughout the session with fingers crossed. Some of them couldn't write for several days thereafter, but they got approval for their new building. That had made the Mascot Club somewhat of a permanent institution in the school.

The actual number of redheads who went to the launching as guests of the Day Line was about fifty, more or less. With the rest of the launching party, they left New York on a special train on the Pennsylvania Railroad, called the "Redheaded Special." The railroad even found a redheaded engineer to handle the throttle. Chief chaperon to the girls was Principal McAndrew, whose hair and beard were still liberally tinged with red.

All of the girls wore white sweaters with "WIHS" in white letters on a red sash, and on their heads had wreaths of ivy from the vine claimed to have been given to Washington Irving by Sir Walter Scott and planted by Irving. They won the

Mrs. Eben E. Olcott, the sponsor of the *Washington Irving*, is surrounded by Washington Irving High School girls with hands raised and fingers crossed. Soon the largest of all the Day Line steamers was sliding into the Delaware River.—*Both: H.R.D.L. coll., Steamship Historical Society of America, Inc.*

affection of the large crowd which had gathered to watch the launching. Amongst representatives of the Irving family present was a Washington Irving.

The launching took place about 1:30 p.m. Mrs. Eben E. Olcott, the sponsor, had brought a white-ribboned bottle of water from the well at Irving's home at Sunnyside. As she raised this for the christening, all of the redheads stood on tip-toe, swung their arms above their heads and crossed their fingers. When the hull commenced to move and Mrs. Olcott, breaking the bottle, said, "I christen thee *Washington Irving*," the girls tossed their ivy wreaths at the vessel. Then they chanted a poem written expressly for the occasion by, of course, Wallace Bruce.

When it was over, Mrs. Olcott breathed a sigh of relief and confessed, "I've had it in my mind and I've been so afraid I'd say, 'I name thee *George Washington*,' but I didn't."

As the big hull slid down into the water, twenty carrier pigeons were released from on deck. Each had a ribbon wound around a leg reading, "I started home when the *Washington Irving* was launched. Time me." Everyone agreed that never — no, never! — had a vessel been launched amidst more omens of good luck than the *Washington Irving*.

Although the shipyard should have been familiar with the temperance launchings of the Day Line through its experience with the *Robert Fulton*, it nonetheless had had ready on the platform a bottle of champagne. This was naturally ignored by Mrs. Olcott, but one wonders if the shipyard did not have its own personal christening, Thomas S. Marvel style. The following week Mrs. Olcott received a letter from an official of the shipyard, reading:

> I am sending you today, under separate cover, the net from the bottle of champagne supplied by this company for the launch of the *Washington Irving* and trust that it will reach you in good condition.
>
> The launch was certainly a great success, and we all of us are indebted to Mr. Olcott & yourself for its many novel and pleasing features. I trust the boat's future career may be as successful as the commencement. . . .

On the afternoon of May 1, 1913, the *Washington Irving* made her official trial trip under sunny skies on the Delaware River, running from the Municipal Pier at the foot of Race Street, Philadelphia, to a point below Chester and then returning. She subsequently went to New York under her own steam. On May 12 a celebrative dinner was held on board and two days later she made an invitation trip on the Hudson, to which came the redheads of the launching. The girls dressed in white and tied blue ribbons in their hair to supply a red, white and blue effect for the occasion. On May 16 the entire student body of Washington Irving High School was invited for an afternoon sail up the river to a point off Irving's home at Sunnyside, giving the girls ample time to consume 75 gallons of lemonade.

Captain David H. Deming commanded the new steamer and was probably the proudest man in the Hudson Valley. The *Washington Irving* was what she was intended to be — a larger version of the *Hendrick Hudson*. The first Day Liner to exceed 400 feet in length, she was more than 20 feet longer than her older sister and nearly two feet wider.

The engine was an inclined compound of the same dimensions and indicated horsepower as the *Hendrick Hudson's*. Since the engines were identical in size and since the *Washington Irving* was considerably larger, one might think that she therefore would not be quite as fast. Actually, the Day Line considered the *Washington Irving* slightly the faster in regular speed. It is said that one point in her favor was that, because of the shape of her hull, she created less disturbance to the water and therefore could be let out a bit more.

The obvious differences in the profiles of the two vessels were that the *Washington Irving* had her hurricane deck extended to the stern and carried a dummy smokestack ahead of her two real smokestacks. At one time a pilot aboard her made a jocular pact with an assistant engineer. If the pilot ever saw smoke coming from the first stack, he would immediately notify the engineer. Then they would both jump overboard!

A less noticeable difference was that the *Washington Irving* had a torpedo or cruiser stern. The *Hendrick Hudson* had a tendency to drag by the stern in such areas of the river as Haverstraw Bay. It was thought that the use of a cruiser stern would prevent this, which it did.

Irving had lived abroad and it was desired that the steamer reflect this portion of his life. As a result there were such things as a lunchroom done in the style of an English tavern and a flamboyant Alhambra writing room. The main saloon blended styles from Knickerbocker to Moorish and off it were located all nineteen of the private parlors, which the Day Line in effect designated as staterooms by having placed on the doors the coats of

The *Washington Irving* is on the Delaware (left) and on the Hudson (below). The latter view has been touched up to show smoke coming from her forward smokestack, which was a dummy. The booths in the lunchroom in the hold were intended to resemble those of an English tavern (left). Passengers who wanted a hearty meal went to the spacious dining room on the main deck (above).—*This page: H.R.D.L. coll., Steamship Historical Society of America, Inc.; opposite above: Albert Gayer coll.*

The ornate Alhambra writing room on this page was an astonishing feature of the saloon of the *Washington Irving;* the forward observation room on the promenade deck (opposite) was adorned by Raphael A. Weed's panorama of the Catskill Mountains. This was at the after end of the room and was set off by vines on either side of it.—*All: H.R.D.L. coll., Steamship Historical Society of America, Inc.*

Above is the saloon of the *Washington Irving*, looking aft. On the housing of the engine-room ventilator is Raphael A. Weed's painting of Golden Hill Inn in New York City. More of Weed's works in the floating art gallery are shown below, with Coxsackie Island the subject of the nearest painting. The doors lead from the saloon to private parlors and are embellished with state coats of arms. Up on the hurricane deck, passengers admire the natural art of Hudson River scenery. The pointed mountain ahead of the first flag-pole on the starboard side is Sugar Loaf. Far away from all of this, the firemen on the *Washington Irving* display the art of feeding coal to the fireboxes. If you bet that they posed for this picture, you would probably win.—*All: H.R.D.L. coll., Steamship Historical Society of America, Inc.*

arms of the first nineteen states to become a part of the Union. Instead of two private parlors beneath the pilothouse as on the *Hendrick Hudson,* the *Washington Irving* had another observation room.

The new steamer was the greatest of the Day Line's "floating art galleries." Originally Samuel Ward Stanton, who had done the steamboat paintings for the *Robert Fulton,* was commissioned to do a series of Spanish views for the *Washington Irving.* Stanton went to Spain to gather material for this project and with his extreme interest in shipping, decided to return to the United States on the maiden voyage of the *Titanic.* With her he was lost. Since Herbert W. Faulkner had earlier sketched in Spain the type of views that were desired, the commission for this work was then turned over to him. Principally, the Faulkner paintings were of the Alhambra, although there was one of Astoria, Oregon, and of Bracebridge Hall in England.

Raphael A. Weed, who had been a close friend of Stanton's, did a series of Hudson River paintings, an Old New York series and other views. A portrait of Washington Irving based on a Jarvis portrait was executed by Harper Pennington, while Victor D. Brenner, who had designed the Lincoln penny, produced a bronze relief portrait of Irving. Also on board were three small paintings by Stanton.

The total cost of this second "million dollar steamer" was somewhat nearer that figure, for it came to $837,618.16. The Day Line had reached its peak so far as size of steamers was concerned.

By a quirk of fate, May of 1913 marked the advent not only of the largest day steamer ever built for the Hudson River, but also of the largest night steamer, the *Berkshire.* This in turn made the latter the largest steamboat ever to be built for the Hudson River and she was advertised as the largest river steamer in the world. The *Berkshire,* 422.4 feet in length, was nearly 22 feet longer than the *Washington Irving.*

The Hudson Navigation Co. had begun to talk about this larger version of the *C. W. Morse* for its People's Line in 1906 and had gotten her launched from the yard of the New York Shipbuilding Co. at Camden, New Jersey, on September 21, 1907, at a time when the Day Line was only toying with what eventually became the *Washington Irving.* The new People's Line vessel was christened the *Princeton,* but financial difficulties caused her completion to be suspended. In fact, the *Princeton* figuratively went into the dead file

when it became more imperative for the Hudson Navigation Co. to build a pair of new steamboats — the *Trojan* and *Rensselaer* — for service on its Citizens' Line in 1909 to replace the aging steamboats then covering the New York-Troy route.

In the meantime, the career of Charles Wyman Morse had somewhat paralleled the career of the *Princeton.* In the shipping field, Morse had gradually built up control of Atlantic coastal shipping until he had in his fold an impressive collection of important lines. He had also been building his interlocking banking interests and was making himself felt in New York banking circles. He naturally figured in the panic of 1907. Finally he was convicted of falsifying books and misapplying funds of the Bank of North America and in 1908 was sentenced to 15 years in the Atlanta Penitentiary. Appeals were futile and in 1910 he finally went behind bars. Relatives and friends failed to arouse in President Taft any desire to pardon him, but when his health was said to be failing a commission of army doctors examined him in prison and reported that he was dying of Bright's disease. The President then pardoned him and he went off to Wiesbaden, Germany, to restore his health. It is reported that he neglected to pay his attorney and word got out that just before his examination by the army doctors he had drunk a hearty combination of soapsuds and chemicals. The resulting symptoms certainly indicated complications.

Morse had gained his freedom about thirteen years ahead of time and when he returned to the United States, was hot to embark on new adventures. As Morse's health was "restored," so was the *Princeton's.* This name, which was never official, had been changed to *Berkshire,* and the vessel made her invitation trial trip on May 20, 1913, just six days after the *Washington Irving's* first invitation run on the Hudson. The Hudson Navigation Co. put the *Berkshire* in service on the New York-Albany night line on May 22, when she made her initial run to Albany. Thereby it stole a march on the Day Line, which hadn't scheduled the *Washington Irving* to go to Albany until Saturday, May 24. Saturday had probably been considered an excellent day for the event, since it was a half-holiday for many people.

There was no disputing the fact that the *Berkshire* was considerably larger, and her arrival in Albany created interest to the point that the coming of the *Washington Irving* would be an anticlimax. Crowds braved the rain on Friday afternoon, May 23, when the newest of the night boats was thrown open for public inspection. Unfor-

With her vertical beam engine and boilers installed, the *Princeton* was laid up for years before she was finally completed as the *Berkshire* of the Hudson Navigation Co. In the spring of 1909 that company brought out the *Trojan* as the first of a pair of sisters for its New York-Troy or Citizens' Line service. The *Trojan* had been on the stocks in the yard of the T. S. Marvel Shipbuilding Co. at Newburgh when the *New York* burned, and is shown here in her earlier years on the Hudson.—*Above: Tracey I. Brooks coll., Steamship Historical Society of America, Inc.; below: Elwin M. Eldredge coll.*

When the *Berkshire* entered service in 1913 as a New York-Albany night boat, she was the largest steamboat ever to be built for the Hudson River. The *Rensselaer* was the running mate of the *Trojan* on the New York-Troy night line.—*Both: Elwin M. Eldredge coll.*

Although this picture is not dated, all signs indicate that it was taken on Sunday afternoon, May 25, 1913, when the new *Berkshire* was thrown open for public inspection at Albany for the second time. Some sightseers in the distance are ogling the *Washington Irving*, which is properly observing the Sabbath without a flag raised.—R. Loren Graham coll.

tunately for the Day Line, the rain persisted through Saturday to make the *Washington Irving's* first trip to Albany somewhat less than a gala event. The heavy downpour kept a great many prospective passengers at home although small crowds did turn out along the way to greet her. One greeter at Poughkeepsie came down to the landing with a saluting cannon. Carried away by his enthusiasm, he forgot to remove the ramrod before a salute, and, but for the quick action of a bystander, would have fired it through one of the plate-glass windows.

That night at Albany an invitation reception was held on board and on Sunday the two largest steamers of their types ever built for the Hudson lay near one another on the Albany waterfront, the center of attraction in the city. While the boats might lie there in apparent harmony, there was soon to be considerably less than harmony between their owners. In 1902 when Morse had first commenced to work his way into Hudson River steamboat operations, it may be remembered that his goal was said to be complete control. Now the goal was again exciting his interest.

In July of 1913 things began to happen. The Hudson Navigation Co. had previously been offering day service Sundays between Troy, Albany and New York with its Citizens' Line steamers *Trojan* and *Rensselaer*. This was a source of easy added income, because the Day Line remained true to its principles and refused to operate on Sundays. The continuance of the old policy so long in an era of changing standards has been said to have been due — like the abolition of bars — to the firm hand exercised by Mrs. Eben E. Olcott in the affairs of the line. There is no question but that it cost the line enormous sums in operating revenue.

The Hudson Navigation Co. was therefore offering added service to the public. Since it owned an icehouse and dock at the upper end of Kingston Point, this was a way landing on Sundays to make Kingston Point Park available to Albanians on that day. One could sail down the Hudson on the southbound steamer for New York, go ashore to enjoy the Park, and return to Albany on the northbound steamer.

The *Washington Irving* had been waiting to go into Poughkeepsie landing and was just getting under way when this picture was taken.—*H.R.D.L. coll., Steamship Historical Society of America, Inc.*

The Hudson Navigation Co. had also offered through day service on Decoration Day in 1913 and did the same thing on the Fourth of July. As neither holiday fell on a Sunday, it was thereby competing directly with the Day Line. On the Fourth of July, too, the *Adirondack,* which had become a spare boat upon the advent of the *Berkshire,* was employed to run a special afternoon excursion from Albany to Kingston Point and return. The Day Line admitted that more people had left Albany on the Fourth on the Hudson Navigation Co. steamers than on its boat.

The Hudson Navigation Co. had announced that it soon planned to operate a day line of its own between New York and Kingston Point, and on July 5 added that this was only a forerunner of regular day service between New York and Albany. The company said it would probably convert the *Adirondack* into a day boat with much of her deckhousing removed, and build another steamer to run with her. The great disadvantage of a night boat for day service was the fact that they were night boats. Their tiers of staterooms limited the open deck space and they had no large-scale arrange-

ments whereby passengers could sit inside in bad weather and still watch the scenery. Hence considerable remodeling would be necessary to make the *Adirondack* into anything like the Day Line steamers, but for the present she would run as she was.

The Day Line claimed it was not at all disturbed. On the surface Eben E. Olcott was either not impressed by Morse, or he felt that he was running such a pious line that Heaven would protect it from the onslaught of a former prisoner! The Day Line let it be known that it had no intention of making the slightest change in its services or its rates, and felt that the steamers by themselves would continue to attract the patronage they always had. But if you probed a little deeper, you found that along the waterfront it was freely predicted by one and all that the greatest steamboat war in the history of the Hudson River was about to start.

The new Morse day line commenced on July 10, when the *Adirondack* made the opening trip of the New York-Kingston Point daily round-trip service. She landed en route at Yonkers, West

Point, Newburgh and Poughkeepsie. Since the fares were the same either one way or round trip, the $1.00 rate to Kingston Point was twenty-five cents less than the Day Line's one-way rate and $1.25 less for the complete trip.

Meanwhile, the Central-Hudson Steamboat Co. had been drawn into the fight when the Hudson Navigation Co. planned to have fencing erected at the entrance to the Main Street wharf at Poughkeepsie, which it was using and which adjoined the Central-Hudson wharf there. Benjamin B. Odell, Jr., an officer of the Central-Hudson Steamboat Co. and an ex-governor of the State of New York, hustled to Poughkeepsie to get a restraining injunction. Then the *Adirondack* struck the steamer *Marlborough* of the Central-Hudson Line while landing at Newburgh. This, the Central-Hudson people implied, was sheer mischief.

It was reported that the Day Line and the Manhattan Navigation Co., operating a cut-rate opposition night line between New York and Albany, were considering a merger. The idea to be conveyed to Mr. Morse was that the resultant organization would build new night boats comparable to the *Berkshire* and the *C. W. Morse* to fight the Hudson Navigation Co. to the bitter end. Then Mr. Olcott officially announced, for his company, that there would be no merger and once again let it be known that he was not fearful of the competition.

Actually he was on solid ground, for the great steamboat war was of short duration. The northern terminus of the *Adirondack* was soon retracted to Poughkeepsie, and after she had made a few more round trips to that place the day service of the Hudson Navigation Co. was again reduced to Sunday operations.

Why Morse pulled out so soon is anyone's guess. Perhaps he had hoped to scare the Day Line quickly into a selling mood. Perhaps he was short on the capital necessary to make the Morse day line a reality. Or maybe he had hotter irons in the fire.

This view of the *Washington Irving* leaving Poughkeepsie gives her a strange appearance, since it emphasizes the extreme width of the main, saloon and promenade decks as compared with the hurricane deck.—*H.R.D.L. coll., Steamship Historical Society of America, Inc.*

The *Mary Powell* is lying at Bear Mountain along with the *Commander* and the *Rose-dale*. The view below of a portion of Bear Mountain Park is a recent one.—*Below: New York State Department of Commerce photograph.*

Chapter 17

THE LAST OF THE *Mary Powell*

THE ADDITION of the *Washington Irving* to the Day Line fleet brought about some operational changes that had been conceived well in advance. Since the *Washington Irving* would run to Albany with the *Hendrick Hudson* during the summer season, the *Robert Fulton* now became the special boat to Poughkeepsie in place of the *Albany.*

The route of the Mary Powell Steamboat Co., the Day Line's third regular service, had been designed to provide early morning transportation from Kingston, Poughkeepsie, Newburgh and other landings to New York, with a mid-afternoon departure from New York to those places. For round-trippers it offered a sail on the river and several hours at New York for shopping, the transaction of business or sightseeing. In deference to the trend toward the Saturday half-holiday and the resultant heavy movement of passengers up the river on Saturday afternoons, the New York sailing time eventually had been moved up to 1:45 p.m. on that day. In 1907, when the Day Line inaugurated the Poughkeepsie special with the *Albany,* the 1:45 p.m. sailing became effective all week long. This enabled the *Mary Powell* to reach West Point before the *Albany* arrived there on her way down from Poughkeepsie and so made it possible for the Day Line to offer New Yorkers an afternoon excursion on the Hudson. At the same time it reduced the available time at New York for up-river patrons to two hours if one went to Desbrosses Street, or 2 hours 40 minutes if he got off at West 42d Street.

As a result of the combination of one-way and excursion services being operated, the Day Line seems to have felt that in 1913 there would be no likely new service to be opened and on which the *Albany* could be employed. Therefore, it decided to place her on the route of the *Mary Powell* during much of the summer season. Since the *Albany's* capacity was greater, she would be better able to handle the traffic, particularly on Saturdays.

During the period when the *Albany* was running on the Kingston route, the *Mary Powell* would be available for excursions or special trips. This would mean that there would be an extra steamer available practically all season, so in 1913 the Day Line looked with a keener eye toward the charter business. That was simply the rental of a vessel to a church, fraternal group, business house or so on for its exclusive use for the day. The organization chartering a vessel could arrange a schedule that best suited its needs and plan activities on board with no fear of disturbing other passengers.

To publicize its facilities in the charter field, the Day Line issued a handbill calling attention to the fact that:

> The addition to the Day Line Fleet of the great, new Steamer *Washington Irving* makes it possible to offer for charter for special parties the Steamer *Mary Powell* during July and August, and in the Spring and Fall the Steamer *Albany.* Ideal outings may be planned for parties at reasonable rates, from New York, Albany and points along the Hudson River.
>
> All Day Line Piers are conveniently situated and up-to-date and the luxury and comfort of the *Albany* and *Mary Powell* may now be enjoyed by private charter parties, especially church societies, patriotic orders, conventions, etc. No bars, and no liquors sold or allowed on either steamer.

On July 7, 1913, the *Albany* commenced regular round trips from Kingston in place of the *Mary Powell* and two days later the latter was off on a Union Sunday School excursion from Kingston to Bear Mountain.

Bear Mountain in the Highlands of the Hudson was then in its infancy as a resort. In 1915 the Day Line made it a regular landing for the Poughkeepsie special and for the northbound run of the afternoon steamer to Kingston. Bear Mountain quickly established itself in popularity and the Day Line thereafter gave it added and ample coverage. Said the *Hudson River Day Line Magazine* in 1915:

Photographed from West Point with Constitution Island in the background, the *Washington Irving* is bound north on a Sunday and flies her church flag above the national flag on her after pole.—*H.R.D.L. coll., Steamship Historical Society of America, Inc.*

The real history of Bear Mountain as a pleasure resort began in 1914. A few years before that public sentiment was so opposed to the project of state officials to relocate Sing Sing Prison at Highland Lake, that they abandoned the site and turned it over to the Interstate Park. In the short time that the tract has been in the hands of the Commission much has been accomplished. A playground which will take care of thousands has been hewn out of the wilderness without materially detracting from the natural charm of the place. Beautiful rustic paths and roads have been laid out and shelter houses, a pavilion and dancing floor constructed. Camp sites, including tent bottoms, have been provided in large numbers and the usual picnic tables, swings, benches, etc., have not been overlooked. A wading pool for children is a unique feature. Rowing enthusiasts can choose from a fleet of nearly one hundred boats to navigate the peaceful waters of the lake. In short, Bear Mountain Reservation is an idealized excursion resort. Its control by the commissioners bars out the cheap tawdriness which is the bane of so many similar places. Man has taken a little bit of one of the Almighty's finest resting places and changed it just enough to satisfy the natural desires of respectable folk out for a pleasant day in the real country.

In 1915, during part of the summer, the *Mary Powell* ran exclusively between New York and Bear Mountain, although in this case her operation was in conjunction with the McAllister Steamboat Co.'s *Highlander*. The *Mary Powell* was laid up for the winter early in September — earlier than ever before — but was soon back in commission. On September 8, as the *Albany* was making the morning run from Kingston to New York, she ran into a heavy fog near Crum Elbow. The *Albany* slowed down, but shortly struck a rock with her starboard paddle wheel, badly damaging it. She whistled for aid and was assisted into Poughkeepsie by the *Homer Ramsdell* of the Central-Hudson Steamboat Co. There the *Albany* discharged her passengers and went on to Hoboken for repairs, while the *Mary Powell* was hastily readied to go into service on her old route until the *Albany* was repaired.

This was the third accident of some moment on the Kingston line in a few years. In 1910 the *Mary Powell* had cracked the crosshead on her piston rod and was replaced briefly by the *Chrystenah*, a smaller sidewheeler but swift enough so that she was sometimes used by the Day Line as a baggage boat. In 1913 the *Mary Powell* had struck an obstruction in the river and stove a hole in her bow on a southbound trip. She was able to continue to New York for temporary repairs.

As a new service to its patrons in the summer of 1916, the Day Line employed the *Mary Powell*, now commanded by Captain Arthur A. Warrington, on a Saturday afternoon special from New York to Albany and continued to do so in 1917. She also saw some further service on her old route and otherwise handled excursions and charters. In June 1917 she made two excursions to New York from Kingston, Poughkeepsie and Newburgh, planned principally for those who wanted to hear the preaching of the famous evangelist, Billy Sunday.

Actually, the Day Line had little occasion to keep the *Mary Powell* busy during either 1916 or 1917. In the latter year she made her first and last trip with passengers on May 30 and September 5 respectively. Between those dates she was idle more than she was running. It came to pass that after 1917 she was not to run again.

In April, 1918, the Day Line announced that the Kingston-New York route would not open until July 6. It was later said that the reason was that the Government had requested a conservation of 30 per cent of the coal normally used. The *Albany* opened the regular season to Albany on May 24, when service flags were unfurled at nine of the company's landings. About the same time the Day Line decided to take what, for it, was a revolutionary step. It would run on Sundays commencing June 16.*

This would be a source of great additional profit, but the Day Line preferred to have it appear that it was going to run on Sundays for the benefit of the traveling public. It announced that the move was being made only after consultation with many prominent clergymen and laymen. These gentlemen, we are told, convinced the management that it should make its boats available on Sundays.

But the line didn't entirely discard its principles. It was largely Mrs. Eben E. Olcott's idea to hold church services on the steamers on Sundays and, while these were in progress the vessels flew church flags from their after flagpoles. As long as Eben E. Olcott lived, or for over a decade, this practice was followed. All during the "Roaring Twenties" the Day Line carried in its literature a paragraph reading somewhat as follows:

In permitting Sunday operation of its steamers, officials of the Day Line feel that they are performing a real public service by furnishing an opportunity for healthful recreation under the best of influence. A cordial invitation is extended to all to attend the divine service, principally of song, conducted by a chaplain on each steamer.

Heretofore, the crews had been assured of at least part of a day of rest each week and it was possible to perform maintenance work that couldn't be done otherwise. Now, in order to continue this practice of having each vessel lay in for one day out of seven, it was necessary to have four boats instead of three available to cover the Albany and the Poughkeepsie services. As an extra boat for this purpose, the *Albany* was needed and could not be used in the Kingston service in 1918. Therefore, the decision to operate on Sundays came to mean the elimination of this service.

The route of the Mary Powell Steamboat Co. was no longer a big money proposition as it had been in days of yore. Closing it under the circumstances was a logical step, and pointing up the coal shortage blocked any possibility of civic protest. Other factors notwithstanding, it was impractical to put the *Mary Powell* back in full-time service on the route. She was over 55 years old and antiquated by the company's standards. Her retirement, rumored on and off since 1910, was now to become a fact.

All during 1918 she remained berthed in Rondout Creek. Then, in the fall of 1919, she was sold to scrapping interests for $3,250 with the stipulation that she was not to be used for further service as a passenger or freight boat on the Hudson River, or for the making of a motion picture. The latter proviso seems to have been inserted as a result of the belief that a motion-picture maker was interested in burning her up for a spectacle. For sentimental reasons, before selling the *Mary Powell* the Day Line removed both her bell and her whistle, and subsequently installed the latter as the main whistle on the *Robert Fulton*. This evidence of the Day Line growing sentimental about the *Mary Powell* must have caused Captain Dave Hitchcock to spin in his grave!

The new owners of the *Mary Powell* decided to try to resell her and in the spring of 1920 disposed of her to John A. Fischer of Kingston. Mr. Fischer, a shrewd trader of the Yankee school, tried to resell her, too, and then broke her up for scrap, appropriately along the shore of Rondout Creek. He found a ready market for many parts of her

---

*West Point did not become a Sunday landing, for steamboats were not permitted to call there on Sunday until 1960.

which were desired as mementoes by those who regarded her with uncommon affection.

The *Mary Powell's* route had been limited, for most of her service was on that portion of the river between Kingston and New York City. For her, that was sufficient. She was fast, safe, dependable and beautiful, and her reputation over the years spread throughout the country and abroad. She was an old friend which during her seasons went to New York every morning and returned every afternoon — except of course on Sunday.

The *Mary Powell* captured the hearts of more people than any other steamboat in the history of Hudson River steamboating and even today, almost fifty years since she last ran, it is not unusual to find her name in print in reminiscing articles in newspapers up and down the Hudson Valley.

The Hudson has often been called the Rhine of America. A foreign-born American in an old novel, after contrasting the two rivers, concluded with a great deficiency of the European river: "... there's no *Mary Powell* on the Rhine."

In the same period in which the *Mary Powell* was retired, the Day Line was participating in transportation changes at Catskill, where it had continued to maintain its interest in the Catskill Mountain Railway and connections. But this route of entry from Catskill landing to resorts in the mountains came on hard times with the growth of the automobile. Reorganization in 1917 failed to stem the serious losses and 1918 was the last year of service.

Before this involvement in Catskill railroading was liquidated, the Day Line became a heavy investor in the Catskill & New York Steamboat Co.,

Ltd., and its subsidiary New York & Hudson Steamboat Co., which operated under the trade name of Catskill Evening Line. The line ran night boats for passengers and freight between New York and Coxsackie, with the principal passenger landings being Catskill and Hudson. It operated two fine beam-engined sidewheelers, the *Clermont* of 1911 and the *Onteora* of 1898, and a wooden-hulled propeller boat, the *Storm King*, built in 1911 for freight only.

The construction of the *Clermont* had been dictated by the need to replace an older steamboat, the *Kaaterskill*, but represented a large outlay of funds at a poor time. The class of people who had previously gone to the Catskills by night boat to Catskill were now going further afield for their summering, and the automobile was making itself felt here, as with the Catskill Mountain Railway. As a counter measure, the Catskill Evening Line had taken to carrying automobiles and advertised that it had excellent accommodations for both them and horses!

By 1916 the financial position of the Catskill Evening Line was not good and early that year the Day Line bought control. Except for economy in administration, this resulted in no change in the operation of either line. The Catskill Evening Line ran as usual through 1916 and 1917 with mounting losses. Receivers, including Eben E. Olcott, were appointed on January 4, 1918, and decided to continue freight service only. The *Clermont* and the *Onteora* were offered for sale.

These two vessels operated in 1918 under charter to the Troy Evening Line, a short-lived attempt of a group of Troy businessmen to oppose the

Speed — Safety — Dignity
in every line of the Day Liners
Washington Irving   Hendrick Hudson   Robert Fulton   Albany
Hudson River Day Line
Daily Except Sunday   Desbrosses Street Pier

entrenched Citizens' Line of the Hudson Navigation Co. Eben E. and Alfred V. S. Olcott were active in this venture.

The *Clermont* and the *Onteora* then went back into idleness and in September 1919 were sold. The next year, stripped of their staterooms and night-boat finery, they were operated by the Commissioners of the Palisades Interstate Park as excursion boats to Bear Mountain Park. On each was a plaque reading in part: ". . . For the service of the public in the enjoyment of the Palisades Interstate Park, the purchase of this steamboat and its companion . . . was made possible by a contribution equalling their cost made in loving memory of Laura Spelman Rockefeller. . . ."

Meanwhile, the Catskill Evening Line continued operating the *Storm King*, and acquired another freight boat, the elderly wooden-hulled propeller *Reserve*. Built in 1864, she was originally the *Transit* and then the *John Lenox*. The line reorganized in 1921 as the Catskill Evening Line, Inc., and in 1923 built a steel-hulled freight boat, the *Catskill*. In 1929 the Day Line's ownership of stock increased to over 90 per cent and the *Catskill* was sold to reduce operating expenses. A mainstay of the business of the Catskill Evening Line, Inc., was transportation of fruit to the New York market. The poor condition of the fruit market in 1929 and succeeding years, increased use of trucks and the depression combined to eliminate the line's fleet from the river. The *Storm King*, its last active vessel, made her final trip in 1932.

The *Clermont* did her bit for the Troy Evening Line; the *Onteora* is shown in the days of her youth.—*Above: William H. Ewen coll.; below: W. du Barry Thomas coll.*

Chapter 18

YEARS OF GREAT EXPANSION

CAPTAIN GEORGE A. WHITE, the assistant general manager of the Day Line, died on March 8, 1917. After the passing of Captain White, Eben E. Olcott decided to become simply "president" instead of "president and general manager," and turned the duties of the general manager over to his son, Alfred Van Santvoord Olcott, who had been treasurer of the Day Line since 1909 and continued to fill that office.

In the period 1915-1917, the Day Line's New York-Albany season was unusually long, for the closing trip from Albany was not made until Election Day. Since Election Day in 1916 — Woodrow Wilson versus Charles Evans Hughes for the presidency — didn't fall until November 7, that season was the longest of the three, with the first up-trip having been made on May 12. In the closing weeks of these seasons the Albany service was covered by the *Robert Fulton* and the *Albany*.

In 1918, with World War I inflation, the old through rate which had been standard almost as long as the Day Line had been operating, went by the board. The one-way fare to Albany rose from $2.00 to $3.00 and the round-trip fare no longer resulted in a saving, since it went from $3.50 to $6.00. Way-landing fares naturally increased, too.

The increased rates of 1918 had no apparent effect on traffic, for Sunday operations were commenced that year and the total number of passengers carried rose to over 880,000. In 1919, the figure soared phenomenally to 1,217,398. In 1920, when 1,460,847 were to be carried by a fleet with a capacity of 18,500 passengers, the Day Line felt that expansion was clearly indicated, and that a more capacious vessel could be fully utilized on the New York-Poughkeepsie one-day round-trip service — the Poughkeepsie special — which had steadily grown in popularity.

Now the Day Line decided to do something it had rarely deigned to do, and that was to buy a steamer. Of course the reason it had seldom done any buying was patently simple: After its initial purchase of the *Armenia* and the *Daniel Drew*

there was no other suitable steamboat available, other than the *Mary Powell*, which was twice acquired. For its latest excursion into the buying market the Day Line chose a vessel that, at first glance, one would think it would not even consider let alone buy. She had been built as a night boat, had done duty as a wartime transport, and she was propeller driven. On the other hand, she had been designed by Frank E. Kirby and J. W. Millard & Brother, and she was fast.

The selected steamer had originally been named the *Manhattan* and had been built in 1913, along with a sister, the *Narragansett*, by the Harlan & Hollingsworth Corp. at Wilmington, Delaware. The twin-screw vessels were 320.2 feet in length, carried four decks, two raked stacks, and two masts — purely masts and not for strengthening purposes — and all the staterooms had running water. This was not then a common feature on night boats.

They were intended as part of a transportation system that never came to be. Charles M. Hays, president of the Grand Trunk Railway, strongly supported a plan for his line to join with the Central Vermont Railroad in building what was to be known as the Southern New England Railway. This was to connect at Providence, Rhode Island, with a line of steamers to New York, thereby offering through service between New York and Montreal. The New Haven Railroad, which ran its own steamboats to Providence, bitterly opposed the scheme and a major conflict between it and the Grand Trunk was in prospect. In 1912 Mr. Hays was lost with the *Titanic* and the project eventually faded away. A major accomplishment, at least, was the building of the *Manhattan* and the *Narragansett*. They lay idle on the Delaware and later at New London, Connecticut. Seldom have such fine, brand-new steamers lain so long without a purpose.

Finally, in World War I, they were acquired by the Government for service as U. S. Navy transports. The *Manhattan* was renamed *Nopatin*, while the *Narragansett* retained her original name. Much

The night boat *Manhattan* was built for a Long Island Sound service in which she never ran. Instead she lapsed into sleepy years of idleness. Then the United States entered World War I and she became the naval transport *Nopatin*.—*Above: Elwin M. Eldredge coll.; below: H.R.D.L. coll., Steamship Historical Society of America, Inc.*

In the promenade-deck bow of the *De Witt Clinton* with Miss Katharine Olcott, De Witt Clinton pours Lake Erie water into the Hudson.—*H.R.L.D. coll., Steamship Historical Society of America, Inc.*

of the interiors were ripped out, sponsons were fitted under the guards, heavy steel cables were run over the top of the deckhouses from guard to guard to secure them, and bracing was installed on the insides. Both vessels made the transatlantic crossing with ease and were then placed on duty as English Channel transports. The navy considered their speed to be 23 knots, which was exceeded by few other naval transports. The *Nopatin* is said to have carried over 150,000 troops across the channel and then, on May 31, 1919, she sailed out of Brest for New York via the Azores. She had been more fortunate than the *Narragansett*, which had stranded off the Isle of Wight during her service, but was subsequently refloated.

This *Nopatin* was the vessel which the Day Line chose to buy for conversion for service in the Poughkeepsie run. Her type of propulsion and deep draft would seem no obstacle, since the channel to Poughkeepsie was of ample depth, but in actual practice the draft was troublesome. She created considerable suction and the number of claims against her for damage to boats tied up at landings was said to have been far in excess of those against the other steamers.

The work of altering the vessel into a day boat was carried out at Hoboken, New Jersey, at the Tietjen & Lang yard of the Todd Shipyards Corp. Since the Poughkeepsie run catered to the one-day excursionists, it was not planned in this case to offer them the lavish type of interiors of the other steamers. Heretofore, the Poughkeepsie steamers had been vessels originally built for the Albany service. The Day Line was more than happy to accept the fares of the one-day excursionists, but it found that they had become less appreciative of interiors than their brethren who patronized the Albany steamers and who fell under the category of travelers. This was especially true of those bent on a hearty day in the out-of-doors at Bear Mountain. Consequently, the interior of the new acquisition was to be comparatively plain.

The main deck was left closed in amidships and also forward. In this latter respect, there was a great departure from the earlier concept that the main deck forward should be completely open. The nature of the steamer, too, resulted in considerably less open deck space generally than was available on the sidewheelers. The Day Line capitalized on that by pointing out that ·the ". . . well-covered decks afford ample shelter in all kinds of weather."

The passenger capacity was to be 5,000, which was 1,000 more than the maximum which the *Robert Fulton* could handle.

The company decided to rename its latest steamer after De Witt Clinton in keeping with the policy to commemorate in its steamers famous men of Hudson River history.

The *De Witt Clinton* made her official trial trip on May 12, 1921, with the usual assemblage of invited guests. Off the 129th Street pier, De Witt Clinton, a great-great-grandson of Governor De Witt Clinton, poured water from Lake Erie into the Hudson, duplicating the act performed by his ancestor at ceremonies marking the completion of the Erie Canal. At the same time, Eben E. Olcott's daugher Katharine intoned, "I rename this ship the *De Witt Clinton*."

The Day Line had arranged to have the student body of De Witt Clinton High School participate in the event, but it kept them at a distance. The De Witt Clinton students were not aboard the steamer. Complete with school band, they watched the rechristening from the 129th Street pier and the adjacent area. Afterwards, the steamer sailed on up the river and in a further ceremony, a por-

146

An artist portrayed the *De Witt Clinton* as she might have looked, but her appearance when she entered service was markedly different. The view in her saloon looks aft and was taken in 1939.—*Above: H.R.D.L. coll., Steamship Historical Society of America, Inc.; below: photograph by R. Loren Graham.*

Right is the *De Witt Clinton* at the time of the rechristening ceremonies that marked the commencement of her Hudson River career in 1921. Above she is steaming up the stream in 1939, her last active year on the Hudson.—*Right: Elwin M. Eldredge coll.*

trait of De Witt Clinton by Rembrandt Peale was unveiled.

And what of her sister ship, the *Narragansett?* She went to Canada and was still running in 1964 on the St. Lawrence and Saguenay Rivers as the *Richelieu* on the popular "Richelieu Cruises" of the Canada Steamship Lines.

With the advent of the *De Witt Clinton,* the Day Line was able to provide added service. In the summer season of 1921, the through boat to Albany was assisted by another steamer which handled the traffic as far as Newburgh on Monday through Saturday. On Saturday, there was an afternoon round trip from New York to Newburgh, and on Sunday two steamers supplemented the Poughkeepsie special. One of these also went all the way to Poughkeepsie, and the other to Newburgh.

Those who remembered the days when the steamers were licensed for well below capacity to avoid undue crowding, now found the Day Line saying:

> In order to provide chairs for all, this company undertakes to furnish ONE chair ONLY for each passenger, and it cannot provide chairs for packages or clothing. Passengers are requested not to appropriate chairs to such use to the discomfort of other passengers. The officers of the boat will enforce this rule.

The Day Line was truly entering the era of "mass transportation of humanity." The total licensed passenger capacity of its five steamers was 23,500 and on a busy summer Sunday when as many as 18,000 might be carried from New York, the task of doing it expeditiously and properly was enormous. Such things as controlling ticket sales, getting the right people on the right boat, disembarking and embarking vast crowds at way landings with a minimum of delay and countless other problems had to be reduced to the point where they were not problems but routine. The Day Line was a specialist in this mass transportation and while there were times when confusion seemed to reign, there was always order in the confusion. Naturally, on week ends the staff at ticket windows and in the purser's department on the steamers was augmented in order to cope with the business.

Instructions to ticket agents seem so fearsome that one wonders whether the applicants for such positions were allowed to read them before they were hired. They were not ordinary instructions, for the general passenger agent of the Day Line at this time was Dr. Edgar Starr Barney, who was also its secretary. Dr. Barney was not a full-time employee. An 1884 graduate of Union College, Schenectady, he received a Doctor of Science degree there in 1904. After graduating, he shortly

In this timetable the verticle date for the last up-boat to
Albany is given incorrectly as October 2, or three weeks
before the last down-boat. Also, the lower right right-hand
column should have been headed "Saturday Only."

joined the faculty of the Hebrew Technical Institute, an early private secondary technical training
school, and in 1893 became its principal. This position he filled until his death in 1938. He was a
pioneer in the advocacy of vocational education
and in that field believed in keeping ahead of the
times. He introduced a course in television in his
school prior to his demise. Joining the Day Line
for summer employment early in his teaching days,
he continued his connection with the company for
the rest of his life.

Dr. Barney's instructions omitted nothing. He
detailed the types of tickets most in use — card,
half, coupon, one-way, excursion, local, foreign,
unlimited, limited, special rate, blank extension,
prepaid order, first class. But it was not as bad as
it looked, for he added that tourist, party, second
class, colonist, coin and signature tickets were
rarely seen on the Day Line. He explained how to
make change, what types of pencils to use, how to
handle passengers who insisted they'd been short-
changed, and what to do with penciled notes made
during the day.

However excited or unpleasant a passenger
may be or seem to be, an agent should always be
pleasant and even-tempered. . . .

An agent should know the times of arrival and
departure of the principal connecting trains at all
of our own landings, and agents in New York City
offices should learn the names of other steamboats
and steamboat lines running to Newburgh, Poughkeepsie, Kingston, Catskill, Albany and Troy, their
piers and schedule leaving times; also the trains
on the New York Central, and the West Shore
roads leaving soon after our boats. Such information will be needed many times a day during the
busy season.

An agent must *not*, under any circumstances,
become *nervous, flustered,* or *excited.* Several hundred, often a thousand tickets must be sold by one
man in an hour, and no man who "loses his head"
during such a rush can regain himself during that
sale. . . .

While an agent must strive to gain speed, he
must be accurate, *absolutely accurate,* first. An
error before a line of people produces a humilia-
tion that cannot be quickly overcome. Unintention-
ally and unwittingly his thoughts, for the next few
minutes, are divided between the error and his
work, and he does not feel sure of himself. . . .

. . . I would urge an agent to strive more and
more to calculate mentally, but *never* at the expense of accuracy. It requires self-possession and
especially as it has to be done while thinking
about the limit of a ticket, cancelling it with a half

punch, answering questions as to where baggage may be found, what to do with a dog, when the [Ulster & Delaware connecting] train leaves Kingston and whether meals are served table d'hote or a la carte.

To determine what to charge for a ticket, Dr. Barney cautioned the agents to keep in mind such little gems as:

Do not quote rates from the Joint Tariff to points North or East via Troy; use the Trunk Line Rate Committees Proceedings book instead.

For rates west of Buffalo, not quoted in the Day Line tariff, deduct $1.00 from the rates in the Joint Tariff for tickets reading over the New York Central R.R. from Albany to Buffalo; but use the rates quoted, without any differential deduction, for tickets over the West Shore R.R.

If, as you waded through the instructions, you suddenly decided that the whole thing was hopeless, Dr. Barney was still one step ahead of you. Said he,

The beginner must not be discouraged by this picture. If he will diligently follow the instructions, he will be amazed at his rapid progress and fascinated by the work.

The Day Line always operated on the principle that the more it offered its passengers, the more passengers it would get. Now it set to work on a plan that would not only get it more passengers, but would give it added revenue in addition to fares and money spent on board the steamers. While the popularity of Bear Mountain was assured, passengers who went ashore there were lost to the Day Line until they boarded a returning steamer for New York. Indeed, they might go to Bear Mountain on boats other than those of the Day Line. If the line had a park of its own in the same general area, it would attract some of the people who now went to Bear Mountain and thereby have captive customers all day long. In addition, it might attract many others who didn't like Bear Mountain.

The Day Line selected a site for such a development on the east shore of the river below Peekskill and there acquired 320 acres of ground. This it converted into a private park which was no more an amusement park in the accepted sense of the word than Bear Mountain. Set in a less rugged terrain than at Bear Mountain, there were facilities for picnicking, dining in a cafeteria, swimming, strolling through the woods or just sitting along the river and enjoying life through relaxation. Claiming that its property had been a meeting place for Indians, the Day Line called the park

This is the playground at Indian Point Park in 1924. Across the river is a laid-up fleet of World War I freighters, with the Dunderberg rising behind them.—*H.R.D.L. coll., Steamship Historical Society of America, Inc.*

Indian Point Park, with its two piers in the foreground, is seen from the air in a view that looks down the Hudson. Verplanck's Point extends off to the right, with wooded Montrose Point to the left of it. Below that the river broadens to its greatest width in Haverstraw Bay, the southern end of which is marked by the long peninsula, Croton Point. In the two Indian Point Park views at left, the *De Witt Clinton* is departing and the *Washington Irving* is at the pier.—*All: H.R.D.L. coll., Steamship Historical Society of America, Inc.*

The *Alexander Hamilton* slides down the ways at Sparrows Point, Maryland.—*Frank O. Braynard coll., Steamship Historical Society of America, Inc.*

Indian Point, a name calculated to have an attractive ring for its younger passengers. In addition to providing outing facilities, the Day Line also established a farm at Indian Point for the raising of vegetables for use on the steamers.

Indian Point opened for business during the season of 1923 and, like Bear Mountain, became a popular resort for excursionists. As a touch of the old Day Line tradition, the bell from the *Mary Powell* was erected near the lower landing there and was sounded five minutes ". . . before steamers take passengers from this pier."

Long before Indian Point was opened, the Day Line was at work on still another steamer. Designed by J. W. Millard & Brother, this vessel was not intended to be a new giant of the fleet. Rather, she was to be in size and capacity a mate to the *Robert Fulton*. This would give the line two well-matched pair of sidewheelers — the other pair being the *Washington Irving* and *Hendrick Hudson* — which, for operational purposes, was important.

The contract for her construction was awarded to the Baltimore plant of the Bethlehem Shipbuilding Corp., Ltd., at Sparrows Point, Maryland. At the launching on October 20, 1923, Mrs. A. V. S. Olcott christened the vessel *Alexander Hamilton*. Although Hamilton had been fatally wounded in the duel with Aaron Burr almost across from the West 42d Street pier of the line, his connection with the Hudson River was less apparent than that of Hudson, Fulton, Irving and Clinton.

The new steamer entered service in May of 1924. While her first trip to Albany on May 29 was not in a class with those of some of her predecessors, her advent did create wide interest in the Hudson Valley. She was the last Hudson River steamboat to make what might be called a "triumphal first trip" to Albany.

The *Alexander Hamilton*, 338.6 feet long, was 1.6 feet/ longer than the *Robert Fulton*. She had an inclined engine, three-cylinder triple expansion in this instance.

The interior followed the same general tried-and-true arrangement of the other large sidewheelers, but it was not decorated on an elaborate scale. Paintings by Herbert W. Faulkner depicted scenes connected with the career of Alexander Hamilton.

This was the first Day Line steamer to be built as an oil burner. The *De Witt Clinton* had been converted from coal to oil between the seasons of 1922 and 1923. The Day Line claimed her fuel cost per mile was thus reduced from $4.00 to $2.27. Some of this saving was attributable to improvements in the efficiency of the boilers made at the time of the conversion.

A particular advantage of oil to the Day Line was that fires could be slackened instantly when slowing or at landings, to eliminate the waste and annoyance of steam blowing off. Labor costs were reduced and the line was no longer subjected to ". . . unreasonable demands on the part of firemen and coal passers." Cleaning fires was a thing of the past and refueling became a simple matter. Although the passengers could not be expected to show a prime interest in whether a steamer burned oil or coal, the greater cleanliness of the former was apparent by the absence of showers of cinders dropping on the deck. The Day Line was so pleased with the result obtained by burning oil in the *De Witt Clinton* that between the seasons of 1923 and 1924 it had the *Washington Irving* and the *Hendrick Hudson* converted to oil. Eventually, only the *Albany* was left as a coal burner.

154

In the construction of the *Alexander Hamilton*, the small size of her paddle-wheel housing is apparent. Since she had an inclined engine, the shaft was set low enough so that the main deck passed over it, the same as in the *Hendrick Hudson* and the *Washington Irving*. The position of the shaft naturally determined the diameter of the paddle wheels. After the building was completed, the *Alexander Hamilton* was photographed on a trial trip on May 10, 1924.—*Both: H.R.D.L. coll., Steamship Historical Society of America, Inc.*

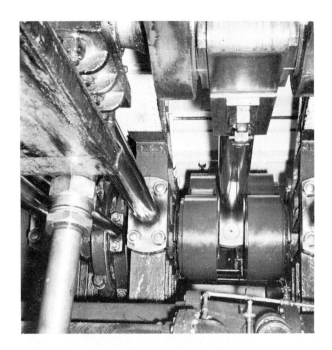

Of these pictures of the engine of the *Alexander Hamilton*, one (left) is a 1960 view under the low pressure cross-head looking aft towards the crank on the paddle-wheel shaft. In the other enthralled passengers are watching the turning cranks and an oiler at work. As the vessel sails along in 1939, the flags on both of the forward side poles are those of the New York World's Fair (right). In an earlier view, with her banners again whipping in the breeze, she is a particularly brave sight.—*This page: photographs by Conrad Milster, Jr.; right below: photograph by Larry Gaillard, William G. Muller coll.*

156

With the coming of the *Alexander Hamilton*, which had a passenger capacity of 4,050, the total passenger capacity of the Day Line fleet rose to 27,550. In 1924 the line carried 1,934,822 passengers, had an operating revenue of $2,441,342, realized a net income of $231,520, and paid $26,541 in dividends.

During 1924 it offered further service by resuming morning trips from up-river points to New York. During part of the week in July and August, a steamer sailed from Poughkeepsie at 7:10 a.m. and returned from New York in the early afternoon. This was a somewhat abbreviated version of the route of the *Mary Powell*.

Between the seasons of 1924 and 1925 the Day Line purchased another steamer. By comparison with the rest of the fleet, the new acquisition was a minor addition, although she was on her own merits a fine little vessel. She was the *Rangeley*, which had been built in 1913 at the Bath Iron Works, Bath, Maine, for the Maine Central Railroad. Her primary service had been between the railhead on the mainland to Bar Harbor on Mount Desert Island. A single-screw, steel-hulled steamer with three decks, she was 185.1 feet long, or almost the same length as the old *Armenia* before her two lengthenings.

The charter business had become increasingly important to the Day Line. With the growing number of steamers, the company was able to offer prospective customers a wider range of accommodations and a longer period over which they were available, than ever before. The charter business was also a healthy source of sure income, since it was not subject to the vagaries of the weather. Once you hired a steamer, you had to use her on the day called for. If the holiest church in all New York decided to have its congregational outing on June 5, and if June 5 turned out to be the coldest and wettest day of the whole season, that was no fault of the Day Line's.

In buying the *Rangeley*, the Day Line had its eye on the many smaller organizations which were likely charterers, but which could not afford to charter one of the larger steamers. She was intended to handle these smaller charters and to serve as an auxiliary in the carrying of the heavy crowds on week ends.

The Day Line, of course, renamed her. Its decision to honor Chauncey Mitchell Depew was somewhat of a throwback to the earliest days of the line, for Depew was closely identified with the New York Central Railroad. He had been its general counsel, second vice-president, president from 1885 to his resignation in 1898 and chairman of the board — a post he continued to fill until his death in 1928. Born along the Hudson at Peekskill of a father who had been active at one time in

The *Rangeley* was purchased by the Day Line from the Maine Central Railroad and renamed the *Chauncey M. Depew.—Jay Allen coll.*

steamboating, he had also been a United States Senator from New York for two terms and had a wide reputation as an orator and after-dinner speaker.

On Chauncey M. Depew's 91st birthday, April 23, 1925, Eben E. and Alfred V. S. Olcott called on him to tell him of their plan to rename the *Rangeley* after him. "The visitors were assured it would afford him deep satisfaction to receive such an honor, particularly as Mr. Depew recalled his long and close intimacy with . . . Commodore Alfred Van Santvoord, the founder of the Albany Day Line, of which the present company is an outgrowth."*

Thus it was that Chauncey Vibbard and Chauncey M. Depew were the only two men who ever saw their names freshly painted on a Day Line steamer — an odd fact when one considers that Chauncey is scarcely a common name. Daniel

*New York *Times*, April 26, 1925.

Here is Chauncey M. Depew in younger years and as he was painted late in life by Orlando Rouland. At the unveiling of the portrait on the *Chauncey M. Depew*, the artist is at the left. Opposite him are Eben E. Olcott with his daughter-in-law, Mrs. Alfred Van Santvoord Olcott and two of her children, Helen Purves Olcott and Alfred Van Santvoord Olcott, Jr.—*Above: Lucius Beebe; below: H.R.D.L. coll., Steamship Historical Society of America, Inc.*

Drew was very much alive when Van Santvoord and his associates bought the vessel named for him, but she had carried that name previously.

The *Chauncey M. Depew* was altered somewhat to fit her better for Day Line service. Since she had been acquired with carpets, she, too, had a carpeted saloon, and for art work a painting of Mr. Depew by Orlando Rouland was hung on board. Her passenger capacity was to be 1,100. Having for so many years stressed the size and capacities of its steamers, the Day Line solved the problem of the contrasting smallness of the *Chauncey M. Depew* by dubbing her the "Day Line yacht."

In 1925 the Day Line fleet had reached its maximum, with a capacity for 28,650 patrons. Passengerwise it was the peak year of operation, for in all 1,968,744 were carried. Of this number, 100,732 had gone all the way through between New York and Albany, or the reverse. Operating revenues peaked at $2,547,100, even though the net income dropped to $147,681. Besides its own private park at Indian Point, the company maintained a chair factory and laundry at Newburgh, had an icehouse at Poughkeepsie, and still retained coal pockets above Newburgh and at Poughkeepsie.

When the summer seasonal business was at full flood in 1925, in addition to the New York-Albany run and the Poughkeepsie special, the Day Line offered a complicated array of other trips. There was a morning boat southbound from Newburgh to New York on Monday and from Poughkeepsie the rest of the week. On Monday through Friday there was an afternoon return from New York to Poughkeepsie; on Saturday and Sunday, an afternoon round trip to Newburgh. On Saturday the Albany boat was assisted as far as Kingston Point by another steamer, which returned from

there. On Saturday afternoon, there was a boat from New York up the river to Catskill. On Tuesday through Thursday, the Poughkeepsie special was aided by another vessel northbound to Newburgh and southbound from Bear Mountain; on Sunday the Poughkeepsie special was operated in what amounted to four "sections."

In September of that year of great business, J. W. Millard & Brother completed the specifications for another giant sidewheeler. She was to be generally a sister to the *Washington Irving* with the same passenger capacity of 6,000, but would be slightly longer so that she could be heralded as the largest vessel of the fleet. She never came to be.

The *Chauncey M. Depew* was dressed in her best when she was photographed in 1925. That year her officers included, left to right, Assistant Engineer Earl Carlette, Chief Engineer Harry P. Harvey, Pilot Grant B. Lezatte, Captain Grant Lezatte and Mate George W. Gray. The saloon (opposite) was comfortable, but certainly not ornate.—*All: H.R.D.L. coll., Steamship Historical Society of America, Inc.*

Chapter 19

CENTENNIAL SEASON AND AFTERMATH

I N 1926 there was to be held in Philadelphia the Sesquicentennial Exposition, to mark the 150th anniversary of the independence of the United States. The Day Line felt that like 1876 — the year of the Centennial Exhibition in Philadelphia — 1926 would be a good year for Hudson River travel. To direct particular attention to its facilities, it planned to make 1926 its own corporate "Centennial Season."

To arrive at this centennial date, the Day Line placed its beginnings in 1826, when Abraham Van Santvoord had been agent at New York for the Steam Navigation Company. Since Abraham's son Alfred and his associates had not founded what became the Hudson River Day Line until 1863, the centennial was actually the 100th anniversary of the participation of the Van Santvoord family in the steamboat business. Indeed, the Day Line later speculated on the possibility that Abraham Van Santvoord might have been connected with steamboating prior to 1826. Centennials have often been observed on a much less firm basis than this one.

The Day Line placed great emphasis on it in advertising and in the first 1926 issue of the *Hudson River Day Line Magazine* devoted fourteen pages to an article called "One Hundred Years of the Hudson River Day Line." This included the information, "And among the passengers carried, numbering 2,000,000 [*sic*] in the year 1925 alone, there has never been a fatality."

Here we must assume that the meaning intended was that there had never been a fatality since 1863. We cannot vouch for the truth of it. Statements of that type have sometimes erroneously been made on behalf of transportation companies because of insufficient study of old records. On the other hand, we have never found anything to contradict it. Considering the number of passengers carried, the safety record was amazing. Disasters to Day Line steamers had been confined to the violent deaths by fire of the *Daniel Drew* and the *New York,* which were then out of service so

that their fire-fighting equipment could not be used with any effect.

Fate was now waiting to send another Day Line steamer to a sudden end. Probably few companies have had a less happy centennial than the Day Line.

The season of 1926 was formally opened on May 12 when a granddaughter of Eben E. Olcott ran up a flag on the *Washington Irving,* which made a special invitation trip on the river. Two days later that steamer opened the regular service by going north to Albany. On the long Decoration Day week end — Saturday, May 29, through Monday, May 31 — the *Washington Irving* made special round trips from New York to Kingston Point and on June 1 was scheduled to go to Albany. The *Robert Fulton* was the down-boat and the old *Albany* was to make the Poughkeepsie special.

Traffic on the day following a holiday week end was not expected to be particularly heavy. As the *Washington Irving* prepared to sail from Desbrosses Street on June 1, she had aboard only approximately 200 passengers, plus her crew of about 110. The morning was somewhat hazy.

It was the practice in the Day Line for the capain to be in the pilothouse until after the vessel had left the uptown pier at West 129th Street and the heavy traffic of New York harbor was safely behind. The first pilot, therefore, would be at the gangway to signal to the pilothouse when all was ready for the departure from Desbrosses Street and would also be at the gangway for the necessary signalling during the landings at West 42d Street and West 129th Street.

Accordingly, as the *Washington Irving* prepared to get under way at about 9 a.m., Captain David H. Deming was in the pilothouse with Second Pilot Frank E. Brown and Quartermaster Herbert Hunter, while First Pilot Harry W. Kellerman was at the gangway. First Mate T. W. Davis and Second Mate Thomas Kraljic were also at their usual positions on the main deck. In the engine room were Chief Engineer Perry H. Banks and Second

Pilots Harry W. Kellerman and Frank E. Brown, and Mate Thomas Kraljic (left to right) were officers of the *Washington Irving* when she was lost. These pictures were taken in the late 1930s when they were officers of the *Hendrick Hudson*.

Assistant Engineer William Van Wie, who was on watch. When all was ready, Pilot Kellerman pulled the gangway bell-pull three times and in the pilothouse the bell tapped out the message that the sailing could be made. The signal to start the engine was transmitted by the engine-room telegraph.

As the *Washington Irving* commenced to move ahead, she sounded one long blast on her whistle to indicate to other vessels in the vicinity that she was getting under way. Harbor traffic was heavy, and coming up the river were a U. S. Army lighter carrying troops, and the tugboat *Thomas E. Moran*. The latter, operated by the Moran Towing & Transportation Co., had on either side of her a loaded oil barge, sitting low in the water and projecting out ahead of her. The two barges were bound for the refueling of a transatlantic liner.

After judging the situation, Captain Deming promptly caused one blast to be sounded on the whistle to indicate that he intended to cross the bow of both the lighter and the tugboat as he came out into the river. The lighter responded and veered to go around the stern of the *Washington Irving*. The tugboat, which had the right of way, continued her course, but allegedly shortly set her engine to hard astern.

Except for a strong ebb tide that was running in the river, all might have been well. But the force of the tide carried the *Washington Irving* downstream sufficiently to alarm Captain Deming, who put the helm ". . . hard a starboard in order to swing my stern clear."* It was not to be, for the starboard corner of the bow of oil barge *No. 415* on the starboard side of the tug, cut into the port side of the hull abaft the paddle wheel. The barge struck into the day boat's number two fireroom and, as the *Washington Irving* moved ahead, sliced through the watertight bulkhead past the fireroom and on into the kitchen. The gash was said to be about twenty feet in length. The steamer had six watertight bulkheads, but the blow had opened up two of the watertight compartments and the water instantly commenced to rush in to flood the hold all the way from the firerooms almost to the stern.

Second mate Kraljic ran for the kitchen stairs, thinking that he might be able to stuff a mattress or blankets in the hole. This was a trick that was often effective in stopping small leaks. The mate

---

*Letter, June 1, 1926, from Captain Deming to the United States Local Inspectors, reporting the collision (HRDL coll., SSHSA).

This picture of the sunken *Washington Irving* was taken when three of her flags were still floating forlornly in the breeze. Lost were three lives—those of two passengers and a former member of the crew.—*Elwin M. Eldredge coll.*

soon realized that this hole was far beyond stopping, for as he looked down the stairs he saw that the water was already coming up fast in the kitchen. A waiter who tried to get back to his quarters to save his money and clothes had his legs badly bruised by floating pots and pans.

Captain Deming sounded the distress signal, and sent Second Pilot Brown to pass the order for all passengers to don life belts. With his steamer already sinking by the stern, Captain Deming studied the watercraft at the piers along the New Jersey shore for a promising haven, but found himself confronted with Hobson's choice. He decided to try to reach the Erie Railroad's Pier 9, Jersey City. Meanwhile, tugboats and other nearby craft rushed toward the stricken vessel to take off passengers and offer assistance.

The captain neatly maneuvered the steamer to the end of Pier 9 so that her forward guard was over some spiles. With the *Washington Irving* rapidly going down by the stern, these spiles helped to hold her on even keel until the last of the passengers had reached the pier. Then the largest steamer ever built for the Day Line sank to the bottom, the water reaching her third deck. Well beneath her was the unfinished Holland Tunnel, through which was to flow the endless vehicular traffic between New York and Jersey City, and there was some fear at first that she might cause a break in the top of the tunnel.

Three persons were found to be missing, two of them passengers. A mother with her three-year-old daughter had remained on a lower deck, waiting for her two older children, ages five and seven, to join her. She did not know that they had already been taken off safely by a tugboat. A recently discharged messboy, still aboard the vessel, was presumed to be trapped in the hold.

The *Thomas E. Moran* was able to continue on her way with the oil barges, although it was later discovered that the one involved in the collision had been considerably damaged.

164

After the disaster to the *Washington Irving* ended so suddenly a routine trip to Albany, some of the officers gather on the hurricane deck. The picture of the vessel once more afloat was taken November 8, 1927, many months after she had been raised. Peaked roofing has been erected over the engine room to provide protection from the weather.— *Above: William H. Ewen coll., below: Elwin M. Eldredge coll.*

Early in his career as a master, Captain David H. Deming is on the then-new *Hendrick Hudson* with other officers and members of the purser's department.—*H.R.D.L. coll., Steamship Historical Society of America, Inc.*

Events transpired so quickly that at first it was difficult to comprehend what had happened. The *Washington Irving* had moved out from Desbrosses Street with her white paint gleaming, flags flying and orchestra playing. She was the picture of everything that meant Hudson River Day Line — a great sidewheeler, immaculate inside and out, speeding away to Albany. A few minutes later she lay sunk on the opposite side of the river.

The *Albany,* instead of serving as the Poughkeepsie special that day, went to Albany in place of the *Washington Irving* and carried those passengers of the lost steamer who chose to continue by boat. The *Albany* made good time and arrived at her destination only about twenty minutes late.

The Day Line at once employed divers to determine the condition of the *Washington Irving* and in view of their report that the hull had been twisted and strained, decided to hold in abeyance the question of salvage, although it did remove many fittings, chairs and so on from the steamer.

Soon the Day Line chose to abandon the *Washington Irving* and her removal became the problem of the U. S. Army Corps of Engineers. Bids were solicited for the vessel and she was acquired by the

Morris & Cumings Dredging Co. Raising her was a difficult task, and it was not until 1927 that she was finally floated and placed in dry dock to have the hull patched. Little remained of the splendor that had once been the *Washington Irving's,* for in the course of the salvaging much of the superstructure had been removed. She remained laid up in the New York area until 1933, when she was at last sold for her metal. We have been told that the tugboat which towed her away to the Delaware River for scrapping was none other than the *Thomas E. Moran.*

Due to the conditions which had existed at the time of the collision, both Captain Deming and the captain of the tug had been exonerated of blame. But those who knew Captain Deming always claimed that he became a fourth victim of the sinking. For a man who had spent his life with the Day Line, the loss of the *Washington Irving* was a deep and personal one and preyed heavily upon him. In 1927 he served as captain of the *Hendrick Hudson,* which had been his first Day Line command. She was to be his last, for on November 24 of that year he died at his home in Albany.

In 1926 passengers fell off to 1,473,556, or almost half a million under 1925, and operating revenues were down by over half a million dollars. The Day Line ended the year — its Centennial Season — with a loss of $174,293.90.

It should not be assumed that half a million people were frightened away from the Day Line because of the sinking of the *Washington Irving.* The weather was not propitious and another important factor was the 6,000-passenger reduction in the capacity of the fleet as a result of the accident. Under completely ideal conditions the *Washington Irving* could account for about 100,000 passengers by her Sunday operations alone in July and August.

The line was not in a position at this point to consider a replacement for the *Washington Irving.* It proceeded with plans for a single-screw steamer designed particularly for the ever-growing charter business. In order to pay for this vessel, to provide itself with working capital, and to retire funded debt, it had to issue $1,500,000-worth of bonds under date of March 1, 1927, secured by a first preferred mortgage on the steamers and the company's real estate. These bonds had a life of twelve years and it was calculated that the sinking fund was sufficient to retire 60 per cent of them at maturity at the rate of $75,000 annually, beginning on September 1, 1927.

On February 2, 1927, the Day Line launched the new vessel which was both the first propeller-driven steamer to be built for the company and the last vessel which it was ever to construct. The name selected was that of Peter Stuyvesant, one of the Dutch governors of New Amsterdam. After summing up its policy of naming steamers for ". . . men whose lives were and are closely bound up with the growth and development to greatness of New York state, the Hudson River and New York city. . . ." the line stated, "It seemed only fitting to us that a similar honor should be paid to the memory of that gallant and interesting character Peter Stuyvesant, whose romantic and picturesque life here has made such an indelible impression upon the history and tradition of this section of our country."

When the *Hendrick Hudson* was named, the decision to use the Dutch form of the English Henry had provoked, it may be recalled, a mild furor. Now the situation was reversed, in that the Day Line elected to use the English form of the Dutch Petrus. This time there were few who disagreed.

Appropriately, Eben E. Olcott's daughter Katharine, who had launched the Day Line into its new era of steamboating when she christened the *Hendrick Hudson* at Newburgh in 1906, again did the honors for the final member. This time the water came from a Saratoga spring because, according to the Day Line, ". . . the Dutch settlement farthest North in the Hudson Valley was at Saratoga."

The *Peter Stuyvesant* was built at the Pusey & Jones Corp.'s yard at Wilmington, Delaware, and was decidedly different from any other steamer in the fleet. J. W. Millard & Brother had designed her to incorporate features attractive to organizations interested in chartering her, and in keeping with the intent that her general service would be almost exclusively on the lower river. On the whole, she was modeled after the Lake Erie steamer *Put-In-Bay*, which had been designed by Frank E. Kirby and which has been considered to be his finest conception in the field of propeller-driven vessels.

The *Peter Stuyvesant's* cabin on the third deck was built on a trunk deck raised well above the outer or promenade deck. Here was located the carpeted saloon and from it the passengers could view the scenery unobstructed by anyone sitting in front of them on the outside deck. Here, too, were the eight private parlors and the writing room — in this case simply a writing table. As a result the second deck cabin was left largely unencumbered and surrounded by plate-glass windows. The bandstand was located abaft the stack housing and from there aft the cabin could be utilized as a spacious dance hall. The dining room was as usual on the main deck aft and the lunchroom in the hold forward. The steamer was not without paintings, for works in oil were executed by Herbert W. Faulkner.

The *Peter Stuyvesant* on May 2, 1927, is at the Pusey & Jones Corp.'s yard, where she was built.—*H.R.D.L. coll., Steamship Historical Society of America, Inc.*

The view from the pilothouse of the *Peter Stuyvesant* (left) was taken in 1961 as she approached Newburgh landing. The Newburgh-Beacon ferryboat *Orange* may be seen. Below (left), bound for Albany in 1937, the *Peter Stuyvesant* is off Castleton-on-Hudson in the upper river. The enclosed area of the second deck served as an auxiliary dining room when an organization chartering the vessel wished to be served lunch or dinner with a minimum of delay (above). It also made a fine dance hall and was particularly fitted for this purpose, with few obstructions and with an air of spaciousness through added

height. This last was due to the fact that the deck overhead was raised above the level of the exterior third deck. The location of the bandstand abaft the stack housing, is marked by potted palms in the distance. In the view looking forward in the carpeted saloon on the trunk deck, the balustraded well through which the music from the bandstand beneath could be heard in the saloon, may be seen by more potted palms.—*Left: Photograph by Conrad Milster, Jr.; below: Photograph by Alexander P. Olcott; both, opposite page: H.R.D.L. coll., Steamship Historical Society of America, Inc.*

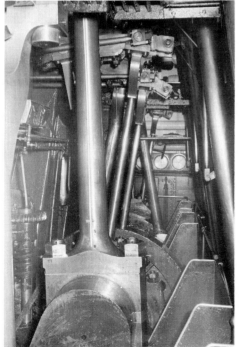

The main engine of the *Peter Stuyvesant* as seen from the upper grating. The lower workings of the same engine are shown at left. Below is the boiler room which can be kept clean because of the use of oil burners.—*All: Photographs by Conrad Milster, Jr.*

Her four-cylinder triple-expansion engine was powered with steam from four Babcock & Wilcox oil-fired water-tube boilers. With but a single smokestack, the 260.5-foot *Peter Stuyvesant* and the much smaller *Chauncey M. Depew* were the only one-stackers of the Day Line. The passenger capacity, set by measurement rules then in force, was 3500, which seems extremely high in view of the fact that it was only 500 and 550 less than the capacities of the far larger *Robert Fulton* and *Alexander Hamilton*. Under later rules, the cited differences were to become far greater.

The *Peter Stuyvesant* entered service in May 1927, but created no great stir on the river. Initially she was afflicted by excessive vibration, but this was later corrected to an extent. Since at first her theatre of operations was the lower Hudson, the Hudson Valley as a whole didn't get a chance to know her until the trend of the times resulted in her being used in the Albany service. As the Day Line itself had said, she ". . . was not primarily designed for through service between New York and Albany . . ." and so she did not gain enthusiastic favor generally with those who traveled on her in that service. To passengers who were used to the broad open decks and roomy interiors of the sidewheelers, she was a bit of a shock. Died-in-the-wool sidewheeler adherents developed a sour aversion to her and there were people who preferred not to sail at all rather than to sail on her. Such a point of view was not as unreasonable as it seems, inasmuch as day boats to Albany had always been sidewheelers ever since there had been Albany day boats.* But here the *Peter Stuyvesant* suffered principally by contrast. Taken for herself alone, she proved a competent steamboat and was well suited for the work for which she was designed.

With the fleet again increased to seven — even though the total passenger capacity of 26,150 was 2,500 below the previous seven-boat figure — the line was able to provide more adequate coverage of the routes on week ends and holidays. Once again it revived part-week morning service from Poughkeepsie from about the second week of July to late August or early September. Passengers increased from 1,594,982 in 1927 to 1,663,926 in 1929, only about 13,000 under 1923. In that year the Day Line had handled the passengers with five steamers with a total passenger capacity of 2,650 less than in 1929.

---

*The *De Witt Clinton* never went to Albany. The *Chauncey M. Depew* once made a trip in through service, New York-Albany, in an emergency when traffic was light.

The through business had been falling off, due to the growth of the automobile. This was offset by heavy excursion traffic out of New York and so made the Day Line less vulnerable to vehicular competition than some other steamboat lines on the Hudson. These were having their own troubles.

Charles Wyman Morse never achieved his goal of dominating Hudson River steamboating. In 1916 he proposed a gigantic ocean combine which to some degree came to be, and during World War I he was awarded a contract to build 36 ships for the Shipping Board. As a result of his activities, he became involved in the courts in the 1920s and in 1926 was adjudged incompetent to manage his affairs. On January 12, 1933, he died at Bath, Maine.

In April of 1921 receivers had been appointed for his Hudson Navigation Co., which had been running the *Berkshire* and *C. W. Morse* to Albany and the *Rensselaer* and *Trojan* to Troy. The *Adirondack* did not operate after wartime duty as a floating barracks and was eventually broken up. The receivers continued business as usual, but later changed the name of the *C. W. Morse* to *Fort Orange*. Morse's name in big letters on the side of a steamboat was no longer considered good advertising for the line. Finally the Hudson Navigation Co. went by the board at a foreclosure sale and its property was acquired by the Hudson River Navigation Corp., which had been incorporated for that purpose in April, 1926.

For a number of years the Hudson Navigation Co., while continuing to use the trade names People's Line and Citizens' Line for its Albany and Troy service, had used Hudson River Night Lines and Hudson River Night Line to describe its overall activities. These latter the new corporation adopted and eventually settled on the singular version — Hudson River Night Line — as its sole trade name.

The Hudson River Navigation Corp. was the eternal optimist, full of great plans for improving and expanding its service. Most of them never came to pass. It realized full well that it would have to take more positive steps to fight the inroads being made into its business by the automobile. An early move in this direction was to acquire two small Long Island Sound screw freight steamers, the *York* and the *Haven*, which were renamed respectively *Green Island* and *Cohoes* and placed in service in 1927. The *Green Island* had been built in 1912, but the *Cohoes* was old — very old, for she had been constructed in 1857 as the *Erastus Corning* for operation on the Hudson

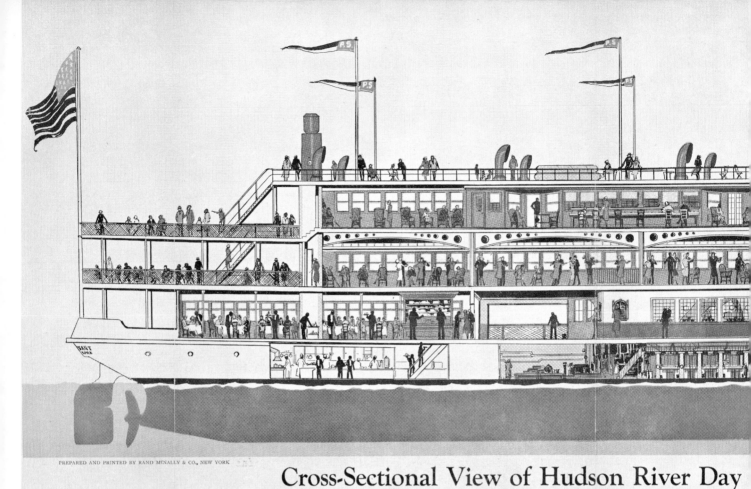

PREPARED AND PRINTED BY RAND McNALLY & CO., NEW YORK

Cross-Sectional View of Hudson River Day

This drawing was used to show the suitability of the *Peter Stuyvesant* for a charter trip or outing. In the hold forward is the lunchroom or cafeteria, followed by the boiler room, engine room and kitchen or galley. The enclosed areas at the bow and stern are crew quarters. At the forward end of the housing on the main deck is the candy and cigar stand; ahead of the stack housing is the baggage room. The four multi-paned windows open into the upper engine room; abaft is the purser's office, with a passenger standing at one of its windows. Aft on the main deck is the dining room. Ahead of the stack housing on the second deck is the news and souvenir stand; abaft the housing

eamer *Peter Stuyvesant* Showing Typical Outing

is the bandstand, occupied by an orchestra which is sending the passengers tripping about. The saloon is on the trunk deck raised above the exterior third deck, and the view partly combines both the saloon and the private parlors on either side of it. Officers' quarters are on the top or hurricane deck in the enclosed areas between the stack and the pilothouse. Below (left) is the *Peter Stuyvesant* at Rockaway on a charter trip in 1956, and (right) being brought out into the river by tugs after a spring drydocking in 1954.—*Below: Photographs by Conrad Milster. Jr.*

River. With these steamers handling much of the freight, the freight space on the passenger boats was now largely available for passengers' automobiles.

The season of 1927 is said to have been the last during which the *Fort Orange* ran. Allegedly she needed new boilers and thereafter remained laid up at Athens, New York, in what developed into permanent retirement. The big *Berkshire* and the smaller *Trojan* and *Rensselaer* had become sufficient to handle the passenger business.

Later the line put into service the sidewheeler *Pioneer* specifically for the carrying of automobiles. Formerly the Maine Central Railroad train ferry *Ferdinando Gorges*, she had only a short career on the Hudson.

By 1927 another important Hudson River freight and passenger carrier was feeling strongly the effects of the automobile. Due to the nature of its route, it was particularly susceptible to competition by trucks. This was the Central-Hudson Steamboat Co., for which receivers were appointed in March of 1927. At the time the line had five steamers, of which two had been constructed expressly for it — the screw steamers *Benjamin B. Odell*, 263.6 feet long, built in 1911, and the *Poughkeepsie*, 206.8 feet, built in 1917. Together with the older propellers *Homer Ramsdell* and *Newburgh*, these boats furnished night freight and passenger service to Newburgh, Poughkeepsie, Kingston and way landings. The fifth vessel, the beam-engined sidewheeler *Jacob H. Tremper*, was employed on the Newburgh and Albany day line. The Central-Hudson Line operated week-end excursion service in connection with its regular business and in an effort to vie with the Day Line briefly offered its patrons a day at Sunset Park, a development a short distance south of Indian Point but far from its quality.

Receivership was no cure for the ills of the Central-Hudson Line and a bankruptcy sale was held in 1929. The buyer was a corporation representing the Day Line and Hudson River Navigation Corp. acting jointly. The steamboat companies were to keep the *Benjamin B. Odell*, *Homer Ramsdell*, *Newburgh* and *Poughkeepsie* and resell much of the real estate and the *Jacob H. Tremper*. The latter, well worn-out, was disposed of to a junk dealer for scrapping.

To operate its acquisitions, the Day Line and the Hudson River Navigation Corp. formed a new corporation in May 1929. Alfred V. S. Olcott of the Day Line was President and E. C. Carrington, President of the Hudson River Navigation Corp., Chairman of the Board. The selection of the name was the Day Line's and became Hudson River Steamboat Co., Inc., to revive the name of the old company of which A. V. S. Olcott's great-grandfather, Abraham Van Santvoord, had become President upon its formation in 1845. The Hudson River Steamboat Co., Inc., continued to provide service between Kingston, Poughkeepsie, New-

The *Peter Stuyvesant* was photographed from the Bear Mountain bridge as she made her way up the Hudson on a charter trip in 1960. The *Fort Orange* was originally the *C. W. Morse*, which Mr. Morse built as a monument to himself, but his checkered career led to a renaming of the vessel.—*Left: Photograph by Conrad Milster, Jr.; below: William King Covell coll.*

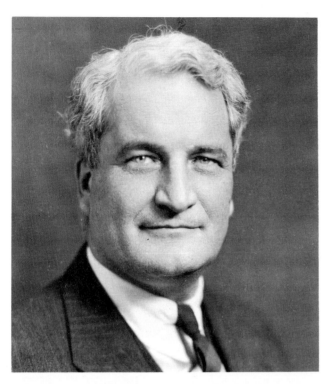

Alfred Van Santvoord Olcott truly loved steamboats and the Hudson River. He died in 1961 in his 76th year.— *Courtesy of Mrs. A. V. S. Olcott.*

burgh, way landings and New York, but did not resume the Newburgh and Albany day line.

With the formation of the Hudson River Steamboat Co., Inc., there was an interlocking of almost all steamboat service on the Hudson River above Peekskill. Its President, A. V. S. Olcott, was then or subsequently President of the Catskill Evening Line, Inc.

The only independent was the Saugerties & New York Steamboat Co., which continued to provide freight and passenger service under the trade name of Saugerties Evening Line between Saugerties and New York with its beam-engined side-wheelers *Ida* and *Robert A. Snyder*. They were hardly new vessels, for the iron-hulled *Ida* had been built in 1881 for service on Chesapeake Bay. As for the *Robert A. Snyder*, she had been constructed in 1848 as the *Ansonia*. A complete rebuilding of the wooden hull had led to her being enrolled as a new boat, the *Ulster*, in 1892. Later on the name was changed to *Robert A. Snyder*. In the early thirties the Saugerties Evening Line quietly expired.

Besides participating in the affairs of other Hudson River lines, the Day Line underwent changes of its own in 1929. This season found the

New York terminus now at the former midtown landing, the West 42d Street pier, for the Day Line had failed to obtain a renewal of the lease of the Desbrosses Street pier. It announced that a survey over several seasons indicated that half of the patrons embarked at 42d Street, with the remainder divided between Desbrosses Street and West 129th Street. Further, it claimed to have found that many of those who boarded steamers at Desbrosses Street did so only to get on ahead of the rush at West 42d Street and so obtain choice seats. The company felt that since most of the Desbrosses Street patrons arrived either by subways or elevated lines, it would be no hardship for them to continue to 42d Street, where they could still obtain choice seats if they arrived early enough. So far as southbound service was concerned the only steamer which had regularly continued on to Desbrosses Street was the down-boat from Albany.

The old scheduled elapsed time of 9 hours 30 minutes between New York and Albany or the reverse, had remained constant, 1885 through 1917. Then there were changes over the years. When West 42d Street became the New York terminus, 9 hours 10 minutes elapsed time was scheduled for the up-boat and 9 hours for the down-boat. In 1931, that was reduced to 8 hours 55 minutes for the up-boat; 8 hours 40 minutes for the down-boat. This shortening of the time was the result of improvements to the channel of the upper river. In 1925 Congress had passed a bill, signed by President Coolidge, providing for the deepening of the channel to 27 feet between Hudson and Albany to permit ocean-going ships to call at the latter place. In 1926 construction of the present Port of Albany was begun, and in 1927 the channel work was commenced and completed in 1931.

The passing of the Desbrosses Street terminus, D. Street, as it was known in the Day Line, was the severing of a link with the past, but it was not the only link that was parted in 1929. On June 5, Eben Erskine Olcott died. The mining engineer who became a steamboatman had been one of the most successful that the Hudson River had ever seen. Building on the firm foundation laid by Commodore Van Santvoord, he had made the Day Line into the greatest organization of its kind.

His son, Alfred Van Santvoord Olcott, now succeeded him as president. The period of postwar prosperity was almost over. For the younger Olcott, the demands of the office were not to be easy ones. Fast approaching were the most perilous days of the company's existence.

In an attempt to retain passenger business being drained away by the automobile, the Hudson River Navigation Corp. for a time operated an automobile transfer vessel, the *Pioneer*. A failing was her lack of necessary speed, since the passengers on the night boats usually arrived at their destination long before the *Pioneer* came in with their automobiles. The night boat *Benjamin B. Odell*, at her landing on Rondout Creek in the Rondout section of Kingston, was the flagship of the Central-Hudson Line and slightly longer than the Day Line's *Peter Stuyvesant.—Above: Frank O. Braynard coll., Steamship Historical Society of America, Inc.; below: Elwin M. Eldredge coll.*

Captain Alonzo Sickles, Jr., is on the *Hendrick Hudson*, Captain Henry B. Briggs is on the *Chauncey M. Depew* and Chief Engineer William Van Wie is in the engine room of the *Hendrick Hudson* (left to right). The *Albany* is sailing up through the Highlands of the Hudson and ahead of her is the Bear Mountain bridge, stretching out from Anthony's Nose on the right. She was an active member of the Day Line fleet for 51 seasons, longer than any other vessel.—*Above, left and center: Mrs. Linwood Rhodes; below: H.R.D.L. coll., Steamship Historical Society of America, Inc.*

Chapter 20

DEPRESSION YEARS

FOR MANY YEARS special timetables had been prepared for the holiday periods of Memorial Day, Fourth of July and Labor Day. Labor Day itself, marking the end of so many vacations, usually produced the heaviest southbound traffic of the year on the through route and additional service was provided from Catskill and Kingston Point. Southbound traffic on the day after Labor Day normally reached considerable proportions, too.

On Labor Day in 1930, the *Hendrick Hudson,* the largest steamer, came down from Albany and was scheduled to return light to Catskill. On Tuesday she was to sail from there and stop at Kingston Point, Poughkeepsie and Newburgh, while the *Albany* — the up-boat on Labor Day — would leave Albany and call at Hudson and Kingston Point. Evidently after considering the state of the traffic, it was decided that the *Albany* would not be needed and consequently the *Hendrick Hudson* was to return light all the way to Albany on Labor Day night in order to depart again on the southbound trip the following morning.

While coming down the river on Labor Day, Captain Alonzo Sickles, Jr., of the *Hendrick Hudson* discussed the return run to Albany with his pilots. They seem to have been filled with a premonition, for out of the talk arose a decision to recommend that the northbound *Albany* remain at Albany until the *Hendrick Hudson* arrived. The *Albany's* orders called for her to land passengers at Albany and then depart. Upon reaching the West 42d Street pier, Captain Sickles spoke to Mr. Olcott about the matter and the latter agreed to have word sent to Captain Henry B. Briggs of the *Albany* to stay at the northern terminus.

As the *Hendrick Hudson* got up the river that evening, it grew hazy and then a light fog set in. After passing Parda Hook, about 6½ miles below the Albany landing, the pilot at the wheel held the steamer over to the westward of the channel in order to keep away from the more hazardous east shore. He clearly saw the navigational light on the east shore at Staats's, and then ran aground in the sand on the west side below Van Wies Point, only about five miles short of his destination. The normal chagrin in such an instance was multiplied by the realization of being so near and yet so far.

Captain Sickles ordered the starboard trim tank filled and the port tank emptied in order to list the steamer towards deep water, and had the engine set at hard astern. This did not move the vessel, but produced the only damage from the mishap by washing sand up in the shaft bearings. At flood tide on Tuesday tugs of the Cornell Steamboat Co. hauled the *Hendrick Hudson* off and she went back down the river. That day the *Albany* made the regular southbound sailing from Albany.

Although the stranding had little effect on the *Hendrick Hudson,* the Day Line itself was beginning to drift steadily towards a stranding of greater consequences. In 1930 the company commenced to feel the business recession which became the Great Depression. The number of passengers dropped by over 214,000 below the 1929 figure.

As a retrenchment step, it was decided to retire the old *Albany* and she was not placed in commission in 1931. In fact, she could have been retired considerably earlier, for the Day Line had had little real need for her in the closing years of her Hudson River career. She remained laid up until 1934 when, on March 6, she was sold at public auction to B. B. Wills for $25,000. In April, she left the Hudson for the Potomac River, where, renamed the *Potomac,* she operated as an excursion boat out of Washington, D. C., through the season of 1948. She was later dismantled and the hull converted to a barge, which is still afloat (January 1965) as the *Ware River.* The walking beam was acquired by the Mariners Museum, Newport News, Virginia, and mounted on the museum grounds.

Traffic continued to decline in 1931 and 1932; in the latter year, total passengers carried fell to 1,250,908 and the net loss soared to $222,486.37. Mr. Olcott was unable to arrange for the usual bank loans to sustain the line between the operat-

Captain J. Rodney Magee stands before the pilothouse of the *Robert Fulton* in 1940, his last season on the river and his 25th year in command of Day Line steamers (left). John Garavan, with suspenders, and Elmont L. Nelson are on the *Hendrick Hudson* in 1938 and were then second and first assistant engineers of the vessel respectively. In the middle is the author, also on the *Hendrick Hudson* in 1938 when he was in the purser's department. The *Potomac*, formerly the *Albany*, is shown near the start of her new career as a Potomac River excursion steamer.—*Above, left: Edward O. Clark coll.; below: B. B. Wills.*

ing seasons of 1932 and 1933. The company was solvent, with assets worth between two-and-a-half and three million and liabilities of about $1,370,-000, the bulk of which was accounted for by the bond issue of 1927. But liquid assets were nil. On the application of the Collier Advertising Service, Inc., a creditor in the amount of $4,125, Federal Judge Robert P. Patterson on January 11, 1933, appointed Mr. Olcott receiver of the Day Line.

Mr. Olcott prepared a plan whereby the line could continue operations and this was authorized in a decision handed down by Judge John C. Knox on May 1. One more steamer was to be laid up to reduce operating expenses by a hoped-for $125,000 and the vessel finally decided upon was the *De Witt Clinton*. To attract more passengers, fares were cut. For example, the one-way fare to Albany was reduced from $3.25 to $2.50 and the round-trip fare from $5.00 to $4.00. Further, the length of the Albany season was to be curtailed, with the last down-trip scheduled for October 1.

In an attempt to gain new patrons in 1932, the Day Line had commenced to run "showboat" trips out of New York. These combined an evening sail on the river with a "gala" revue, dining and dancing, and were operated several nights a week during part of the season. Expanding further in this direction, in 1933 the company became involved in the one-time barkentine *Buccaneer*, originally the *City of Beaumont*. Earlier owned by the Buccaneers Club of New York and Famous Story Pictures, she was acquired by a group which included James A. Kenyon of the Day Line and anchored in the Hudson off Dobbs Ferry. Except on Sundays and holidays, in showboat season the down-boat from Albany became a moonlight cruise vessel and sailed back up the river to the *Buccaneer*, which the passengers boarded to see a "rollicking" revue. At its conclusion they returned to New York by steamboat.

The *Buccaneer* shows were continued through 1935 and in lieu thereof in 1936 moonlight sails were operated. That ended the Day Line's efforts in the field as a permanent attraction, although later on moonlight sails became a regular feature on Saturday nights.

After repeal, beer and liquor appeared on the steamers, for now the pressing need to make money overrode any vestiges of the old feeling regarding it. But on regular trips there were still no bars. Bottled beer could be had in the lunchroom, (the cafeteria), and liquor was served only in the dining room.

In 1936 the Day Line filed a petition for reorganization under the National Bankruptcy Act and submitted a required plan dated August 1, 1936. On August 20, 1937, the final reorganization was signed by the court. In that year reduced fares descended to the level of the late 1860s through 1917 — $2.00 for a one-way passage between New York and Albany and $3.50 for a round-trip.

But, like vultures, deficits remained inseparable from the Day Line's financial statements. Passengerwise, the worst season of the 1930s was 1938, when the total passengers carried dropped close to 1,080,000.

The pattern of service in 1933 and onward was fairly constant. In brief, it might be said that the Albany service usually operated from latter May until latter September, with the Poughkeepsie special service beginning about the same time and ending trips on the week end after Labor Day. Thereafter the Poughkeepsie special was operated on Sundays until mid-October, with Saturdays added after the through route closed. In October the fall foliage was a prime attraction. During part of the season, an afternoon round trip to Newburgh was available on Saturdays and Sundays; on Sundays there was a morning boat to Indian Point at 8:30 from West 42d Street; and, still during part of the season, the down-boat from Albany usually returned to Indian Point Sunday evenings to provide a late return from there to New York. Sometimes this was a necessity to handle the remainder of the excursionists who had been unable to board the earlier steamers because of the crowds. In addition, during July and August — roughly — the *Chauncey M. Depew* sailed from Poughkeepsie for New York every morning and returned in the afternoon.

The *Hendrick Hudson*, with the largest passenger capacity, came to be employed principally on the Poughkeepsie special. During a midsummer Sunday, when the excursion business out of New York was heaviest, the *Peter Stuyvesant* would be the through boat to Albany, while either the *Alexander Hamilton* or the *Robert Fulton* would make the 8:30 a.m. trip to Indian Point, return light and leave again at 1:45 p.m. for a round trip to Newburgh. Again, either the *Alexander Hamilton* or *Robert Fulton* would come down from Albany and then make the evening round trip to Indian Point.

Further to plague the Day Line during the 1930s was new legislation which resulted in a reduction of the passenger capacities of the steamers. This legislation came about primarily as a result of the burning of the *Morro Castle* off the New

This picture of officers of the *Alexander Hamilton* was taken in 1929 or 1930, and includes (front row, left to right) First Mate John H. Courtrey, Chief Engineer Oscar W. Bedore, Captain Ralph Van Woert and Purser E. J. Bailey. Second Pilot Maurice A. Howard is standing directly behind the captain; First Pilot George C. Reitnauer, behind the purser. In 1937 the *Alexander Hamilton* herself, bound north, is leaving Newburgh.—*Below: Photograph by Arthur Helmke.*

Jersey coast in September 1934. Under the new regulations, in 1935 the passenger capacity of the fleet was cut by over 10 per cent, an important consideration on week ends and holidays. Later on, by minor alterations to three vessels, the Day Line was able to have the reduced figure increased by over 2 per cent.

As the number of passengers who patronized the Day Line in the thirties changed, so did the type of passenger. Many now were attracted to the line as a means of cheap transportation. The era when the Day Line had catered to the best had faded; the passengers who appreciated the style of the interiors grew fewer. In fact, the interiors were not what they had been. The steamers were kept in the best of operating condition, but there was not enough money to replace such things as worn carpeting.

There was, of course, a hard core of Day Line patrons who traveled on the boats because they loved them and because they loved a trip on the river. It was not unusual to find such people making at least a trip per week all during the season. Some of these had been sailing the river for decades and were strongly partisan toward a particular vessel. Indeed, some would travel on their favorite and no other. Shortly after World War II we ran across a man in Bear Mountain Park who had been especially fond of the *De Witt Clinton*. He was seated on a rock, staring intently down the river and waiting for the ecstatic moment when she would come into view. Since the *De Witt Clinton* had not run on the Hudson since 1939, he was a singularly sanguine mortal. Perhaps he's still there on his rock.

The travelers most representative of the better days of the line were those going all the way from one terminus to the other. This they often did to enjoy fully the varied beauty of the river—a beauty that was endlessly changing. Probably their fathers and grandfathers had done the same thing before them.

Then there were passengers who still went to the writing room immediately upon embarking and stayed there to send post cards to an inexhaustible list of friends and relations. The only scenery they saw was that depicted on the post cards, but they had a fine time. And there were always passengers who could never find the washrooms and at least one a day who vainly searched for a telephone.

From time immemorial many passengers have boarded steamboats under the self-conceived delu-sion that their landing was the end of the route. On the Day Line a porter went around the vessel well before each landing, singing out the stop loud and long and, when appropriate, adding, "This steamer goes on up the river." But there were those who never heeded him. In the 1930s, Poppa and Momma and a brood of nine out for a Sunday holiday at Bear Mountain with six colossal lunch boxes, would suddenly find the family budget thrown all out of kilter when they realized that the steamer really was going on up the river and that they would have to pay additional fares to Newburgh.

Other people were more worried about how to get on than when to get off. Prospective passengers often called the Day Line office at New York for directions to the pier and it was not unknown to have one display indignation when he was asked where he was. That was a violation of personal privacy!

Between the "getting on" and "getting off" passengers were some who set out for destinations which they could never reach by water. Elderly people occasionally appeared, bound for a landing at which no steamboat had called for many a long year.

Steamboats have been called the most pleasant means of transportation ever devised by man. With that we concur. But we would be forced also to concur with the theory that they seem to have been the most attractive form of transportation ever devised for eccentrics. And of these the Day Line had its share.

Some regular passengers derived their primary amusement from going around the steamer and pointing out spots of interest to their fellow travelers. One old gentleman, always attired in a frock coat, a derby hat and an ascot tie, carried this to the extent of lecturing to captive audiences. He passed out his card and was glad to receive some slight monetary recompense. Those who knew he was spending his declining years in a home for the elderly were sympathetic. These unofficial guides were most unhappy when in the 1930s the Day Line commenced to employ cruise directors on the Albany service. Primarily, their duties were to lecture on the passing scene.

Operationally, probably the most unusual incidents of the 1930s came about as a result of the great hurricane of 1938. On Wednesday, September 21, the *Alexander Hamilton* was northbound to Albany and the *Robert Fulton* southbound for New York.

The *Robert Fulton*, thwarted in a first attempt to land at Bear Mountain, headed out in the stream. When she was crossways in the river, the wind listed her over and carried her broadside on down the Hudson. Because of the narrowness of the stretch of the river in which she was, there was nothing her officers could do except to go ahead with the engine when the stern got too close to the west shore, and go astern when the bow neared the east shore. Finally, when she was literally blown out of the Highlands and into the broader waters off Peekskill, it was at last possible to maneuver her. There was now no thought of going to New York and she was headed back for Bear Mountain. This time she was successfully landed and remained there overnight. The passengers, about 180 in number, continued by train.

The *Alexander Hamilton*, going up, broke three lines holding to Catskill landing, but continued on to Hudson and then to Albany. She arrived off the Recreation Pier at 6:37 p.m. with about 20 passengers aboard and backed into the Day Line landing.

For safety's sake, thirteen lines were put out to make sure she was secure. The water in the river was about one foot ten inches below the gangway cuts in the landing. By early Thursday it was over the wharf. Later it was decided that it was neither safe nor practical to attempt a sailing that day, for the flood continued to grow in strength. At 7 p.m. it was at its peak and the water was almost six feet over the Day Line wharf.

Meanwhile, the *Robert Fulton* had left Bear Mountain about 5 a.m. Thursday and on that day and Friday made round trips between New York and Poughkeepsie. It would take more than a hurricane to stop the Day Line completely.

On Saturday morning the *Alexander Hamilton* was at last able to leave Albany on her regular sailing, which was also the last trip of the year from that place. Because of the freshet still running in the upper river, the *Robert Fulton* was scheduled to go only as far as Catskill on Saturday and to close the up-river service from there on Sunday, September 25.

The *Alexander Hamilton* was unable to sail from Albany on September 22, 1938, when these pictures were taken, due to the high water which followed in the wake of a hurricane. In the small boat maintaining contact with the shore, Second Pilot Maurice A. Howard is at the steering oar with Captain Ralph Van Woert (light suit), Chief Engineer Oscar W. Bedore and Stewardess Minnie Mittelmayer. "Entrance to Broadway" marks a pedestrian tunnel beneath the railroad. At its peak the water was even with the top of this tunnel.

Chapter 21

THE NIGHT LINE SAYS "GOOD NIGHT"

W HILE THE DAY LINE was not forced into receivership until 1933, the Hudson River Navigation Corp., operating the Night Line, had reached that point a year earlier, in January 1932. This was hard on the heels of a court order for the sale of its freight steamers *Green Island* and *Cohoes* and its tugboat *A. H. Hanscom* to satisfy a repair bill balance.

At that point the Hudson River Steamboat Co., Inc., of which the ownership was still shared jointly by the Night Line and the Day Line, had only the *Benjamin B. Odell* and the *Poughkeepsie*. The other half of its fleet, the *Homer Ramsdell* and the *Newburgh*, had been sold in 1930 for use as excursion boats between Boston and Nantasket Beach, Massachusetts, and were renamed respectively the *Allerton* and the *Nantasket*.

In December 1931 the Hudson River Steamboat Co. had completed an agreement with the Night Line whereby the *Benjamin B. Odell* and the *Poughkeepsie* were placed in service between New

York, Albany and Troy to run during the winter months when the Night Line's sidewheelers were laid up. Then, in April 1932 the Night Line's half interest in the Hudson River Steamboat Co. was sold.

In May Judge John C. Knox accepted the offer of the McAllister Navigation Co. to operate the Night Line. This company was controlled by Captain D. F. McAllister, who had a long background of excursion boat operation, including years of service to Bear Mountain. In his fleet were the *Clermont* and the *Onteora*. The Commissioners of the Palisades Interstate Park of New York, having run them at a loss, turned their operation over to him and eventually sold them to him. To keep his management of the Night Line separate from his other activities, Captain McAllister formed the McAllister Night Line, Inc.

The Hudson River Steamboat Co., headed by A. V. S. Olcott, had also attempted to gain the lease of the Night Line, but withdrew in the face of

The marked squareness of the after end of the *Benjamin B. Odell* was utilitarian design. It enabled her to use fully the freight gangways at the New York pier from which she originally operated, without sacrificing staterooms aft.—*Young coll.*

McAllister's better offer. Now it elected to maintain its own service between New York, Albany and Troy. So, when the *Berkshire*, *Rensselaer* and *Trojan* went back in commission they were opposed by the *Benjamin B. Odell* and the *Poughkeepsie*.

While the *Benjamin B. Odell* was an adequate night boat, she was smaller than the Night Line steamers and lacked their more luxurious and ample interiors. The still smaller *Poughkeepsie* had almost nothing in the way of passenger accommodations. To make up for what it lacked in overall facilities, the Hudson River Steamboat Co. scaled its fares considerably below those of the Night Line and, in an attempt to draw its passengers on the sailing nights of the *Benjamin B. Odell*, spelled them out in advertisements and called her the "popular steamer." Both the Night Line and the Hudson River Steamboat Co. continued to carry freight as usual, and in this category the latter company had won a round through gaining control of Troy wharfage and so forcing the Night Line to terminate its route at Albany. All Troy freight handled by the Night Line now had to be hauled to or from Albany by truck.

In 1932 any competition hurt. Captain McAllister commenced to oppose Mr. Olcott's Day Line by running a day line of his own on week ends — up on Saturday and down on Sunday, with landings en route at Newburgh, Poughkeepsie and Catskill. Briefly he used his excursion steamers *Clermont* and *Onteora* and then covered the service with the Night Line boats. In addition, he ran Saturday night moonlight sails out of Albany.

In the summer of 1932 the Day Line's fare was $3.25 for a one-way trip between New York and Albany or $5.00 for a round trip. The Night Line on its week-end day line charged $2.00 one way, and for its regular Night Line service had rates of $3.00 one way and $5.00 round trip, plus the stateroom charge if you wanted to sleep in comfort. The Hudson River Steamboat Co. would carry you for $2.00 one way or $3.00 on the round trip, again with the stateroom cost extra. It was a strange situation that in the depths of the depression there should spring up a bitter steamboat war for business that, by its absence, now resulted in keen competition.

In the fall of 1932, new offers for continued operation of the Night Line were submitted. This time the Hudson River Steamboat Co.'s proposal was the more attractive and it was accepted, to become effective November 1, 1932, and to continue for one year. The company planned to use its own steamers throughout the winter, for by

construction they were well suited for that purpose. In fact, the *Benjamin B. Odell* was probably the finest vessel for ice operations that ever ran on the Hudson River.

McAllister, in anticipation of the continuance of his lease of the Night Line, had chartered the steamers *Hartford* and *Middletown*, which had been built to run as night boats between New York City and Hartford, Connecticut. This route had been suspended in 1931. The *Hartford* and *Middletown* were screw steamers, 243.3 feet long, and considered suitable as replacements for the Night Line's sidewheelers in the anticipated winter service. When McAllister lost control of the Night Line to the Hudson River Steamboat Co., he decided to run the *Hartford* and *Middletown* as opposition boats under the banner of the McAllister Night Line, Inc.

The desirable landings at Albany — those of the Night Line, the Hudson River Steamboat Co. and the Day Line — were now all controlled by Olcott, so McAllister was forced to settle for an out-of-the-way wharf at the upper end of the Albany waterfront.

As far as the passenger trade was concerned, Mr. Olcott was still faced with the scanty facilities available on the *Poughkeepsie*. In advertising "limited staterooms," the line admitted the deficiency and later stated that steamer chairs would be furnished gratis to anyone who had no stateroom.

At a February 1933 meeting of creditors and attorneys of the Hudson River Navigation Corp., Judge Knox was asked to approve an immediate sale of the Night Line boats to satisfy the claims. "If there is any hope under heaven of a reorganization," the judge replied, "let it proceed. I don't want these boats to be sold at the present time. If we have to have a forced sale at this time, we might as well take the boats out and sink them." He had in mind the disastrous sale, earlier in the month, of the assets of the Iron Steamboat Co. Its seven notable iron-hulled sidewheelers had for decades connected Manhattan and Coney Islands. The whole fleet brought a total of $15,050. There was no forced sale of Night Line boats.

Also in February Judge Knox accepted McAllister's offer for the operation of the Night Line after the receivers objected to the fact that the pier used as a terminus by the Hudson River Steamboat Co. was too narrow for the loading and unloading of automobiles. Later in the year McAllister put the Night Line sidewheelers back on the route in place of the *Hartford* and *Middletown*.

The Hudson River Steamboat Co. maintained firm opposition. As a more suitable running mate for the *Benjamin B. Odell* it chartered for the summer season the spare boat of the Norfolk & Washington Steamboat Co., the *Southland*, a screw steamer somewhat larger than the *Benjamin B. Odell*.

At the coming of the winter of 1933-1934, the *Poughkeepsie* and the *Benjamin B. Odell* were operating in the service of the Hudson River Steamboat Co., with the *Middletown* and *Hartford* on the Night Line, still under lease to McAllister. The *Hartford* had been restored to the route prematurely when the *Rensselaer* was damaged in a collision with an ocean freighter off Poughkeepsie early on September 27.

That winter was an extremely severe one. On December 30, 1933, the *Poughkeepsie* arrived at Albany after a battle of 22 hours with river ice. Following off her stern came the *Middletown*. Under the command of Captain George Carroll and with Howard Eaton as chief engineer, the *Poughkeepsie* had left New York shortly before 6 p.m. on December 29, with the *Middletown* sailing a little later. The *Poughkeepsie* lost time in making several landings, but went out of the track through the ice to break her way past both the *Middletown* and a Coast Guard cutter, which accompanied the steamers on the final stretch, and victoriously led the way into Albany. The *Poughkeepsie* finished with her engine there at 3:58 p.m. on the 30th and, after discharging passengers and freight, went on to Troy.

Early in January a new contract for the operation of the Night Line was awarded to the Hudson River Steamboat Co. McAllister had asked to be relieved on the grounds that there was not enough business for two lines — a fact that had been obvious for a long time — and the receivers were complaining of unsettled rentals for the two previous months. By early February the river ice was anywhere from one to three feet in thickness, but still the *Benjamin B. Odell* and the *Poughkeepsie* continued to run. There had been nothing like this in the history of the Hudson.

On Thursday night, February 8, 1934, the *Benjamin B. Odell*, Captain John H. Dearstyne, broke her way out of the ice at her New York pier and started northward for Albany. The cold was bitter and at 7:25 the next morning the temperature at New York dropped to the lowest there in the history of the Weather Bureau, 14.3 degrees below zero. Sceptics along the river claimed that the *Benjamin B. Odell* would never get anywhere near Albany. The Hudson was covered by a solid sheet of ice for almost its entire length and the steamer track was tightly locked. On the last previous up-trip the *Poughkeepsie* had gone only to her namesake city. With power less than half that of the *Benjamin B. Odell* it was felt advisable to keep her in service only on the lower river, so she unloaded all of her freight and returned to New York.

The *Benjamin B. Odell* bucked her way up the stream to Poughkeepsie, loaded the up-river freight left there by the other boat, and kept right on going. At times her speed dropped to almost nothing,

The pictures on this page were taken on February 10, 1934, as the *Benjamin B. Odell* neared Castleton-on-Hudson on the final lap of a memorable trip to Albany. Here she has paused to permit some of the officers and members of the crew to descend to the ice by way of the ladder from the open freight gangway, so that they might take a chilly constitutional. Opposite is the *Poughkeepsie* making her way through the ice.— Above: Elwin M. Eldredge coll.; others: Captain William O. Benson coll.

The mighty *Berkshire* (above) on September 8, 1937, is making the final trip of her career under steam and is near Athens, where she was laid up. The picture was taken from the *Hendrick Hudson*, which thereafter through 1948 held the honor of being the longest steamboat operating on the river. The *New Yorker*, originally the *Trojan* and shown at Albany, was the last night boat to ply between New York and Albany. She covered the route alone in 1939, the final year of the service.

190

but the important thing was that she kept moving. When she reached New Baltimore Saturday morning, only about 14 miles from the Albany wharf, some of those who thought she would never make it now walked out on the ice to greet her. Members of the crew later climbed down onto the ice for a wintry stroll. On Saturday afternoon she arrived at Albany.

The next afternoon, departing from the Albany landing, the *Benjamin B. Odell* broke a propeller blade. Since it was impossible to have her towed through the ice to New York for repairs, she was laid up and the New York-Albany service suspended. For a time after that, the *Poughkeepsie* still ran as far north as Poughkeepsie, but eventually had to be withdrawn. In the spring both steamers resumed full service.

Mr. Olcott continued to operate the Night Line with the Hudson River Steamboat Co. as lessee and put the *Rensselaer*, *Trojan*, and *Berkshire* in commission in 1934 as usual. Finally, March 28, 1935, the Hudson River Navigation Corp. was auctioned to a representative of Samuel Rufus Rosoff — "Subway Sam" — for $100,100. Included

in the sale was the *Fort Orange*, originally the *C. W. Morse*. Still laid up at Athens, she was sold late in the year for scrap.

Rosoff had been born in Russia and arrived in New York as a child. He fought his way upward and became best known as a subway contractor. His secret of success came to be, "I haven't got any education. What I got is what it takes to make guys with an education do the job I want done." Attributed to him, too, is, "I'm a member of Tammany Hall and proud of it. I'm also a Republican and proud of that."

He gave as his reason for buying the Night Line, "I am interested in the welfare of the good old Night Line and I love the Hudson River." And then, in true Hudson River Navigation Corp. tradition, he stated that he planned to build new vessels. Again in true Hudson River Navigation Corp. tradition, he didn't. But he did eventually add to his fleet two more vessels, the *Benjamin B. Odell* and the *Poughkeepsie*. Right after his acquisition of the Night Line there came a new meshing of its affairs with the Hudson River Steamboat Co. to eliminate competition. That company was

Lying at Albany is the night boat *Southland*, chartered by the Hudson River Steamboat Co., Inc., for several months in 1933.—*Edward O. Clark coll.*

now in financial difficulties and late in March 1936, Rosoff's offer for it was approved.

The previous year, 1935, was the last in which the sidewheelers *Berkshire*, *Rensselaer* and *Trojan* were all in commission, for the *Berkshire* did not run in 1936. The *Benjamin B. Odell* and the *Poughkeepsie* operated well into the fall of that year, providing their usual service to way landings, but were withdrawn before the onset of winter. It was rumored that this withdrawal was permanent and that in 1937 the Night Line would not provide service to way landings. The Night Line issued a denial and countered by saying it had almost completed the specifications for two large diesel vessels which it hoped to have on the river in the spring of 1938.

In January 1937, the *Poughkeepsie* was transferred to the Meseck Steamboat Corp. to be rebuilt into an excursion steamer for service between New York City and Rye Beach on Long Island Sound. She was renamed *Westchester*. On February 22, 1937, the *Benjamin B. Odell* took fire in winter quarters at the dock of the Rosoff Sand & Gravel Co. near Marlborough, New York, and except for the after end of the superstructure, burned to the hull.

The Night Line advertised it would open for business in 1937 on April 30. The *Rensselaer* was not put in commission, reportedly because of the condition of her boilers, and so the *Berkshire* came out of her short retirement to run with the *Trojan*. Service to Troy was maintained by the latter vessel, which continued on to there from Albany. The *Berkshire*, as always, terminated her trips at Albany. In late August the Night Line announced it would close its season on the premature date of September 7. The next day the *Berkshire*, the largest steamboat ever built for the Hudson, sailed to her winter berth at Athens. It was the last trip under steam she would ever make.

The following January the Hudson River Navigation Corp. petitioned to reorganize under the bankruptcy laws. With eternal Night Line optimism, it later announced that the boats would not run in 1938. They were going to be modernized completely for service in 1939, when the World's Fair would be a leading attraction at New York.

In 1938, therefore, aside from the excursion trade on the lower river, there was nothing left of Hudson River steamboating but the Day Line.

The situation was not unique, for during the thirties many other lines on other waters had breathed their last. Primarily responsible were the automobile and the depression, but in some cases other factors hastened an inevitable demise. In 1938 only two passenger-carrying night lines moved on Long Island Sound — the Eastern Steamship Lines to Boston and the Colonial Navigation Co. to Providence. During the summer season, the Colonial also served New Bedford with one steamer. In the spring and summer of 1937, the New York, New Haven & Hartford Railroad had closed both its Providence and Fall River Lines. The death of the Fall River Line silenced forever the greatest sidewheel night boats ever built to run out of New York.

By the end of 1938 plans for reorganizing the Night Line were still pending. In the spring of 1939 the *Trojan* was refurbished, renamed the *New Yorker* and went into service between Battery Park, New York, and the World's Fair under the management of the New York Harbor Steamship Corp., a Rosoff-controlled operating company. Except for the fact that she rammed her pier at the Fair grounds on one of her trips, the venture was not a smashing success. On June 16 the *New Yorker* resumed Hudson River Night Line service between New York and Albany.

She was advertised to make her final sailing from Albany on September 9 and this time the Night Line died. The *New Yorker* went into winter quarters at the Rosoff Sand & Gravel Co. dock where were lying the *Rensselaer* and the hulk of the *Benjamin B. Odell*. The latter was eventually sold for scrap.

Early on March 1, 1940, the *New Yorker* was found to be afire, and like the *Benjamin B. Odell*, burned to the hull. On March 4 she turned over and sank to the bottom.

In 1941 the Government took an option on the *Berkshire* and the *Rensselaer* and they were hastily towed through winter ice to Hoboken, New Jersey. On June 25 the *Berkshire* was towed out of New York Harbor and away to Bermuda for use as quarters. Later returned to the United States, she was dismantled at Philadelphia. The *Rensselaer* was rejected as unsuitable. Afterwards she was dismantled at Providence, Rhode Island, and her hull ultimately converted into the barge *James River*, which was scrapped only recently.

In a flurry of governmental activity, the *Berkshire* was towed from her lay-up berth at Athens to Hoboken, New Jersey, in 1941. Above she is making her last trip down the Hudson near Silver Point on January 31, in charge of the *Comanche* of the U. S. Coast Guard. The tow lay overnight in the ice, so it was not until the next day that the *Berkshire* passed Poughkeepsie (below, left). She and the *Rensselaer*, which was also towed down, are shown at Hoboken on February 9, 1941.

The *Chauncey M. Depew* and the *De Witt Clinton* are lying at the Day Line's New York terminal, Pier 81, on May 7, 1939. This was the West 42d Street pier, actually at the foot of West 41st Street. The *Hendrick Hudson* is at Pier 80; ahead of her may be seen the after end of the *Alexander Hamilton*, with an oil barge alongside. Not a passenger landing, Pier 80 was used to provide additional berthing room when necessary. Ten days later, May 17, the *De Witt Clinton* departed on a trial trip, her first trip under steam since 1932. The spectators are some of the crew on the *Hendrick Hudson*.

Chapter 22

THE LAST LANDING

THE ACTIVITIES of the Day Line in 1939 were much more reminiscent of better days than those of the Night Line. In anticipation of heavy business as a result of the World's Fair, which was to have a two-year stand on the Flushing Meadows, the Day Line completed arrangements to run a regular service whereby out-of-towners could combine a nautical sightseeing trip with a day at the Fair. Again it needed a six-boat fleet, so the *De Witt Clinton* at long last came out of the second major retirement of her career for refurbishing and with a revised passenger capacity of 4,297. In the spirit of going all out, the Day Line ordered stack markings, metal plates emblazoned with a reproduction of the house flag, for all the steamers.

The new service consisted of round trips between the West 42d Street pier and Whitestone in Queens, where passengers could go ashore and continue to the Fair by bus. At one time or another, all the boats were employed on the run. In order to afford the patrons a complete view of Manhattan from the water, the Whitestone steamer first sailed up the Hudson to the George Washington bridge and then called again at West 42d Street for an hour-later departure for those who preferred to spend less time afloat. After the second departure, the steamer went on down the Hudson, around the Battery and up the East River to the destination. A morning and afternoon trip were operated from April 30 through October 1, with an added evening trip during June, July and August. As far as the Fair business was concerned, this third run was largely for returnees, but at the same time it provided a pleasant evening sail for New Yorkers who enjoyed such diversion. It was advertised as a moonlight cruise, with dining, dancing and bar service.

This is the *Chauncey M. Depew* as she appeared while being operated by the War Department.

The Hudson River routes were maintained as usual and in fact the service from Albany continued until Columbus Day. Both the up and down boat were now scheduled for an elapsed time of 8 hours 55 minutes between termini.

Unfortunately, the result of all this activity was that at the end of the fiscal year, the Day Line's deficit was at a new high of $318,035.

In 1940 the *De Witt Clinton* was laid up; the round-trip service from Poughkeepsie to New York, down in the morning and back in the afternoon, was discontinued; and the connecting trips to the World's Fair via Whitestone were not resumed. The sightseeing feature of the latter was retained by running a steamer over almost the same route as before, without landing at Whitestone. Two trips a day were scheduled and were generally made by the *Chauncey M. Depew*. During 1940, for the first time since 1918 when circumstances were entirely different, the Day Line carried less than a million passengers.

On October 12, 1940, the *Chauncey M. Depew* was taken over by the War Department under charter, to run from New York to Sandy Hook. She was released in the spring of 1942 and laid up; on August 1, 1942, she was requisitioned by the War Shipping Administration for the War Department. She continued to be used at New York and carried

the army designation FS-89. After the war, she was initially acquired by B. B. Wills, who at that time still owned the *Potomac,* formerly the *Albany.* The *Chauncey M. Depew's* postwar career included excursion service from Boston to Provincetown on Cape Cod; from Providence, Rhode Island, to Block Island; from New York City to Atlantic Highlands, New Jersey; then, in 1950, she was purchased by the Government of Bermuda to serve as a passenger tender to ships too large to come into the wharves.

When she arrived in Bermuda under her own steam on June 8, 1950, she carried *Chauncey M. Depew* on her bow and stern, and *Somers Isle* on the upper nameboards. The last was intended to be her new name, but it was never adopted and she remained the *Chauncey M. Depew.* She has done well there. In addition to her duties as a tender, she is used for excursions and moonlight sails, and even serves occasionally as an emergency tugboat to push ships into berths. In 1952 her main deckhouse was cut off forward so that, with less wind resistance, she would be easier to handle when going alongside ships. In 1963 she was extensively repaired and refurbished, after which she was considered good for another ten years.

In February 1942, the *De Witt Clinton* was drafted for her second tour of wartime duty, being

The *Chauncey M. Depew* is still in service in Bermuda.—*Photograph by Alan J. Staight*

The *De Witt Clinton* had served the navy in World War I as the *Nopatin;* in World War II she became the *Frederick C. Johnson* (below) and was operated by the army. The vessel ended her days in the Mediterranean as the *Galilah.—Right: Frank O. Braynard coll.; below: Steamship Historical Society of America, Inc.*

The *Alexander Hamilton* adorns this song cover.

requisitioned by the War Shipping Administration several months before the *Chauncey M. Depew.** In World War I she had served with the navy; now she was to change to the army. Rebuilt into a transport with refrigerated cargo space and renamed *Frederick C. Johnson,*** she was operated by the War Department as an inter-island troopship and remained under army control until about July 1946.

In 1947 she was sold by the Maritime Commission to Samuel Derecktor. For over a year, the vessel lay at Norfolk, Virginia, part of the time under the surveillance of the Coast Guard apparently because the British Government was convinced that she was going to attempt to run the

---

*The Day Line was later paid $305,000 for the *De Witt Clinton* and $101,000 for the *Chauncey M. Depew.*

**Her wartime name may be found in listings of the American Bureau of Shipping and of Lloyd's, as well as in much of the considerable writings about her, as *Col. Frederick C. Johnson.* Her nameboards when she was sold by the Government read simply *Frederick C. Johnson.* According to the Office of the Chief of Military History, Department of the Army (1958), this was indeed her correct name, without the "Col."

Palestine blockade. Then, carrying the name *Derecktor* and flying the Panamanian flag, she finally left the United States via New York for the Mediterranean. Later on, as the *Galilah* of the Zim Israel Navigation Co., Ltd., she arrived at Haifa loaded with former inmates of British detention camps. Her career on the Mediterranean was largely that of an immigrant ship, and according to reports, ended in a shipbreaking yard in Italy in 1953.

In 1942, the violent change in the national transportation pattern brought about by World War II, resulted in a healthy resurgence of Day Line passengers. With gasoline rationing making a drive in the country an impossibility, people again turned to the Day Line as a way to spend pleasant hours out-of-doors. Vacationists were forced to limit their horizons and their way of going. Anew the Day Line was a primary route to the Catskills.

The losses were wiped out and in 1942 there was a reported profit of over $20,000, which increased to almost $74,000 in 1943. In that boom year about 1,431,000 passengers were carried, more than at any time since 1930, and traffic at the upriver landings was remarkably good. This happy state of affairs was not to last, though, for in 1944 and 1945 passengers fell off and small net losses were realized.

The service during the war years and afterwards changed little. The Albany route was operated at first from late May until shortly after Labor Day, but beginning in 1943 was maintained until about mid-September. The Poughkeepsie special service started at nearly the same time as the Albany run and continued on a daily basis until about Columbus Day or the week end after that holiday. For part of the season there were afternoon round trips to Newburgh on Sundays and through 1942 also on Saturdays; the early run to Indian Point on Sundays; depending on traffic, the Sunday evening return of the down-boat to Indian Point to pick up those passengers who could not be transported by the other steamers. Because of the war, two landings were affected. Due to the operation of a shipyard at Yonkers, calls there were discontinued after 1943 and not resumed until during the season of 1947. West Point service, 1942 through 1945, was limited.

In 1946, with the nation returning to the ways of peacetime, the reported net loss soared to almost $168,000, even though passenger traffic had increased over 1945. In 1942, 1943 and 1944, fares had been raised, and in 1947 they again moved

The *Hendrick Hudson* is returning to New York on August 21, 1940. The preceding day she had made a special round-trip excursion from Indian Point and way landings to Albany, and had lain overnight at Indian Point. The *Robert Fulton* on her way to Albany is arriving at Kingston Point on a regular through run in 1939; the same year the *De Witt Clinton* is in the Highlands, bound for Newburgh on a Sunday afternoon round trip from New York.—*Above, lower: Photograph by Elwin M. Eldredge.*

The *Chauncey M. Depew* in 1939 is bound up the river for Poughkeepsie on the return half of her morning down trip from Poughkeepsie to New York. She was employed in this service for many years. The *Peter Stuyvesant* is slicing her way through the water in 1937; the *Alexander Hamilton* is landing at Bear Mountain.—*Above, lower: Photograph by Arthur Helmke; below: Photograph by Stephan Gmelin.*

upward, but the deficit rose, too. A final fare increase in 1948 brought the one-way rate between New York and Albany to $3.00 and the round-trip, $5.00, without affecting the deficit appreciably.

To the Day Line, the size of the losses of 1946-1948 made it painfully apparent that there would be no change unless the company drastically altered its services and limited itself to purely excursion operations from New York. Allegedly, too, the City of New York was contemplating an increase in the rental for the West 42d Street terminus and was proposing repairs to both that pier and the 125th Street landing, for which it apparently intended to assess the line.

In 1948 the *Robert Fulton* made the last sailing from Albany on September 13, and on October 17 the *Alexander Hamilton* closed the Poughkeepsie service. The latter steamer made chartered trips on October 18 and 20, and on October 22 went to the Day Line landing at Poughkeepsie to lay up for the winter.

There had been strong rumors that something was about to happen to the Day Line. It happened soon, for on November 8 announcement was made that the company had decided to give up. And somewhere along the way, Mr. Olcott took time to scribble on his calendar-pad record of the *Alexander Hamilton*'s charter of October 20, "Last Day Line Passenger Trip. 25 years to the Day after RPO [Ruth Purves Olcott, his wife] Christened the *AH*."

To the security holders he wrote, "Your directors have for some time been devoting intensive consideration to the question of the advisability of discontinuing operations. They regret to inform you that at their last meeting it was unanimously voted to discontinue further operations and to proceed with the liquidation of the company and the sale of its assets."

He also said, "Your company operated at a substantial loss during 1946 and 1947. It was hoped that an increase in the rate of fares . . . which your directors decided to put into effect in 1948 would enable your company to operate at a profit this year. Unfortunately, however, increased cost of fuel and other operating expenses and the continued decrease in the number of passengers carried have more than offset the increased rate. . . ."

An indication of the economic change over the years is best shown by the fact that while the reported operating revenues of over a million-and-a-half dollars per year in 1946-1948 were higher than at any time since 1930, the loss on operations in the financial statement for the year ending December 31, 1948, stood at $134,275.35.

The news of the ending of the Day Line came as a shock up and down the Hudson valley. Newspapers devoted columns to it and carried editorial laments bolstered by letters from the incredulous. Even those who had been convinced that doomsday was at hand, couldn't believe it when it came. To picture the Hudson River without the Day Line suddenly became an impossibility. But many of those who wailed the loudest hadn't traveled on the steamers for years. The world was changing and the age of steamboat travelers was almost over.

For many years the Day Line steamers were laid up for the winter at the New York terminal. After the season of 1948, the *Alexander Hamilton* sailed up to Poughkeepsie to go into winter quarters. By then the rest of the fleet was laid up at New York, but the *Peter Stuyvesant* was subsequently towed to Newburgh, and the *Robert Fulton* and the *Hendrick Hudson* to Indian Point, where the last two were photographed. The view shows solid woodwork across the paddle housing of the *Hendrick Hudson* on the saloon deck. This was substituted for the decaying dummy windows before the vessel entered service in 1946.—*Photographed by Captain William O. Benson.*

201

The *Hendrick Hudson* (above) is at the scrap yard where she was broken up. Chief Engineer George H. Mowers and First Assistant Engineer Alvin Mowers (left to right) are on the *Robert Fulton* in 1954. On September 12, 1954, the *Robert Fulton* made the last trip of her career under steam and is shown (below, left; both views) arriving at Indian Point that day with a charter. Light snow covers her walking beam as she lies idle at New York during the winter of 1955-56. Finally she is in her present landlocked berth in the Bahamas.—*Photographs by: Edward O. Clark (above, left), Conrad Milster, Jr. (above, right; center, right), William G. Muller (center and lower left); lower right: Courtesy of C. G. McLaren, Owens-Illinois.*

Chapter 23

SUCCESSOR DAY LINES

NOT LONG AFTER announcing the demise of the Day Line, Mr. Olcott observed, "A private company could operate profitably if a limited number of boats were used on the run to Bear Mountain and Poughkeepsie only, but since this line would primarily be in the public interest, it should receive a subsidy in the form of free pier rental and repairs."

One of the first people to contact him concerning the purchase of the Day Line was Samuel Rufus Rosoff, but nothing materialized. Eventually George Sanders and associates opened negotiations and early in March, 1949, the stockholders approved the sale of the four steamers and the landings at Newburgh and Poughkeepsie to the Sanders group which had filed a certificate of incorporation as the Hudson River Boat Co., Inc. The Day Line retained the rest of the real estate which was later offered for sale, filed a certificate of change of name to Indian Point Corp. on April 8, 1949, and eventually filed into voluntary dissolution.

As soon as the Hudson River Day Line had freed its name, the Hudson River Boat Co., Inc., took the name of Hudson River Day Line, Inc., April 11, 1949, thus continuing the name of the old company with the addition of the word "incorporated."

Mr. Sanders was also interested in the Sutton Line, Inc., of which he had formerly been president. This was the only line besides the Day Line running regularly on the Hudson in 1948. It operated the sidewheeler *Bear Mountain*, originally the *Clermont* of the Catskill Evening Line, to Bear Mountain. This vessel, in need of extensive repair, was not placed in commission in 1949 and the Sutton Line service was covered by the Day Line. Next year the *Bear Mountain* was sold for scrap.

The plan of Mr. Sanders and his associates was to run up the river only as far as Poughkeepsie, calling at 125th Street, Yonkers, Bear Mountain, West Point and Newburgh. Indian Point had not been purchased, but by 1950 arrangements had been made so that the Day Line resumed landing

there and continued to call through 1956. It is now the site of a nuclear power station of the Consolidated Edison Co.

Curtailment of the route meant the new company would not need all the steamers it had acquired and those commissioned in 1949 were the *Robert Fulton, Alexander Hamilton* and *Peter Stuyvesant*. The *Hendrick Hudson*, largest and oldest of the fleet, remained laid up and on June 4, 1951, left New York under tow for a Delaware River shipbreaking yard. Her last active trip had been made on September 12, 1948, a little over 42 years after her now long-forgotten triumphal first run to Albany which had marked the beginning of the greatest days of the Day Line.

To inaugurate the activities of the new owners, the *Alexander Hamilton* made an invitation sail on May 25, 1949, and on May 28 the *Robert Fulton* opened the regular season by going to Poughkeepsie and return. This was the old Poughkeepsie special and it was to be the mainstay of the Hudson River Day Line, Inc. Changes were made in the steamers in accordance with the changing character of the service. The dining rooms on the main decks aft were altered into what became combination lunch rooms and dining rooms, with refreshment stands; the old lunch rooms or cafeterias in the holds forward were subsequently closed. Liquor and beer bars were established on the decks.

In 1952 the company experimented with very limited service to Catskill and in 1953 again offered some trips to that place. Also for a few seasons it covered a route to Atlantic Highlands, New Jersey, from where passengers could continue by bus to the race track at Monmouth Park.

In 1953 the company entered the sightseeing business around Manhattan Island with two converted infantry landing craft, the *Knickerbocker* and the *Gotham*. To manage this phase of its business, there was formed Day Line Sightseeing, Inc., a wholly owned subsidiary of the Hudson River Day Line, Inc. The vessels themselves were in turn

The *Robert Fulton* is a strange sight in the Bahamas. A vestige of better days is the name still over the after gangway.—*C. G. McLaren, Owens-Illinois.*

owned by separate corporations. The *Gotham* was subsequently renamed *Knickerbocker II* — her fourth name — and in 1957 a third converted landing craft was added with the new name of *Knickerbocker VII*. Seven was said to have been selected because she was the seventh passenger vessel to be owned by Mr. Sanders since his acquisition of the Day Line.

After the season of 1954, the line felt that the *Alexander Hamilton* and the *Peter Stuyvesant* were adequate for its steamboat service, and the *Robert Fulton* was not placed in commission in 1955. In that year, regularly scheduled service consisted of daily round-trips to Poughkeepsie, trips to Atlantic Highlands, and moonlight sails on the Hudson on Saturday nights.

In 1956 the *Robert Fulton* was sold to the National Container Corp., which had leased timber-cutting rights in the Bahamas and which was subsequently acquired by Owens-Illinois. On June 28, 1956, she left New York Harbor in tow of the tugboat *Peggy Sheridan* for Jacksonville, Florida, where she arrived on July 3. The *Robert Fulton* was almost the last of the once great fleet of beam-engined steam vessels to operate in the United States. As she made her way up and down the Hudson in 1954 with her three tall smokestacks athwartship and her walking beam moving in stately cadence, she must have seemed to the casual observer to be the strangest steamboat imaginable. To old-timers she was a beloved reminder of the better days of steamboating.

When she was sold by the Day Line, there was but one other active vessel left in the United States with a beam engine. This was the ferryboat *Eu-*

reka, in the service of the Southern Pacific Railroad between San Francisco and Oakland, California. Her retirement in 1957 as the result of the breaking of her crankpin, silenced completely in this country the beam engine which had once been so common.

At Jacksonville, the motive power of the *Robert Fulton* was removed and she was converted into a floating community center, badly needed for use at the site of pulpwood-cutting operations in the Bahamas. When she arrived at Riding Point on Grand Bahama Island, she became a combination general office, apartment house, supermarket, infirmary and school, with a snack bar, kitchen, dining room, soda fountain, laundry, television room and motion picture facilities. Later she was moved to another timber-harvesting area on Great Abaco Island, and is now completely surrounded by fill and land-locked about midway between Marsh Harbour and Wilson City on Snake Cay, adjacent to the wharf from which the Forest Products Division of Owens-Illinois ships pulpwood to its Jacksonville mill. Here her supermarket serves about 5,000 people. Ownership of the *Robert Fulton* is held by Owens-Illinois of the Bahamas, Ltd.   .

In September 1956, the Day Line revived the pleasant Hudson River custom of running an excursion from Newburgh and Poughkeepsie to Albany. The *Peter Stuyvesant* made the trip and was the first Day Line steamer to appear at Albany since the *Robert Fulton* sailed away on September 13, 1948. The only passenger-carrying steamboat in between had been the *Westport*, which ran excursions out of Albany in the summer of 1954 — a happy summer for dyed-in-the-wool steamboaters in that area.

The year 1957 marked the sesquicentennial of the introduction of steam navigation to the Hudson by Robert Fulton. The Day Line commemorated the event by running the *Peter Stuyvesant* — complete with costumed crew and strolling entertainers — from New York to Albany on June 1 and back the following day. This was the first trip of a Day Line steamer between the old termini since 1948. Also for the first time since 1948, a side-wheeler arrived at Albany in September 1957 when the *Alexander Hamilton* landed with an excursion from Newburgh and Poughkeepsie.

In 1958-1962, the Day Line ran an annual Labor Day week-end cruise between New York and Albany, on which the steamer went up on Saturday and returned on Labor Day. The *Alexander Hamilton* was assigned to this happy duty four times, and the *Peter Stuyvesant* once, in 1960.

The *Peter Stuyvesant* (above) is bound for Albany on June 1, 1957, on a special trip
to mark the sesquicentennial year of Hudson River steamboating. The top of her stack
is shrouded by steam from the whistle as she answers a salute. Off the old Livingston
estate of Clermont, a memorial wreath to Robert Fulton was cast overboard by a des-
cendant of Robert R. Livingston. In 1960 the *Peter Stuyvesant* is departing from Bear
Mountain with a charter as the *Alexander Hamilton* lands on her way from Poughkeepsie
to New York.—*Above: Photograph by Ira V. D. Warren; below: Photograph by Conrad
Milster, Jr.*

The *Alexander Hamilton* is carrying a special Sunday excursion from Albany in connection with her Labor Day week-end cruise to that place. The black bands were first painted around the tops of the smokestacks in 1957; the *Peter Stuyvesant* was similarly treated at the same time. Chief Engineer Elvoid E. Post is at the throttle as the *Alexander Hamilton* lands at Pier 81 at the end of her final trip of the 1964 season. In the uniform of the old Day Line he is on deck in 1947, the year he became chief engineer. At right (left to right) are Captains Edward M. Grady and George Carroll, master and pilot respectively of the *Alexander Hamilton* in 1964.—*Photographs by: Edward O. Clark (above), Conrad Milster, Jr. (far left), William H. Ewen (left) and Franklin B. Roberts, Jr.*

SUCCESSOR DAY LINES

Famed as an operator of sightseeing vessels at New York, Francis J. Barry is the present head of the Day Line.—*Fabian Bachrach.*

In 1962 the Hudson River passenger season closed in September. The steamboats had scarcely gone into winter quarters when the Day Line was purchased by the Circle Line, headed by Francis J. Barry. The Circle Line has specialized for many years in water sightseeing at New York City, and its activities in this field are widely known.

Included in the sale were the three converted landing craft used in around-Manhattan service, the *Day Line I, Day Line II* and *Day Line VII* (renamed respectively from the *Knickerbocker, Knickerbocker II* and *Knickerbocker VII* in 1961), and the *Alexander Hamilton* and the *Peter Stuyvesant.* Ownership of the last two was transferred to the Circle Line-Sightseeing Yachts, Inc., on October 1, 1962. The Circle Line continued Hudson River service under the style of Hudson River Day Line, and has in its fold corporations named Day Line, Inc., and Hudson River Day Line, Inc. The latter corporation assumed that name upon the dissolution of the former Hudson River Day Line, Inc., in September 1963.

After considering business needs and the expense of putting both the *Alexander Hamilton* and the *Peter Stuyvesant* in prime condition, the latest Day Line decided to run only the former in 1963. She was extensively refurbished; the *Peter Stuyvesant* remained laid up and continued so in 1964.

The Newburgh and Poughkeepsie piers were badly in need of costly repairs. In 1963 the Day Line eliminated these landings, but as a substitute it scheduled the *Alexander Hamilton* to sail up the river as far as Poughkeepsie and there turn around without landing. Passengers not interested in visiting either Bear Mountain or West Point were thus enabled to spend a full day on the river in proper steamboating fashion.

In 1964 the landings at West 125th Street in New York, and Yonkers were eliminated, so the timetable for that year called for departure from Pier 81 at the foot of West 41st Street, New York, at 10 a.m.; arrive at Bear Mountain at 12:15 p.m.; arrive at West Point at 12:35 p.m. (except during graduation ceremonies May 30-June 3); cruise to off Poughkeepsie and back; leave West Point 4:00 p.m.; leave Bear Mountain 4:30 p.m.; arrive New York 6:45 p.m. Daily service was maintained from Memorial Day through Labor Day, except on Fridays in June. Poughkeepsie cruises did not commence until June 20. In addition to regular business, the *Alexander Hamilton* handled a few charters. Similar service is in prospect for 1965.

The *Alexander Hamilton* sails from Yonkers.—*Photograph by William G. Muller.*

In 1964 the *Alexander Hamilton* was licensed for 3675 passengers, with a total allowed of 3741 including crew. Her master was Captain Edward M. Grady, her pilot Captain George Carroll.* Her chief engineer was Elvoid E. Post, the only officer aboard who had been an officer in the Olcott-managed Day Line. His service of over 30 years on one steamboat is remarkable, and through it all his continuing affection for the *Alexander Hamilton* is in the highest tradition of steamboating.

A link with the earlier days of Hudson River steamboating was provided by another member of the 1964 crew of the *Alexander Hamilton*. This was Alexander McKinney, hallman, who had joined the Day Line about 1905 on the old *Albany* and was head porter on the *Washington Irving* when she sank in 1926. Newspapers at the time noted how long he had been with the line, and this was almost 40 years previously! In the summer of 1964 the writer visited with Alex to find him reminiscing fondly about the old towing steamer *Oswego*, a vessel built in 1848 for the Hudson River Steamboat Co. of Abraham and Alfred Van Santvoord, and which last ran in 1918.

Great changes have come to the river since the *Oswego* was new; since Alfred Van Santvoord be-

*Captain Carroll will be recalled as the officer in command of the *Poughkeepsie* at the time of her battles with the ice in the winter of 1933-1934.

Alexander McKinney (right) was head porter on the *Hendrick Hudson* when this picture was taken in 1939. With him are Bert (left) and Thomas Crowell.

The *Alexander Hamilton* is on dry dock after the close of the 1964 season; on the next page she is seen from the George Washington bridge, July 1964.—*Both Photographs this page by Conrad Milster, Jr.*

gan his Day Line over a century ago; and even since Alfred Van Santvoord Olcott, with his great love for steamboats and his pride in the traditions of his family's company, saw that the passing of a way of life cannot be countered by the best efforts of any man. The Hudson flows on and can be best appreciated only from the deck of a steamboat. But the world about it and the type of traffic on its waters have changed beyond the wildest dreams of Captain David H. Hitchcock, Captain John F. Tallman, or any of their contemporaries who knew the river when steamboats were legion and when a fast passage was top news.

All things considered, it seems almost miraculous that at least one steamboat has plied the Hudson during every year since Robert Fulton first sailed to Albany in the *North River Steam Boat* in 1807. Paddle wheels moved him on his way then. And if you sailed up the Hudson on the *Alexander Hamilton* in 1964, paddle wheels still moved you along.

When this long continuity will be broken no man knows. We can only hope that a steamboat whistle will echo along the Hudson for awhile yet, for a lingering while.

The *Alexander Hamilton* carries a Sunday crowd upriver,
under the George Washington Bridge.—*Conrad Milster*.

APPENDIX

Appendix A-1

MEASUREMENTS

Statutory length, breadth and depth of hold, frequently mentioned in the text and listed in the following tables, are the official dimensions of a vessel as carried in Government records. In order that they may be uniform, the method of taking measurements is prescribed by law.

When the *North River Steam Boat* was enrolled, the law directed that the length be taken from the fore part of the main stem to the after part of the stern-post, above the upper deck; the breadth, at the broadest part above the main wales; the depth, from the underside of the deck plank to the ceiling in the hold. The resultant measurements were expressed in feet and inches. Tonnage was obtained by using these figures in a formula, with 95 as a divisor.

By an act of 1864, these definitions applied: "The length from the fore part of the outer planking on the side of the stem to the after part of the main stern-post of screw steamers, and to the after part of the rudder-post of all other vessels measured on the top of the tonnage-deck shall be accounted the vessel's length. The breadth of the broadest part on the outside of the vessel shall be accounted the vessel's breadth of beam. A measure from the under side of the tonnage-deck plank, amidships, to the ceiling of the hold (average thickness), shall be accounted the depth of hold." All measurements were to be taken in feet, with fractions expressed as decimals.

At the same time, the method of computing tonnage was changed and was then based on separate measurements, with 100 as a divisor. This tonnage figure was designated as gross tonnage after the United States in 1882 adopted net tonnage, which was arrived at by making allowable deductions from gross.

It should be borne in mind that these tonnages were cubic measurements. A common fallacy is to assume that they indicate the weight of a vessel, which would be displacement in tons.

Likewise, the depth of hold is not the draft of water, and the statutory length is not generally the same as other possible measurements such as the length overall. As its name implies, the latter is the entire length of a vessel and usually a figure released by the owner. Consequently it does not have the reliability for comparative purposes that statutory length has. Because steamboating was a highly competitive business each major new steamboat, particularly in the 19th century, was expected to be superior to her predecessors. Therefore it was not unusual to find considerable liberty taken with the overall length.

The statutory breadth of beam of Hudson River steamboats was in most cases measured over the hull only, with the overall breadth again being a figure of the owner. The latter was measured from the outside of the guards at the widest point, and on Hudson River sidewheelers often approached almost twice the width of the hull proper.

Appendix A-2

PASSENGER STEAMBOATS OWNED BY THE PROPRIETORS OF THE DAY LINE OF STEAMERS, HUDSON RIVER LINE OR HUDSON RIVER DAY LINE AND OPERATED 1863-1948.

Daniel Drew 6609* Sidewheel.

Built: 1860, New York City, Thomas Collyer.
Hull: Wood; as built, 244' x 30'6" x 9'3"
670-25/95 tons.
    Lengthened 1863-64, new measurements,
260' x 30' x 10'.
930.35 gross, 841.06 net tons.
    Altered 1884-85, 880.89 gross, 622.19 net tons.
Engine: Vertical beam, erected by Neptune Iron Works, constructed by Morgan Iron Works for *Titan*, built 1852. Cylinder as built, 60" x 10'; new cylinder installed 1873-74, 68" x 10'; 2 boilers.

*Official number 475 hp (nominal).

Daniel Drew, Continued

History: Purchased by Van Santvoord, Davidson and Vibbard for Day Line, 1863, for about $78,000. Regular operation 1863-1880 until advent of *Albany,* then used as spare boat. Burned 1886, Kingston Point, N. Y.

Armenia 1706   Sidewheel.

Built: 1847, New York City, Thomas Collyer.
Hull: Wood; as built, 181'9" x 27'6" x 8'4"
                      398-59/95 tons.
    Lengthened 1859-60, 200' x 28' x 8'6"
                      458-91/95 tons.
    Lengthened 1860-61, 214'3" x 28' x 8'6"
                      494-63/95 tons.
    New measurements, 212' x 30' x 9'
               528.29 gross, 347.34 net tons.
Engine: Vertical beam, Henry R. Dunham & Co. Cylinder as built, 34" x 14'; new cylinder, 40" x 14'. 1 boiler as built, later 2 boilers. Dates of these changes not known.   350 hp (nominal).
History: Purchased for Day Line, 1863, for about $53,000. Regular operation 1863 season only, then used as spare boat. Sold 1883; operated on Potomac River. Burned 1886, Alexandria, Va.

Chauncey Vibbard 5664   Sidewheel.

Built: 1864, Brooklyn, N. Y., Lawrence & Foulks.
Hull: Wood; as built, 267' x 34' x 9'   794-29/95 tons.
    New measurements, 265' x 35' x 9.6'   1027.07 tons.
    Lengthened 1871-72, 281' x 35' x 9.6'   1066.98 tons.
    Altered 1879-80   1158.27 gross, 789.31 net tons.
Engine: Vertical beam, Fletcher, Harrison & Co. Cylinder as built, 55" x 12'; new cylinder installed 1871-72, 62¼" x 12'. 2 boilers on guards as built; 3 boilers installed in hold 1879-80.   500 hp (nominal).
History: Built for Day Line, cost about $144,000. Regular operation 1864-87 until advent of *New York,* then used as spare boat. Sold 1890, operated on Delaware River. Officially abandoned, 1900, broken up.

Albany 105908   Sidewheel.

Built: 1880, Wilmington, Del., Harlan & Hollingsworth Co.
Hull: Iron; as built, 284' x 40' x 10.1'
              1346.53 gross, 854.19 net tons.
    Lengthened 1892-93, 314' x 40' x 10.1'
    (overall, 325'6" x 73'3", 7'6" draft loaded aft.)
              1415.42 gross, 919.63 net tons.
    Net tonnage changed 1895,   815.03 net tons.
Engine: Vertical beam, Fletcher, Harrison & Co., Cylinder 73" x 12'. 3 boilers.   3200 hp.

History: Built for Day Line, cost about $187,000. Operated 1880-1930, then withdrawn. Sold 1934, renamed *b. Potomac,* operated on Potomac River 1934-1948. Hull converted to barge *Potomac,* renamed *c. Ware River.* Still afloat January 1965.

New York 130373   Sidewheel.

Built: 1887, Wilmington, Del., Harlan & Hollingsworth Co.
Hull: Steel; as built, 301' x 40.2' x 11'
            1552.52 gross, 1091.89 net tons.
    Lengthened 1897-98, 335' x 40.4' x 11.2'
            1974 gross, 1261 net tons.
Engine: Vertical beam, W. & A. Fletcher Co.
                Cylinder 75" x 12'.
3 boilers.   3850 hp.
History: Built for Day Line, cost about $242,000. Operated 1887-1908.
Burned 1908, Newburgh, N. Y.

Hendrick Hudson 203424   Sidewheel.

Built: 1906, Newburgh, N. Y., T. S. Marvel Shipbuilding Co.
Hull: Steel; 379.1' x 45.1' x 13.4' (overall, 390'6" x 82', 10'4½" draft, loaded, aft). 2847 gross, 1598 net tons.
Engine: Inclined compound, W. & A. Fletcher Co. Cylinders, 45", 70", 70" x 7'. 6 boilers.   6200 hp.
History: Built for Day Line, cost about $621,000. Operated 1906-1948. Acquired 1949, Hudson River Day Line, Inc. Not returned to service. Sold for scrap 1951.

Robert Fulton 206288   Sidewheel.

Built: 1909, Camden, N. J., New York Shipbuilding Co.
Hull: Steel; 337' x 42' x 11.5' (overall, 346' x 76'2", 8'2½" draft, loaded, aft). 2168 gross, 1344 net tons.
Engine: Vertical beam, rebuilt from *New York,* W. & A. Fletcher Co.
    Cylinder, 75" x 12'. 3 boilers.   3850 hp.
History: Built for Day Line, cost about $500,000.
                  Operated 1909-1954.
Acquired 1949, Hudson River Day Line, Inc.
Sold 1956 for conversion to a "community center," Bahamas. Still in use, 1964.

Washington Irving 211170   Sidewheel.

Built: 1913, Camden, N. J., New York Shipbuilding Corp.
Hull: Steel, 400.5' x 47' x 13.7' (overall, 414'1" x 86', 10'1" draft, loaded, aft). 3104 gross, 1664 net tons.
Engine: Inclined compound, W. & A. Fletcher Co. Cylinders 45", 70", 70" x 7'. 6 boilers.   6200 hp.
History: Built for Day Line, cost about $838,000. Operated 1913-1926. Sank 1926.

De Witt Clinton   211734   Twin screw.

Built: 1913, Wilmington, Del., Harlan & Hollingsworth Corp.

Hull: Steel;   as built, 320.2' x 48.1' x 22'.
                                    3539 gross, 2134 net tons.
   Rebuilt 1920-21, 320.2' x 48.1' x 19' (overall, 332' x
   66', 16'10" draft, loaded, aft).
                                    3899 gross, 2246 net tons.

Engines: Two triple expansion, Harlan & Hollingsworth Corp.   Cylinders 23½", 37½", 42", 42" x 3'.
   6 boilers.   4000 hp.

History: Built as night boat *a. Manhattan;* in U.S.N.,
   World War I, as *b. Nopatin.* Purchased by Day
   Line, 1920, for about $226,000, reconstructed and
   equipped at cost of about $401,000, renamed *d. De
   Witt Clinton* from *c. Manhattan,* to which she had
   reverted. Operated 1921-1932 and 1939. Requisitioned 1942 by U. S. War Shipping Administration.
   Rebuilt and renamed *e. Frederick C. Johnson.* Sold
   by government after World War II. Renamed *f.
   Derecktor* and then *g. Galilah.* Operated in Mediterranean.   Scrapped 1953.

Alexander Hamilton   223775   Sidewheel.

Built: 1924, Sparrows Point, Md., Bethlehem Shipbuilding Corp., Ltd.

Hull: Steel;   338.6' x 77' (molded 42') x 13.6' (overall, 349'5" x 77', 8'4" draft, loaded, aft).
                                    2367 gross, 1252 net tons.

Engine: Inclined triple expansion, Bethlehem Shipbuilding Corp., Ltd.
   Cylinders 36½", 56", 85" x 6'.   4 boilers.   3900 hp.

History: Built for Day Line, cost about $852,000.
   Operated from 1924 on.   Acquired 1949, Hudson
   River Day Line, Inc.; 1962, Circle Line-Sightseeing
   Yachts, Inc.   Still in Hudson River service 1964.

Chauncey M. Depew   211290   Single screw.

Built: 1913, Bath, Maine, Bath Iron Works.

Hull: Steel;   185.1' x 35.6' (molded 30.5') x 13.5'
   (overall, 194'11" x 37'4", 11'7" draft, loaded, aft).
                                     652 gross, 282 net tons.

Engine: Triple expansion, Bath Iron Works.   Cylinders, 16", 26", 30", 30" x 2'.   1 boiler.   1198 hp.

History: Built as *a. Rangeley.*   Purchased by Day
   Line for about $150,000; reconditioned and equipped
   for about $40,000; operated 1925-1940.   Chartered
   by government. Requisitioned 1942, U. S. War Shipping Administration.   Sold by government after
   World War II.   Operated as excursion boat.   Sold
   1950 to government of Bermuda for use as tender.
   Still in service 1964.

Peter Stuyvesant   226565   Single screw.

Built: 1927, Wilmington, Del., Pusey & Jones Corp.

Hull: Steel;   260.5' x 60' (molded 46') x 15.8' (overall, 269'6" x 60', 13'5½" draft, loaded, aft).
                                    1721 gross, 633 net tons.

Engine: Triple expansion, Pusey & Jones Corp.
   Cylinders, 25", 40", 47", 47" x 3'.   4 boilers.   2700 hp.

History: Built for Day Line, cost about $728,000.
   Operated 1927-1962.   Acquired 1949, Hudson River
   Day Line, Inc.; 1962, Circle Line-Sightseeing Yachts,
   Inc.   Last operated 1962.   Laid up.

Mary Powell   16982   Sidewheel.

Built: 1861, Jersey City, N. J., Michael S. Allison.

Hull: Wood;   as built, 267' x 34'6" x 9'2".
                                       819-81/95 tons.
   Lengthened 1862-63, 288' x 34'6" x 9'2".
                                       889-78/95 tons.
   New measurements, 288' x 34.6' x 9.2'.
                              983.57 gross, 877.16 net tons.

Engine: Vertical beam, Fletcher, Harrison & Co.
   Cylinder as built, 62" x 12'; new cylinder installed
   1874-75, 72" x 12'.   2 boilers.   1560 hp.

History: Operated by Van Santvoord and Davidson,
   seasons of 1869-71. Operated by Mary Powell Steamboat Co. as subsidiary of Hudson River Day Line,
   seasons of 1903-1917. Operated 1861-1917. Laid up.
   Sold to scrapping interests 1919.   Later broken up.

NOTES

   Built: The year shown here is that used in official documents.

   Hull: Statutory dimensions are from official documents
or from *MVUS* (the Government's annual *List of Merchant Vessels of the United States:* see Bibliography) for
various years. Figures change for lengthenings or alterations, of course, or for "new measurements" taken under
revised statutes. Even in official sources variations may
sometimes be found over a period of years, and so the
dimensions used here have been weighed. In the case of
the vessels listed, with three exceptions, the words of the
law requiring that the statutory breadth be "the broadest
part" were interpreted to be the broadest part of the hull.
The exceptions: The statutory breadth in *MVUS* for the
Alexander Hamilton and the *Peter Stuyvesant* is the overall breadth; for the *Chauncey M. Depew,* slightly less than
that. For these three vessels, the molded breadth of hull
from Day Line figures is included in parentheses following
the statutory breadth, to provide a basis for comparison
with the other vessels. Hyphenated years indicate operating seasons between which the vessel was lengthened or
altered.

   Although we have mentioned the sometimes question-
able nature of owners' overall measurements, those listed
here are from the Day Line. In this case they are valid,
since they are the company's "official" figures, used for
operational purposes. With them are the Day Line's figures for "draft, loaded, aft."

Tonnages, too, are from official documents or *MVUS*, with variations weighed. For vessels built before the adoption of net tonnage, that figure has been entered on the line corresponding with the dimensions and gross tonnage of the vessel at the time its net tonnage was first computed.

Engine: Information as to engine builder for the *Armenia* and the *Daniel Drew* is from John H. Morrison's *History of American Steam Navigation* (see bibliography). From the same source are the original cylinder dimensions for these same vessels; enlarged diameters are from inspection certificates. Figures for engines built by Fletcher, Harrison & Co. and its successor, the W. & A. Fletcher Co., are from a list of engines prepared from records of the firm. All other figures are from Day Line records.

Nominal horsepower, given for the *Daniel Drew*, the *Armenia* and the *Chauncey Vibbard*, is from *MVUS*, and was recorded when the *Armenia* alone had an enlarged cylinder. Nominal horsepower, computed on measurements, is not comparable with indicated horsepower, computed on measurements and tests, which is given for the other vessels. For the *New York* and the *Mary Powell* (enlarged cylinder), indicated horsepower is from *MVUS*. For the rest it is from Day Line records.

History: Costs of construction and purchase are rounded off to the nearest thousand dollars.

General note: While the Day Line sometimes chartered vessels to fill transitory needs, such vessels are not within the scope of this listing.

Appendix A-3

OTHER STEAMBOATS ON THE HUDSON RIVER

Besides the steamers of the Day Line, many other vessels are named in the text. While a detailed or comprehensive roster of all Hudson River steamboats is far beyond the scope of this book, a selection of boats which figure predominantly in the narrative is briefly listed here. Statutory dimensions and motive power are detailed as a basis for comparison of these vessels with the Day Line steamboats listed in Appendix A-2 above.

Adirondack   107230   Sidewheel.
Built: 1896.
Hull: Wood;   388.2' x 50.0' x 12.1'.
Engine: Vertical beam;   cylinder 81" x 12'.   4 boilers.
Operation: New York-Albany night boat (People's Line).

Alida   866   Sidewheel.
Built: 1847.
Hull: Wood;   as built, 249'5" x 28'6½" x 9'9"; later lengthened and readmeasured, 272' x 29' x 10'.
Engine: Vertical beam;   cylinder 56" x 12';   later fitted with cylinder 62" x 12'.   2 boilers.

Operation: Originally day boat; also operated as night boat; ended career as a towing steamer.

Benjamin B. Odell   208448   Screw.
Built: 1911, for Central-Hudson Steamboat Co.
Hull: Steel;   263.6' x 48.8' x 17.3'.
Engine: Triple expansion;   cylinders 26", 41", 68" x 3'.   4 boilers.
Operation: Night boat.

Berkshire   211149   Sidewheel.
Built: Launched 1907 as the *Princeton* but never so enrolled. Completed and enrolled as the *Berkshire*, 1913.
Hull: Steel;   422.4' x 50.6' x 12.9'
Engine: Vertical beam;   cylinder 84" x 12'.   4 boilers.
Operation: New York-Albany night boat (People's Line).

C. W. Morse   200894   Sidewheel.
Built: 1903.
Hull: Steel;   411.1' x 50.8' x 12.8'.
Engine: Vertical beam;   cylinder 81" x 12'.   4 boilers.
Operation: New York-Albany night boat (People's Line).
New name: Renamed b. *Fort Orange*, 1922.

City of Albany   1986   Sidewheel.
Built: 1863.
Hull: Wood;   200' x 30' x 8'.   *MVUS*, 1886 and ff. gives breadth at 32'.
Engine: Vertical beam;   original engine, measurements unknown;   new engine built 1868, cylinder 48" x 12'.   1 boiler.
New names: Redocumented as b. *Adelphi*, 1867; renamed c. *City of Albany*, 1885.

Clermont   208651   Sidewheel.
Built: 1911.
Hull: Steel;   271.5' x 39.2' x 11.5'.
Engine: Vertical beam;   cylinder 55" x 11'.   2 boilers.
Operation: Night boat (Catskill Evening Line). Became excursion boat, 1920, New York—Bear Mountain.
New name: Renamed b. *Bear Mountain*, 1947.

Dean Richmond   6264   Sidewheel.
Built: 1865.
Hull: Wood;   348' x 46' x 10.6'.
Engine: Vertical beam;   cylinder 75" x 14'.   2 boilers.
Operation: New York-Albany night boat (People's Line).

Drew   6249   Sidewheel.
Built: 1866.
Hull: Wood;   366.5′ x 47.5′ x 10.9′.
Engine: Vertical beam;   cylinder 81″ x 15′.   2 boilers.
Operation: New York-Albany night boat (People's Line).

Francis Skiddy   No official number.   Sidewheel.
Built: 1851.
Hull: Wood;   312′7″ x 37′10″ x 10′3″.
Engine: Vertical beam;   cylinder 70″ x 14′.   4 boilers.
Operation: Built as day boat;   staterooms added for night service.

Hendrik Hudson   Enrolled as the *Hendrick Hudson*. No official number known.   Sidewheel.
Built: 1845.
Hull: Wood;   as built, 329′9″ x 35′4″ x 10′4″; readmeasured, 327′ x 35′ x 9′.
Engine: Vertical beam;   cylinder 72″ x 11′.   2 boilers.
Operation: New York-Albany night boat (People's Line).

Isaac Newton   No official number.   Sidewheel.
Built: 1846.
Hull: Wood;   320′7″ x 40′ x 10′8″ as built; after 1855 season lengthened perhaps by about 59′; not reenrolled.
Engine: Vertical beam;   cylinder 81½″ x 12′.   2 boilers.
Operation: New York-Albany night boat (People's Line).

New World   No official number.   Sidewheel.
Built: 1848.
Hull: Wood;   as built, 352′8″ x 35′5″ x 10′7½″; enlarged in 1855 to 356′ x 47′ x 10′4″.
Engine: Vertical beam;   cylinder 76″ x 15′.   2 boilers.
Operation: New York-Albany day boat; later night boat, same route (People's Line).

North River Steam Boat   No official number.
Built: 1807, for Robert Fulton.   Sidewheel.
Hull: Wood;   142′ x 14′ x 4′. Enlarged 1807-08, 149′ x 17′11″ x 7′
Engine: Cylinder 24″ x 4′.   1 boiler.
Remark: Popularly known to history as the "Clermont."

Onteora   155322   Sidewheel.
Built: 1898.
Hull: Steel;   236.7′ x 35.2′ x 10.1′.
Engine: Vertical beam;   cylinder 55″ x 10′.   2 boilers.
Operation: Night boat (Catskill Evening Line.) Became excursion boat, 1920, New York-Bear Mountain.

Poughkeepsie   215041   Screw.
Built: 1917 for Central-Hudson Steamboat Co.
Hull: Steel;   206.8′ x 47′ x 14.2′.
Engine: Triple expansion; cylinders 18″, 29″, 47″ x 2½′.   3 boilers.
Operation: Night boat. Rebuilt into excursion boat, 1936-37.
New name: Renamed *b. Westchester*, 1937.

Rensselaer   206501   Sidewheel.
Built: 1909 for New York-Troy Citizens' Line.
Hull: Steel;   317.3′ x 42.5′ x 12.5′.
Engine: Vertical beam;   cylinder 70″ x 12′.   2 boilers.
Operation: Night boat.

Rochester   No official number.   Sidewheel.
Built: 1836.
Hull: Wood;   as built, 201′9″ x 24′9″ x 8′7″; lengthened 1838-39 to 237′ x 25′ x 7′6″; lengthened 1841-42 to 264′ x 25′ x 7′6″.
Engine: Vertical beam; cylinder 43″ x 10′; later fitted with cylinder 50″ x 10′.   2 boilers.
Operation: New York-Albany night boat (People's Line).

St. John   22787   Sidewheel.
Built: 1864.
Hull: Wood;   393′ x 51′ x 10′.
Engine: Vertical beam;   cylinder 84″ x 15′.   2 boilers.
Operation: New York-Albany night boat (People's Line).

Swallow   No official number.   Sidewheel
Built: 1836.
Hull: Wood;   not enrolled as built; withdrawn after first trip, New York-Albany, and lengthened to 225′ x 23′ x 8′4″; lengthened 1842-43, 249′9″ x 23′ x 8′4″.
Engine: Vertical beam;   cylinder 46″ x 10′, later fitted with cylinder 52″ x 10′.   2 boilers.
Operation: Night boat.

Trojan   206129   Sidewheel.
Built: 1909 for New York-Troy Citizens' Line.
Hull: Steel;   317.2′ x 42.5′ x 12.5′.
Engine: Vertical beam;   cylinder 70″ x 12′.   2 boilers.
Operation: Night boat. Last night boat to ply between New York and Albany, 1939.
New name: Renamed *b. New Yorker*, 1939.

NOTES

The awarding of official numbers to vessels of the United States for purposes of identification was instituted by an act of July 28, 1866. Consequently, vessels which had passed away before the effective date of this act did not have official numbers.

Built: The year shown is that used in official documents.

Hull: Statutory dimensions, both original and for changes, are from official documents or *MVUS*. (See note in Appendix A-2.)

Engine: Sources of information were: John H. Morrison, *History of American Steam Navigation (Alida, Dean Richmond, Drew, New World)*; advertising prints *(Francis Skiddy, Hendrik Hudson, St. John)*; David Stevenson, *Sketch of the Civil Engineering of North America (Rochester, Swallow*, original cylinder); Morrison, *op. cit. (Rochester, Swallow*, larger cylinder); American Bureau of Shipping *(Benjamin B. Odell, Poughkeepsie)*; Samuel Ward Stanton, *American Steam Vessels (Isaac Newton)*; engine drawings courtesy of Cedric Ridgely-Nevitt *(North River Steam Boat)*; Elwin M. Eldredge *(City of Albany)*; the Fletcher list provided information on all others.

Information concerning number of boilers for vessels with boilers in the hold is from lists of the American Bureau of Shipping and Eads Johnson.

Appendix B-1

ASSIGNMENT OF CAPTAINS ON DAY LINE STEAMERS: 1863-1948

Daniel Drew
David H. Hitchcock, 1863
John F. Tallman, 1864
W. H. Peck, 1871
Ferdinand Frost, 1872

Armenia
John Perry Smith, 1863

Chauncey Vibbard
David H. Hitchcock, 1864
Ferdinand Frost, 1880
Jacob B. Odell, 1882

Albany
David H. Hitchcock, 1880
Ferdinand Frost, 1882
Jacob B. Odell, 1887
George A. White, 1899
George E. Post, 1907
William Van Woert, 1913
Henry B. Briggs, 1921
Ralph Van Woert, 1924
Henry B. Briggs, 1927

New York
Ferdinand Frost, 1887
J. Benjamin Briggs, 1892
Alfred H. Harcourt, 1901

Hendrick Hudson
George A. White, 1906
David H. Deming, 1906
George E. Post, 1913
Alonzo Sickles, Jr., 1921
David H. Deming, 1927
Alonzo Sickles, Jr., 1928
Frank E. Brown, 1940

Robert Fulton
Alfred H. Harcourt, 1909
J. Rodney Magee, 1916
Walter M. Magee, 1921
Henry B. Briggs, 1924
Walter M. Magee, 1927
Henry B. Briggs, 1931
J. Rodney Magee, 1933
John C. Jones, 1939
J. Rodney Magee, 1940
George C. Reitnauer, 1941

Washington Irving
David H. Deming, 1913

De Witt Clinton
J. Rodney Magee, 1921
J. Rodney Magee, 1939

Alexander Hamilton
Walter M. Magee, 1924
Ralph Van Woert, 1927
Frank E. Brown, 1939
John C. Jones, 1940
Maurice A. Howard, 1947

Chauncey M. Depew
Grant Lezatte, 1925
Frank D. Briggs, 1928
Grant Briggs Lezatte, 1929
Henry B. Briggs, 1933
Arthur W. Van Schaick, 1939

Peter Stuyvesant
Alonzo Sickles, Jr., 1927
Grant Lezatte, 1928
Frank D. Briggs, 1929
De Forest Rainey, 1939
Frank D. Briggs, 1941

Appendix B-2

SOME REPRESENTATIVE DAY LINE OFFICERS

The following biographical sketches are in no sense a complete record of Day Line officers. In 1925, for example, Day Line captains, pursers, engineers and pilots alone totaled 46. Hence, these sketches feature most of the captains, with a few other officers included. Many prominent officers with long service had to be omitted through necessity.

E. J. BAILEY was a long-time purser. He succeeded A. H. Harcourt in that office on the *New York* in 1901 and subsequently moved to the *Robert Fulton* in 1909 and the *Alexander Hamilton* in 1924. Here he served into the 1930s.

OSCAR W. BEDORE was a chief engineer in the classic mold. As a young man he was electrician on the *James W. Baldwin*, a notable boilers-on-the-guards, beam-engine Kingston-New York night boat. Later he went to sea with the Morgan Line. He was with the Erie Railroad's marine fleet at New York before accepting appointment as chief engineer of the *Hendrick Hudson* in 1920. In 1927-28 he was chief of the new *Peter Stuyvesant*, and then went to the *Alexander Hamilton* to remain until his retirement after the season of 1946. A big man with a deep voice, he did not always see eye-to-eye with management. Not unusual was his bellowing at a high official of the line who once made the mistake of ordering a hose disconnected while Chief Bedore was taking on water. He never permitted chairs in his engine room, but his assistants may have been somewhat consoled by the fact that he spent most of his time standing too, either in the engine room looking out, or on the main deck looking in. He loved

216

gladiolas and dogs. Any passengers who shared these fancies became his friends.

FRANK D. BRIGGS, a younger brother of Captain Henry B. Briggs, was first pilot of the *De Witt Clinton* when she entered Day Line service in 1921. In 1928 he succeeded his brother-in-law, Captain Grant Lezatte, in command of the *Chauncey M. Depew;* again in 1929 he succeeded him as master of the *Peter Stuyvesant.* In 1939, when the *De Witt Clinton* was restored to service, Captain Briggs elected to return to her as first pilot for that season, and then left the Day Line to vary his career by becoming a tugboat pilot. He reassumed command of the *Peter Stuyvesant* in 1941 and remained with that vessel through 1948.

HENRY B. BRIGGS was appointed first pilot of the *Albany* in 1912. Nine years later, at age 47, he became her captain, then moved to the command of the *Robert Fulton,* the *Albany* again, back to the *Robert Fulton,* and finally to the *Chauncey M. Depew.* Then he retired from steamboating and died in 1952. He was related to four other Day Line captains: his brother Frank, brothers-in-law Grant Lezatte and J. Rodney Magee, and to his nephew Grant Briggs Lezatte.

J. BENJAMIN BRIGGS secured the position of first pilot on the *Chauncey Vibbard* in 1874, later holding the same berth on the *Albany* and then the *New York.* Breaking temporarily with its previous practice of promoting pursers, the Day Line advanced him to command of the *New York* in 1892. He retired after the 1900 season, well past his mid-seventies. He had been a pilot on the Hudson-New York night boat *Berkshire,* not to be confused with the giant 20th century *Berkshire,* at the time of her burning June 8, 1864. He was mentioned in the press as having remained steadfast at the wheel until the flames drove him from the pilothouse. According to the late Captain Grant Briggs Lezatte, J. Benjamin Briggs was not related to him or therefore to Captains Frank D. and Henry B. Briggs.

FRANK E. BROWN was second pilot on the *Washington Irving* 1924-26, then was 12 years a pilot on the *Hendrick Hudson.* In 1939 he was promoted to captain of the *Alexander Hamilton,* where he remained for a season, followed by nine more in command of the *Hendrick Hudson.* "Brownie" was a captain for a number of years with the Hudson River Day Line, Inc. He died in 1962.

DAVID H. DEMING was regarded as a highly skilled steamboat man and as such he was entrusted for more than two decades with the command of the Day Line's largest steamers. His career as Day Line captain was preceded by an even longer career as pilot, much of it with his father, whom he finally succeeded in 1898 as first pilot of the *Albany.* In 1906 he was selected to command the brand-new *Hendrick Hudson* after she had been broken in by Captain George A. White. In 1913 he brought out the *Washington Irving,* largest of all the day boats, and was the only master she had. A strict disciplinarian he ruled her in what was then described as "battleship style" and is said to have inspected the main saloon daily with white gloves in search of dust. He was commodore of the Day Line fleet and his opinions carried great weight with Eben E. Olcott. Captain Deming's recommendation was considered tantamount to a ticket for a job for "life" with the Day Line at a time when such positions were eagerly sought. After the loss of the *Washington Irving* he went back to the *Hendrick Hudson* in 1927, but the disaster weighed heavily on him. Those who knew him felt that it shortened his life which ended at 70 in his Albany home, November 24, 1927.

LEWIS D. DEMING, David's father, had been a veteran officer on New York-Troy night boats and in 1876 was captain of the Citizens' Line's brand-new *City of Troy* with his son David aboard as quartermaster or apprentice pilot. This seems to have been a high point in Captain Lewis Deming's career since, for some reason, he and the Citizens' Line came to a parting of the ways. Being in the select category of Hudson River passenger boat captains who were also pilots, he went to the Day Line as a pilot. He was first pilot of the *Chauncey Vibbard* during part of the 1880s with David under him as second. David next became second pilot of the *Albany,* which Lewis later joined as first, remaining there through most of the 1890s. After his death or retirement, David succeeded him as first pilot of the *Albany.*

LEWIS ENSIGN began his boating career in proper Hudson River fashion serving as a cabin boy on his father's sloop. Then he became a sloop pilot and inevitably a steamboat pilot, serving on many of the well-known early steamers. He left the river for a time, became a port pilot on ocean ships and got around the Horn to San Francisco more than once. When he returned to the Hudson he reportedly piloted the *Daniel Drew* for awhile, left her and then came back in 1869 to remain with her pilot wheel for the rest of his active life. In the late 1870s he was considered the oldest pilot on the Hudson and was referred to as the "veteran pilot." This led some passengers to go up to the *Daniel Drew's* pilothouse to stare at him as some extraordinary attraction. Such attention infuriated the old man. He probably did not particularly appreciate his nickname of "Drew" Ensign, either, for he was a staunch admirer of the *New World* of 1848 which he considered the finest steamboat that had ever been on the river. And that was that. He died in January, 1880.

FERDINAND FROST had been master of the *Mary Powell* for three years before her purchase by Van Santvoord and Davidson in 1869 and continued to hold that position through 1871. His original appointment to the *Mary Powell* gave rise to a witticism of the day which ran, "Have you noticed that the mornings are quite cold on the *Mary Powell* this season?" The proper reply was, "That's because there's Frost on board." After Van Santvoord and Davidson sold the *Mary Powell* Captain Frost was placed in command of the *Daniel Drew* in 1872 and his salary raised from $1800 to $2000 per year, the amount paid his senior colleague, Captain Hitchcock on the *Chauncey Vibbard*. Frost followed Hitchcock on the *Chauncey Vibbard* and the *Albany* and was the first captain of the *New York*. Because of failing health he left the river after the 1891 season. Counting his three years on the *Mary Powell* under Van Santvoord-Davidson ownership, he had been a Day Line captain for 23 years, a record that was to stand for nearly half a century.

ALFRED H. HARCOURT, born in Albany in 1843, became second captain or purser of the *Chauncey Vibbard* when that vessel was practically brand new. He later held the same position on the *Albany* and then the *New York* of which he was named captain in 1901. Captain Harcourt was the last Day Line commander to be appointed under the old "deck captain" rules, for he never held a pilot's berth. After the *New York* burned he was master of the *Robert Fulton* for seven years and then retired with over half a century of service to the Day Line behind him. He died at his Albany home in November 1918.

DAVID H. HITCHCOCK was born at Poughkeepsie October 9, 1816, moved with his family to West Troy in 1829, then to Albany where his father, Captain "Jack" Hitchcock, was harbormaster for a time. "Dave" and his three brothers all took to the river at an early age. He seems to have been a pilot as well as a captain, and for a considerable period served as master of the *Anna*, a towing steamer in which he owned an interest and which was operated by the Hudson River Steamboat Co. A genial man with the knack of properly

blending courtesy and garrulity, he once had his occupation listed in a city directory as "skipper," and again as "mariner." He produced four sons, all steamboatmen. At one time on the *Chauncey Vibbard* he had with him two sons, as cashier and baggagemaster, and a brother, William P. Hitchcock, as second pilot. His sons did not stay with the Day Line, because he needed them elsewhere. Captain Hitchcock operated small steamboats between Albany and nearby places, and eventually all four of his sons were captains on these vessels. As long as David H. Hitchcock was with the Day Line, he was its senior captain, commanding the *Daniel Drew*, the *Chauncey Vibbard* and the *Albany*. He died June 16, 1882, at his Albany home.

MAURICE A. HOWARD was a downeaster. You only needed to hear him speak to know it. He was born in Maine, April 3, 1896. In his youth he went on coastal schooners and during World War I trained at the merchant marine school in Boston. He was then assigned to the Hudson Navigation Co., a vital carrier in those days, and because of his prior practical experience almost immediately became a quartermaster on the *Trojan*. He liked the Hudson River and stayed on after the war, joining the Day Line in 1924 as second pilot on the *Albany*. In 1927 he moved to the *Alexander Hamilton* to begin two decades as a pilot on her. He was appointed captain in 1947 and went on commanding her under the new owners for two years after the sale of the old Day Line. Altogether he was on this vessel for 24 years. He was later a representative for insurance underwriters at the Port of

Albany and died December 26, 1958. Captain Howard's personal love for steamboating and shipping as a whole has probably been exceeded by few. When his steamer lay in for a day he generally went off to watch other steamboats or to sail on some other line. Old Day Line passengers will well remember his call, "All aboard the North Rivah flyah, tha palatial steamah *Alexander Hamilton* for Albany."

old mother on her arm. Captain Jones was equal to the occasion. At his order, a couple of deckhands dashed up the sidewalk with a Windsor chair, seated the old lady on it, and carried her aboard, with her bulky daughter bringing up the rear as fast as she could. The maneuver was not completely successful, for the *Robert Fulton* was slightly late leaving Newburgh that day. A kindly man, Captain Jones seldom left his steamboat except to go home.

JOHN C. JONES, after serving as first pilot on the *Robert Fulton* and the *Alexander Hamilton,* commanded those vessels until his retirement. A steamboatman of the old school, Captain Jones had a greater respect for a timetable than most people and was eternally consulting his impressive pocket watch to see if his vessel was on schedule. In his first year as a Day Line captain, his *Robert Fulton,* southbound from Albany, lay at Newburgh one day awaiting departure time. Captain Jones stood in the gangway, one hand on the bell-pull, the other holding his watch, waiting for the minute hand to reach 2:50 p.m. so that he could signal the pilothouse to get the steamer under way. The time was drawing close when to his horror he saw, approaching at a snail's pace on the long sidewalk from the ticket office on shore, a 300-pound woman with her 97-year-

S. M. KEYS came east from Detroit in 1900 to take what he thought would be only a summer's job as ticket collector on the *New York.* But he stayed on and later became a baggagemaster, and then a purser. The latter berth he filled successively on the *Albany,* the *Hendrick Hudson* and the *Alexander Hamilton.* When the old line ceased operations after the season of 1948, Mr. Keys was the senior Day Line officer in point of service. Truly it had been a long "summer's job."

GRANT LEZATTE had been master of the Catskill Evening Line's *Clermont* before he came to the Day Line in 1921 as second pilot of the *Albany,* under the command of his brother-in-law, Henry B. Briggs. When Briggs took command of the *Robert Fulton* in 1924, Lezatte went there as first pilot. He was himself given command of the Day Line's "yacht," the *Chauncey M. Depew* when she entered service in 1925, and in 1928 became master of the almost-new *Peter Stuyvesant*. He died in 1929.

GRANT BRIGGS LEZATTE, son of Captain Grant Lezatte, was pilot of the *Chauncey M. Depew* under his father and then his uncle, Captain Frank D. Briggs. While still in his twenties he became captain of that vessel in 1929 and continued through 1932. Depression circumstances shrank the Day Line fleet and he lost his command. Later he became second pilot of the *Robert Fulton*, and was first pilot from 1939 through 1948. In 1949 he was briefly captain of the *Chauncey M. Depew*, then running as an excursion boat at New York. Afterwards he was captain of the Kingston-Rhinecliff ferry *George Clinton* (1949-57) and at the time of his death was master of Newburgh-Beacon ferryboats. Born with a deep steamboating background, Grant B. Lezatte carried on the tradition well.

JOHN RODNEY MAGEE was born along the Hudson at Smith's Landing, June 1, 1869. He became second pilot of the *New York* in 1902 under his father, Peter Magee, who had been first pilot on that vessel for a number of years. From 1907-11 J. Rodney Magee was first pilot of the *Albany*. After the loss of the *New York*, Peter Magee was assigned as first pilot of the *Robert Fulton* and retired after the season of 1911. "Rod" was then transferred to the *Robert Fulton* to take his father's place, and in 1916 became her captain. When the twin-screw *De Witt Clinton* was commissioned in 1921, she was a marked departure in handling in a line that heretofore had operated only sidewheelers. Captain Magee was selected to command her and did it so successfully that he was the only master the vessel had on the Hudson. After her withdrawal, the captain went back to the *Robert Fulton*, returned to the *De Witt Clinton* upon her one-year re-emergence in 1939; and again to the *Robert Fulton* in 1940. That was his last season on the river, for he did not return in 1941 and died in August of that year. Captain Magee was a genial man, popular with his employers, crew and passengers. A Day Line chef once created and named in his honor, "Filet d'Mignon Magee." The fractured French cannot be blamed on the good captain. It comes from the recipe as carried in a marine magazine many years ago. In his younger days, Rod sported a moustache, but when those facial adornments went out of fashion, he became smooth-shaven. After Alfred E. Smith became widely known, some passengers used to fancy that Captain Magee resembled Al. If they got around to telling this to Magee, he would stoutly deny it. He maintained that Al Smith resembled him. Captain J. Rodney Magee commanded Day Line steamers for 25 years, or longer than any other man.

WALTER M. MAGEE's early career rather paralleled that of his brother J. Rodney whom he followed in piloting positions on the *New York* and the *Robert Fulton*, and as captain of the latter. Death ended his Day Line service after the 1930 season.

ELMONT L. NELSON served as assistant and chief engineer of the *Hendrick Hudson* in the 1930s and 1940s. In 1949 "Elmer" was chief engineer of the *Chauncey M. Depew*. He was engineer of the ferryboat *Dutchess* when she made the last ferry crossing between Newburgh and Beacon in 1963.

JACOB B. ODELL was said to have been the "obliging" second captain or purser of the *Daniel Drew* at the time she was purchased by Van Santvoord and associates. He continued to hold that post until in 1880 he became purser of the *Chauncey Vibbard*, of which he was appointed captain in 1882, moving to the *Albany* in 1887. Bright's disease forced him ashore early in the 1898 season and he died in October of that year.

ELVOID E. POST joined the engine room crew of the *Alexander Hamilton* in the fall of 1931 and worked his way up to become her chief engineer in 1947, a position he still held in 1964. In the intervening years "Posty" was off her only a single season, 1939, when, newly assigned as second assistant engineer, he was placed on the *Peter Stuyvesant*. His remarkable continuity of service on the *Alexander Hamilton* demonstrates his affection for that vessel and his devotion to the tradition of steamboating. He has often played host to steamboat enthusiasts on his vessel, and they and many other Day Line passengers have happy recollections of the friendly chief.

GEORGE E. POST was master of the *C. W. Morse*, then the largest steamboat on the Hudson, before he came to the Day Line in 1906. He was slated to become captain of the *Albany* after the fleet was expanded

Captain George C. Reitnauer and his officers stand on the *Robert Fulton's* hurricane deck. Left to right: First Mate John Boyle, Purser Ira W. Brandies, the Captain, First Pilot Grant B. Lezatte, Second Mate Joseph Fox, and Second Pilot William H. Burlingham.—*Collection of William H. Ewen.*

with the addition of the *Hendrick Hudson*. In the meantime he was assigned to his future command as first pilot. Since David H. Deming who was to command the *Hendrick Hudson* was the regular first pilot, the *Albany* thus briefly carried two officers with the same title. Still a pilot, Captain Post was on the *Hendrick Hudson* when she entered service and then returned to the *Albany* as captain. In 1913 he was transferred to the *Hendrick Hudson* and remained with the Day Line through 1920.

GEORGE C. REITNAUER decided to become a deckhand on the Day Line in his youth when, for reasons of health, an outdoor life was suggested to him. He advanced in responsibility and in 1913 was appointed first mate of the *Hendrick Hudson*. In 1916 he became second pilot on the *Robert Fulton*. Twenty-five years of piloting this boat, the *Albany* and the *Alexander Hamilton* led him to the top, when he was selected in 1941 to command the *Robert Fulton*.

PHILIP ST. PIERRE, one of the best-known Hudson River engineers of his day, was born December 1828 in Canada, and was brought to the United States

about four years later. Engineering ran in his family and when old enough he went to work on steamboats and rose to the post of engineer. He is said to have been an engineer on the *Daniel Drew* when she came out in 1860. In 1862 he went to China with the *Fire Cracker*, a wooden sidewheeler built in the United States for Chinese service. After some time in the Far East as a marine engineer, he returned to the United States and went back to the *Daniel Drew*. By 1866 at the latest he was first (chief) engineer and remained in charge of her engine until he was transferred to the new *Albany* in 1880. Ill health forced him to leave this vessel in June 1891. He died at his Nyack home in March 1892 at the age of 63.

ALONZO SICKLES, JR. had been quartermaster on the *C. W. Morse* under Captain George E. Post and came to the Day Line in 1907 to serve as second pilot on the *Albany* under his old commander. "Lon" was soon transferred to the *Hendrick Hudson* and in 1913 became first pilot of the *Washington Irving*. In 1921 he succeeded Captain Post in command of the *Hendrick Hudson* and except for 1927 when he brought out the new *Peter Stuyvesant*, remained master of the big steamer until September 1939. The active career of this quiet, unassuming man ended on the *Hendrick Hudson's* last down trip from Albany in 1939. The condition of the captain's health obliged him to go ashore at Kingston where he lived and the vessel proceeded to New York without him, lashed on the way by an extremely severe summer storm. Two days later the *Hendrick Hudson* made her last trip of the year and the next day, September 11, began the work of laying her up for the winter. That evening Captain Sickles died with his first pilot, Harry W. Kellerman, at his bedside.

JOHN PERRY SMITH, a man early in his thirties, was captain of the *Armenia* for the remainder of the season after his father, Captain Isaac P. Smith, sold the vessel to Van Santvoord and Davidson in the fall of 1863. It is said that Smith was engineer of the *Armenia* before he took command. While this line of promotion was far from common, Smith was certainly not the only practicing marine engineer to become captain of a steamboat on the Hudson.

JOHN F. TALLMAN was an investor in steamboats and one of the original owners of the *Armenia*. He commanded this vessel and other New York-Albany day boats including the *Metamora* and the *Henry Clay*, on which he was master at the time of her disastrous fire while racing in 1852. He was captain of the brand-new *Daniel Drew* in 1860, again in 1862, and returned to her in 1864 after she had come under Day Line ownership. His nickname for her was the "Honey Cooler" and he remained her master through 1870.

RALPH VAN WOERT was second pilot of the *Albany* in 1912. Next year he moved to the pilothouse of the

Washington Irving; in 1924 he was given command of the *Albany*. An efficient and thorough master, he served as captain of this and the *Alexander Hamilton* until he left the Day Line after the season of 1938.

WILLIAM VAN WIE came to the Day Line from the Cornell Steamboat Co.'s tugboat fleet in 1917 as assistant engineer of the *Albany*. He moved to the *Washington Irving* in 1920 and was on watch in her engine room when that vessel was sunk in 1926. Next year he was on the *Hendrick Hudson* on which he remained, finally as chief, through the 1940 season. He died soon afterwards.

WILLIAM VAN WOERT, the father of Ralph, commanded the *Albany* for eight years. He was later a captain with the Albany night line and died in 1962 in his mid-nineties.

GEORGE ANDREW WHITE was born in Shelburne, Vermont, November 9, 1855, the son of L. S. White, a Lake Champlain boatbuilder. He graduated from the University of Vermont in 1877 with a degree in civil engineering. For several years he was purser of the steamboat *Horicon* on Lake George. Here he so impressed Charles T. Van Santvoord that he was engaged by the Day Line and in 1883 was appointed purser of the *Chauncey Vibbard*. In 1887 he went to the *Albany* as purser and 12 years later officially became her master. This gave the Day Line the rare distinction of having a full-fledged college graduate as a steamboat captain. In 1906, after briefly commanding the new *Hendrick Hudson* he went ashore to devote full time to his new position as assistant general manager which he continued to fill until his death on March 8, 1917.

STAATS WINNE came to the Day Line in 1898 as second pilot of the *Albany*. He was doubtless the same Staats Winne who had earlier been wheelsman (quartermaster) and second pilot on the *Daniel Drew* under Lewis Ensign. He now remained on the *Albany* until the *Hendrick Hudson* was commissioned. After David H. Deming assumed command of that vessel, Winne became the first pilot, a post he filled for a comparatively short time. It has been said that he always wore red flannel underwear. On hot days he would remove his uniform coat and roll up his shirt sleeves. His friends on other vessels were quite used to seeing a red arm waving a greeting from a Day Line pilothouse, but it must have looked a bit odd to the passengers.

CHARLES N. WRIGHT was appointed purser of the *Albany* in 1900. He moved in 1906 to the brand-new *Hendrick Hudson* and likewise in 1913 to the new *Washington Irving*, where he remained through her entire career until she was lost.

BIBLIOGRAPHY

Braynard, Frank O. *Lives of the Liners*. New York: Cornell Maritime Press, 1947.

Bruce, Wallace. Hudson River guidebooks.

Bugbee, Gordon P. *The Lake Erie Sidewheel Steamers of Frank E. Kirby*. Detroit: Great Lakes Model Shipbuilders' Guild, 1955.

Callender, James H. *Yesterdays in Little Old New York*. New York: Dorland Press, 1929.

Covell, William King. *A Short History of the Fall River Line*. Newport, R. I.: A. Hartley G. Ward, 1947.

Curtis, George William. *Lotus-Eating: A Summer Book*. New York: Harper & Brothers, 1852.

Dictionary of American Biography. New York: 1928 *et seq.*

Elmendorf Papers. Clippings, pictures, etc. collected by William B. Elmendorf, in the Manuscript Division, New York State Library, Albany, N. Y.

Farwell, Raymond F. *The Rules of the Nautical Road*. Annapolis, Md.: United States Naval Institute, 1941 ed.

Flexner, James Thomas. *Steamboats Come True: American Inventors in Action*. New York: The Viking Press, 1944.

Haviland, Edward Kenneth. "American Steam Navigation in China, 1845-1878." *The American Neptune*, Vol. xvi, No. 3 - Vol. xviii, No. 1.

Holdcamper, Forrest R. "Biography of the *List of Merchant Vessels of the United States*." *The American Neptune*, Vol. xxiv, No. 2.

Hudson-Fulton Celebration, 1909, The. 2 vols. The Fourth Annual Report of the Hudson-Fulton Celebration Commission to the Legislature of the State of New York. Prepared by Edward Hagaman Hall. Albany: 1910.

Hudson River Day Line Collection. The New-York Historical Society, New York, N. Y. The major collection of Hudson River Day Line material, presented by Alfred V. S. Olcott. See acknowledgments.

Hudson River Day Line Collection. The Steamship Historical Society of America, Inc., reference library, Staten Island, N. Y. Additional material retained by Mr. Olcott during his lifetime. Presented by Mrs. Alfred V. S. Olcott.

Lane, Wheaton J. *Commodore Vanderbilt: An Epic of the Steam Age*. New York: Alfred A. Knopf, 1942.

List of Merchant Vessels of the United States, 1868-1924. *Merchant Vessels of the United States, 1925-present*. Annual list. Washington: U. S. Government Printing Office.

Lossing, Benson J. *The Hudson, from the Wilderness to the Sea*. Troy: H. B. Nims & Co., c. 1866.

Lyman, John. "Register Tonnage and Its Measurement." *The American Neptune*, Vol. v, No. 3-4.

McAdam, Roger Williams. *The Old Fall River Line*. New York: Stephen Daye Press, 1955 ed.

Merchant Steam Vessels of the United States, 1807-1868: "The Lytle List." Publication No. 6, the Steamship Historical Society of America, 1952, with supplements.

Merchant Vessels of the United States. See *List of Merchant Vessels of the United States*.

Miller's New Guide to the Hudson River. New York: James Miller, 1872.

Moody's Analyses of Investments and Security Rating Books. Moody's Manual of Investments and Security Rating Service. New York: Moody's Investors Service. Various years.

Morrison, John Harrison. *History of American Steam Navigation*. New York: W. F. Sametz & Co., Inc., 1903.

Morrison, John Harrison. *Iron and Steel Hull Steam Vessels of the United States, 1825-1905*. Reprinted from *Scientific American Supplement*, October 21 - November 25, 1905, as Reprint Series No. 3 of the Steamship Historical Society of America, 1945.

Murdock, George W. Collection. Extensive collection of pictures and biographies of Hudson River and other steamboats in the New-York Historical Society, New York, N. Y.

National Archives and Records Service, General Services Administration, Washington. Files of documents of American vessels.

National Cyclopedia of American Biography, The. New York: 1892 *et seq.*

Newspapers. Files of newspapers of New York, Albany, Kingston, Newburgh, Poughkeepsie, etc., in the New York State Library, Albany; the Kingston City Library, Kingston; the Newburgh Free Library, Newburgh; the Adriance Memorial Library, Poughkeepsie.

Periodicals. Files of *The American Neptune*, Salem, Mass.; *The Nautical Gazette*, New York; *Ships and the Sea*, Milwaukee; *Steamboat Bill*, journal of the Steamship Historical Society of America, Inc., Staten Island, N. Y.

Poor's Rating Service. New York: Poor's Publishing Co. Various years.

Roberts, R. S. "Amphibious Logging." *Seafarer*, Vol. vii, No. 2.

Stanton, Samuel Ward. *American Steam Vessels*. New York: Smith & Stanton, 1895.

Stevenson, David. *Sketch of the Civil Engineering of North America*. London: John Weale, 1838.

Sutcliffe, Alice Crary. *Robert Fulton and the "Clermont."* New York: The Century Co., 1909.

Tourist's Guide Through the Empire State, The. Albany: Mrs. S. S. Colt, editor and publisher, 1871.

INDEX OF VESSELS

Vessels which had more than one name are indexed by the name which appears on the page indicated.

*Indicates illustration.

— A —

A. H. Hanscom, 186
Adelphi, 81
Adirondack, 92, 93*, 97, 136, 137, 171
Albany (1826), 109
Albany (1880), 59-61*-65, 67-73*, 75*-78*, 80, 81*, 83, 87-89*, 92, 95, 97, 107, 109, 110, 114, 115, 118, 120, 123, 139-141, 144, 154, 162, 166, 178*-180, 196, 209
Alexander Hamilton, 69*, 154*, 155*, 156*, 157*, 158, 171, 181-182*-184*, 185*, 194*, 198*, 200*, 201, 203-205*, 206*, 207*, 208*, 209*, 210*
Alida, 14*, 15, 17, 45
Allerton, 186
Anna, 20
Ansonia, 176
Armenia, 8, 14*-17, 20, 21*-23, 25, 36, 44, 45-48, 50, 51, 57, 60*, 93, 144, 158
Arrow, 15
Atlantic, 100*

— B —

Bay Queen, 99
Bear Mountain, 203
Benjamin B. Odell, 175, 177*, 186*-189*, 191, 192
Berkshire, 132, 133*, 134*, 135*-137, 171, 175, 187, 190*-193*
Broadway, 15
Buccaneer, 181

— C —

C. W. Morse, 97, 98*, 107, 132, 137, 171, 175, 191
Catskill, 143
Charles A. Shultz, 67
Charmary, 99, 103
Chauncey M. Depew, 158, 159*, 160*, 161*, 171, 178*, 181, 194*, 195*, 196*, 198, 200*

Chauncey Vibbard, 25, 26*-28, 30-34, 36*, 44, 45*-49*-51*, 56-61*-63*, 67, 68, 76*, 77, 115
Chrystenah, 140
City of Albany, 18*, 20, 21, 23, 81, 82*, 83
City of Beaumont, 181
City of Brockton, 68
City of Fall River, 68
City of Hudson, 19
City of Lowell, 120
Clermont (1807), Misname for North River Steam Boat, which see.
Clermont (1892), 82*, 84, 92, 99
Clermont (1909), 120, 121*, 122
Clermont (1911), 142, 143*, 186, 187, 203
Cohoes, 171, 186
Comanche, 193*
Commander, 138*
Commerce, 12*, 13
Commodore, 100*
Cygnus, 82*

— D —

Daniel Drew, 15, 16*, 17, 20*-23, 25, 26*, 27, 30-34, 36, 44-46*-51, 57-61, 66*-68, 83, 89, 113, 144, 162
Day Line I, 208
Day Line II, 208
Day Line VII, 208
Dean Richmond, 24*, 25
Derecktor, 198
De Witt Clinton, 146*, 147*, 148*, 149*, 152*-154, 171, 181, 183, 194*-199*
Drew, 25, 28*

— E —

Eagle, 19
Erastus Corning, 171
Eureka, 204
Express, 7

— F —

Ferdinando Gorges, 175
Fishkill-on-Hudson, 100*
Fort Orange, 171, 175*, 191

Francis Skiddy, 8, 10*
Frederick C. Johnson, 197*, 198

— G —

Galilah, 197*, 198
Gloucester, 120
Gotham, 203, 204
Green Island, 171, 186

— H —

Half Moon (Henry Hudson's ship) See Halve Maene
Half Moon (replica), 120, 121*, 122
Halve Maene, 106*, 109
Hartford, 187, 188
Haven, 171
Hendrick Hudson (1845) See Hendrik Hudson
Hendrick Hudson (1906), 96*, 99*, 100*-102*-104*, 105*, 106*-108*, 109*, 110, 114, 115, 118, 120*-123, 125, 132, 139, 154, 155, 163*, 166*, 167, 178*-180*-181, 190, 194*, 199*, 201*, 202*, 203, 209*
Hendrik Hudson, 7-9*, 11, 99
Henry Clay, 8
Hercules, 101
Highlander, 140
Homer Ramsdell, 140, 175, 186

— I —

Ida, 176
Isaac Newton, 7, 8, 11*, 25

— J —

Jacob H. Tremper, 175
James Kent, 4*
James River, 192
Jesse Hoyt, 19, 94
John Lenox, 143

— K —

Kaaterskill, 142
Knickerbocker, 203, 208
Knickerbocker II, 204, 208
Knickerbocker VII, 204, 208

— L —

Lady Clinton, 12*, 13
Lady Van Rensselaer, 13

GENERAL INDEX

People's Line, 5, 7-9, 11, 13, 16, 24,
    25, 28, 42, 61, 92-94, 97, 107, 132,
    171
People's Line Association, 7, 8
Perry, Hiram, 59
Peterschen, F. W., 80
Peterschen's Orchestra and Military
    Band, 80
Post, Elvoid E., 206*, 207, 209, 220*
Post, George E., 220
Post, John, 13
Poughkeepsie Transportation Co., 93
Power, George H., 19
Princhart, Emile, 109
Providence Line, 192
Pusey & Jones Corp., 167

— R —

Ramsdell Transportation Co., Homer,
    93
Redfield, W. C., 12
Reitnauer, George C., 182*, 221*
Renfrew, Lord, 17
Richardson, J. O., 120
Richmond, Dean, 25
Robins Co., John N., 74
Rockefeller, Laura Spelman, 143
Rogers, Stephen, 27
Romer & Tremper, 19, 94
Romer & Tremper Steamboat Co., 93
Root & Davidson, 22
Rosoff, Samuel Rufus, 191, 192, 203
Rosoff Sand & Gravel Co., 192
Rouland, Orlando, 159*, 160
Rowland, Thomas F., 58

— S —

St. John, A. P., 25
St. Pierre, Philip, 50, 221
Sanders, George, 203, 204
Saratoga & Hudson River Railroad,
    39, 42
Satterlee, Walter, 109
Saugerties & New York Steamboat
    Co., 93, 176
Saugerties Evening Line, 176
Schuyler Line Towboat Association,
    47
Scott, Sir Walter, 123
Scott, Winfield, 36
Sedgwick, F. J., 101
Sennett, Mack, 111
Sharpe, George H., 50
Shupe, Walter H., 81, 83
Sickles, Alonzo Jr., 178*, 179, 221

Sinn's, Colonel, Orchestra, 77
Sloane, W. & J., 72
Smith, Abraham P., 15
Smith, D. D., 15
Smith, Isaac P., 15, 20, 21, 23
Smith, John Perry, 23, 222
Smith, Tunis, 15
Snyder Hose, 39
Southern New England Railway, 144
Southern Pacific Railroad, 204
Stanton, Samuel Ward, 101, 118, 122,
    132
Stark, H. R., 120
Staten Island Shipbuilding Co., 120
Steam Navigation Co., 12, 13, 162
Stony Clove & Catskill Mountain
    Railroad, 85
Stuyvesant, Peter, 167
Stuyvesant, Petrus
    See Stuyvesant, Peter
Sunday, Billy, 141
Sutton Line, Inc., 203

— T —

T. S. Marvel Shipbuilding Co.
    See Marvel Shipbuilding Co., T. S.
Taft, William Howard, 132
Tallman, John F., 8, 15, 17, 25, 32,
    33, 35, 50, 209, 222
Taylor, Stephen G., 71
Terry, D. C., 19
Tietjen & Lang, 146
Todd Shipyards Corp., 146
Townsend & Downey Shipbuilding
    & Repair Co., 95
Townsend, Absalom, 15
Troy Evening Line, 142, 143

— U —

Ulster & Delaware Railroad, 60, 85,
    89-91*, 151
United States Army Corps of
    Engineers, 166
Utica & Schenectady Railroad, 22

— V —

van Benthuysen, Charles, 57
van Benthuysen, Clarence R., 57,
    62, 71
Van Santvoord, Abraham, 13, 15,
    162, 175, 209
Van Santvoord, Abraham (Son of
    Abraham above), 13
Van Santvoord, Abraham (Grandson
    of Abraham first above), 57

Van Santvoord, Alfred, 13, 15, 17,
    19-23, 27, 28, 32, 46-50, 57-59, 61,
    62, 64, 65, 67, 68, 71, 81-83*, 84,
    87-89, 92-95, 97, 99, 101, 109,
    159, 162, 176, 209
Van Santvoord, Anna Margaret
    Townsend, 15
Van Santvoord, Charles Townsend,
    57, 58*, 59, 62, 84, 87, 109
Van Santvoord, Cornelius, 13, 57
Van Santvoord, Sarah Hitchcock, 13
Van Wie, William, 163, 178*, 222
Van Woert, Ralph, 182*, 185*, 222*
Van Woert, William, 222
Van Wyck, Robert A., 94
Vanderbilt, Cornelius, 5, 39, 42
Vaux, Downing, 90
Vibbard, Chauncey, 21, 22, 25, 27,
    159

— W —

W. & A. Fletcher Co.
    See Fletcher Co., W. & A.
Wales, Prince of (King Edward VII),
    17
Wallkill Valley Railroad, 60
War Department, 195, 196, 198
War Shipping Administration, 196,
    198
Warrington, Arthur A., 141
Washington, George, 109
Washington Heights Chemical Engine
    Co., 111, 113
Washington Steamer Co., 111
Weed, Raphael A., 118, 128, 130, 132
Welch, E. S., 104*, 105
West Shore Railroad, 90, 97, 150,
    151
White, Alfred, 44
White, George A., 92, 97, 107, 120,
    122, 123, 144, 222
White, Mrs. George A., 115*
Wickes, I. C., 95
Williamson Steam Steerer, 72
Willis, Nathaniel P., 37, 109
Wills, B. B., 179, 196
Wilson, Woodrow, 144
Winne, Staats, 104*, 105, 222
Wright, Charles N., 166*, 222

— Y —

Yzquierdo, 109

— Z —

Zim Israel Navigation Co., Ltd., 198